FRANKLIN'S THRIFT

From the Center for Thrift and Generosity
at the Institute for American Values

For A New Thrift: Confronting the Debt Culture
A Report to the Nation from the Commission on Thrift

Thrift: A Cyclopedia by David Blankenhorn

www.newthrift.org

FRANKLIN'S
THRIFT

The Lost History of an American Virtue

Edited by David Blankenhorn,
Barbara Dafoe Whitehead,
and Sorcha Brophy-Warren

TEMPLETON PRESS

Templeton Press
300 Conshohocken State Road, Suite 550
West Conshohocken, PA 19428

www.templetonpress.org

Designed and Typeset by ION Graphic Design Works

Library of Congress Cataloging-in-Publication Data

Franklin's thrift : The lost history of an American virtue / edited by
David Blankenhorn, Barbara Dafoe Whitehead, and Sorcha Brophy-Warren.
    p. cm.
  ISBN-13: 978-1-59947-148-8 (alk. paper)
  ISBN-10: 1-59947-148-5 (alk. paper)
  1. Saving and investment--United States--History. 2. Thrift
institutions--United States--History. 3. Franklin, Benjamin,
1706-1790--Philosophy. I. Blankenhorn, David. II. Whitehead, Barbara
Dafoe, 1944- III. Brophy-Warren, Sorcha.
  HC110.S3F73 2009
  332.10973--dc22

                                    2008041135

Printed in the United States of America

09 10 11 12 13 14   10 9 8 7 6 5 4 3 2 1

To tomorrow's thrift visionaries
and
in memory of Sir John Templeton
(*November 29, 1912–July 8, 2008*)

Contents

Introduction   ix
David Blankenhorn, Barbara Dafoe Whitehead,
and Sorcha Brophy-Warren

Part One: Franklin's Thrift: The Creation of an American Value

1. Franklin's Way to Wealth   3
   Barbara Dafoe Whitehead

Part Two: Thrift after Franklin: Institutions and Movements

2. U.S. Mutual Savings Banks and the "Savings Bank Idea":
   The Virtue of Thrift as an Institutional Value   29
   Sorcha Brophy-Warren

3. Thrift for a New Century: Public Discussions about Thrift
   in the 1910s and 1920s   57
   Sara Butler Nardo

4. A Century of Thrift Shops   97
   Alison Humes

5. In Savings We Trust: Credit Unions and Thrift   127
   Clifford N. Rosenthal

**Part Three: For a New Thrift: Meeting the Twenty-First Century
   Challenge**

6. Confronting the American Debt Culture   145
   Barbara Dafoe Whitehead

7. Crafting Policies to Encourage Thrift in Contemporary America   165
   Alex Roberts

8. Private Enterprise's Role in Increasing Savings 187
   Ronald T. Wilcox

   Conclusion 207
   David Blankenhorn, Barbara Dafoe Whitehead,
   and Sorcha Brophy-Warren

   Notes 211
   Contributors 243
   Index 247

Introduction

*David Blankenhorn, Barbara Dafoe Whitehead, and
Sorcha Brophy-Warren*

THIS VOLUME OF ESSAYS is dedicated to enlarging and enriching our
historical understanding of thrift. Thrift is one of the oldest American
values, but its long and ample history is unfamiliar to most people
today. It is not hard to figure out why. The study and teaching of thrift
have all but disappeared from American life. Children seldom learn
about this value in school. Civic and youth organizations that once
championed thrift have moved on to other things. National campaigns
for thrift have vanished from public life altogether. Everyday thrift
objects and images—advertisements, poster art, piggy banks, children's
games, savings passbooks, budget cookbooks, bank promotions—have
become curiosities for collectors. Even today's historians fail to exhibit
much interest in the history of thrift, except as a foil for critiques of
capitalism, "Coolidge-ism," and Main Street boosterism.

Lost from history and living memory, thrift is commonly viewed as
nothing more than tight-fisted economizing. Say the word *thrift* and
people think of Dickens' Ebenezer Scrooge or Dell Comics' Scrooge
McDuck. Or perhaps they conjure up images of Depression-era privation and home-front hardships of World War II. Or they think of obses-
sive string savers and coupon clippers. Whatever image comes to mind,

it is likely to be one of joyless self-denial. Thrifty people, it seems, may be good at pinching pennies, but they are not much fun to be around.

The essays contained in this volume challenge and confound this reductive and unappealing view of thrift. The picture of thrift that emerges in these pages is the opposite of small and small-minded. Thrift, the historical evidence suggests, is big and big-hearted. It is big in several ways. It is rooted in a broad conception of social thriving. It encompasses two classic, and sometimes competing, traditions in American life—self-help and mutual aid. From Benjamin Franklin to the philanthropist Edward Filene, thrift advocates have believed in giving people the opportunity to achieve independence through their own efforts and initiative. At the same time, they rejected a radically individualistic notion of "do-it-by-yourself." Cooperative institutions and associational bonds were central to their broad conception of thrift. By building institutions of mutual aid, thrift leaders believed, Americans from poor and "middling" ranks could do better together than they could do apart.

Thrift thinks big. Like the environmental movement today (which is itself connected to the thrift ethic), thrift has tended toward a national or even global perspective. Its leaders borrowed from the world's traditions, ideas, and models of thrift. Benjamin Franklin did not make up Poor Richard's famous sayings; he borrowed and often improved upon the world's treasury of thought and lore on thrift.[1] Likewise, the nineteenth-century founders of mutual savings banks patterned their institutions after the "savings and friendly societies" in Great Britain. In the twentieth century, leaders of the American credit union movement built upon the models of the German "people's banks" and the French Canadian *caisse populaire*.

Thrift is generous. The men and women who set out to create thrift campaigns and institutions were far from skinflints. Some, like the credit union philanthropist Edward Filene, devoted substantial portions of their self-made business fortunes to establishing cooperative thrift institutions. Others, like the community leaders who founded and often ran nonprofit mutual savings banks, insisted on working as unpaid volunteers.

Finally, and perhaps most surprisingly, thrift is a source of pleasure. For one thing, it produces an abundance of good things to savor in life. Benjamin Franklin famously enjoyed rich food, fine wine, elegant carriages, and luxurious living. This indulgence was not a lapse from thrift on Franklin's part; it was one of the rewards of thrift. As Poor Richard said, "Wealth is not his who has it but his who enjoys it." Thrift also offers a second great pleasure. It is fun to give. In the essay on thrift shops, readers will find a portrait of three generations of avid thrift shopping women who enjoy the giving as much as the getting.

But if these essays enlarge our understanding of thrift, they also identify the countervailing forces that have worked to limit and undermine a sustained culture of thrift. Prosperity is one. Thrift has a hard time in good times. Somehow, Americans find it easy to forget about the rewards of thrift in a boom economy. Another is regionalism. Historically, thrift has been more deeply rooted in the institutions and culture of the Northeast and upper Midwest than in the rest of the country. Yet another obstacle is the recurrent challenge from "antithrift" institutions. Today's state lotteries, the leading public antithrift, resurrect the state-sponsored gambling practices of the legally banned nineteenth-century lottery; payday lenders, the leading private antithrift, follow in the tradition of the salary lenders and loan sharks of the early twentieth century.

Yet thrift has demonstrated great resilience over time. For more than three centuries, it has served as a renewable source of social energy and institutional creativity. Franklin established a legacy of thrift for future generations, but it has not been a legacy frozen in time. On the contrary, each generation has had to invent a new case for thrift and to come up with institutions that fit contemporary conditions. Today, as the nation faces the failure of major financial institutions, a crisis of overindebtedness, and the depletion of our natural resource wealth, our generation is called to the task of renewing thrift once again. How we might begin to make such change is the concern of the final section of this book.

With this brief preview in mind, we invite you to dig in for yourself. And enjoy!

PART ONE

Franklin's Thrift
The Creation of an American Value

Chapter 1

Franklin's Way to Wealth

Barbara Dafoe Whitehead

THE TRICENTENNIAL CELEBRATION of Benjamin Franklin's birth brought forth a fresh crop of scholarly articles, popular biographies, and museum exhibits. For the most part, however, the tributes to Franklin's life and work focused on his contributions as a scientist, statesman, and international superstar. Almost entirely neglected was the one contribution for which Franklin has been most widely known: his thought and writing on thrift.

Franklin did not invent the value of thrift, but he made it an American value. For at least two centuries, he stood as the emblem and exponent of thrift. He personified it, practiced it, promoted it, and, through his writings, exported it to the rest of the world. He produced two hugely popular works: *Poor Richard's Almanack* (1732–57) and *The Way to Wealth* (1757). Both were filled with sayings on thrift. Both were reprinted, excerpted, anthologized, and translated into many languages. Both were taught to schoolchildren throughout the world. Indeed, it is fair to say that few Americans—living or dead—have done more to promote the value and practice of thrift than Benjamin Franklin.

Franklin also produced a record of his life. Published first in Europe and then posthumously in the United States, the *Autobiography* (1817) was the classic American self-help book. In it, Franklin offered moral instruction and how-to advice for practicing thrift and achieving wealth. He also revealed dispositions that reflected not just his own character but the American character itself: the passion for freedom, the aspiration for self-improvement, the pragmatic approach to problems, the desire to do good, and the confident outlook on the future.

Franklin's thrift became the cornerstone of a new kind of secular faith in the individual's capacity to shape his or her own lot and fortune in life. For Franklin's Calvinist forebears, it was God who had the power to elect those who would gain worldly fortune. For Franklin, it was the common man and woman who had the potential to gain worldly fortune through his or her own efforts. No longer would the distribution of material blessings be subject to the mysterious workings of God's grace nor to the mere accidents of fortunate birth. The way to wealth rested in the cultivation of habits of "industry and frugality:" "All Men are not equally qualified for getting Money," he wrote as Poor Richard, "but it is in the Power of every one alike to practise [Thrift]."[1]

A fresh appraisal of Franklin's thrift is especially timely today. In the aftermath of the boom years of the late 1990s, twenty-first century Americans face a sobering reality. The personal savings rate has dipped below zero in recent years. Consumer debt is sky-high. Home ownership has dropped, and foreclosures have shot up as a result of the subprime mortgage debacle. Retirement savings are falling short. The natural wealth of the planet is being consumed at an unsustainable rate.

In his own day, Franklin confronted similar problems: a nation drowning in debt; a society living on credit; and a people burdened by bankruptcies, overindebtedness, and real estate deals gone bust. Like Americans today, he also worried about the trade-offs between helping one's adult children and saving enough for one's own old age.[2] Franklin's proposed solutions sound familiar as well. He believed that Americans should save more and spend less; conserve rather than consume; and sacrifice for the common good rather than accumulate more luxury goods for oneself—notions that echo today's public calls for reducing consumer debt, curbing hyperconsumerism, encouraging public service, and promoting good stewardship of the nation's natural and human resources.

That said, it is not easy to retrieve the meaning of Franklin's thrift for the twenty-first-century American reader. For some people today, the word *thrift* connotes stinginess; for others, it conjures images of grinding privation and joyless self-denial; for still others, it simply sounds musty and old school. This negative response is not new. It has roots in a long intellectual tradition. In the nineteenth century, even as Franklin became the workingman's hero and the schoolchild's role model, his image and reputation inspired a backlash among some of the literary luminaries of the day. Herman Melville called him a "maxim-monger," a "professor of housewifery," and an "herb-doctor." Mark Twain wrote that Franklin inflicted suffering on generations of boys who had to live by his maxims. Twentieth-century writers continued the tradition. D. H. Lawrence called Franklin a "snuff-colored little man" who corralled all the unruly passions of humankind into a narrow moral accounting system of credits and debits. Most famously, the German sociologist Max Weber attacked Franklin as a "colourless Deist" who preached the gospel of "earning of more and more money" as an end in itself and who promoted a secular philosophy of avarice and crude utilitarianism. Even Carl Van Doren, Franklin's eminent twentieth-century biographer, explained that his mission was to rescue Franklin from the "dry, prim people" who revered him for his ideas on thrift.[3]

This essay takes issue with Franklin's critics and their characterization of his idea of thrift. Specifically, it rejects the claim that Franklin promoted an outmoded, crabbed, and narrowly economistic vision of human purpose and possibility. Instead, it offers an alternative claim: namely, that Franklin's thought and writings on "industry and frugality" set forth a social philosophy of human flourishing and freedom rooted in social mobility, economic opportunity, and generosity to others. Indeed, Franklin's ideas about economic independence remain as central to American identity as the ideas of political independence inscribed in the founding documents. If Jefferson wrote the Declaration of Independence and Madison crafted the Constitution, then Benjamin Franklin, it might truly be said, invented the American Dream.

FRANKLIN'S THRIFT: A WAY OF LIFE

Franklin is, as one historian has noted, "one of the most massively symbolic figures" in American history.[4] His life and work have been used to exemplify larger themes and ideologies. Over the years, he has been variously portrayed as a noble savage; canny self-promoter; home-spun humorist; scientific genius; cracker-barrel philosopher; bourgeois moralist; secular rationalist; and—yes—a small-minded, penny-pinching protocapitalist. Franklin himself contributed to this symbolizing impulse. He was a subtle, many-sided, shape-shifting figure. As a writer, he adopted many personas, identities, and voices. He had serious things to say, but he often said them in a playful way—favoring the lampoon, the spoof, and the hoax as ways to make his point.

Yet beneath Franklin's changing masks and literary guises are the plain facts of his life. Here, we can begin to see the consistent core of his ideas of thrift—or "industry and frugality," as he more commonly called it.[5] Franklin earned his reputation for thrift the old-fashioned way. He lived it.

Franklin's life can be divided into two parts. Before he became a philosopher-king, he was a colonial tradesman. From his teens to his early forties, he worked as a provincial printer—first as an apprentice in Boston and then as the owner of a printing shop and dry-goods store run out of his house in Philadelphia. During these years, he worked hard and lived simply. Two years after he set up his own business, he was able to pay off all his debts—a remarkable achievement at a time when colonists were beset by chronic currency shortages, overindebtedness, and bankruptcies. He became a substantial creditor, landholder, and land speculator. He was also something of a paper baron. He established eighteen paper mills at one time or another and may have been the largest paper dealer in the English-speaking world.[6]

By the time Franklin was forty-two, he had become a wealthy man. He was able to retire from business for good. In the second half of his life, he left the management of his affairs in the hands of his wife and son-in-law and spent much of the next four decades abroad, pursuing scientific interests, transatlantic friendships, and international diplomacy.

Franklin gave much of the credit for his early business success to his wife, Deborah. Though she brought no dowry into the marriage, she enriched the family in other ways. She proved a highly competent manager of the Franklin enterprises. She ran the general store connected to the printing shop. She kept accounts, dealt with suppliers, and expanded the inventory. She helped with the printing business as well, folding and stitching pamphlets and buying "old Linen rags for the Papermakers." She sold a homemade "itch cream." She managed the Post Office. In addition, she ran the household, kept house without servants, and lived within the family's means. For her contributions, Franklin remained deeply grateful: "Frugality is an enriching Virtue, a Virtue I could never acquire in myself," he later admitted, "but I was lucky enough to find it in a Wife who thereby became a fortune to me."[7]

Another source of Franklin's success was his ability to win the support of powerful patrons. In the eighteenth century, ambitious but obscure young men needed sponsors and patrons to help them get ahead in the world. Franklin got such help from colonial governors and influential public officials who paved the way to profitable government printing contracts. In 1737, he became the postmaster for Pennsylvania. This office gave him free use of the mails, and as a consequence he was able to boost the circulation of his newspaper, the *Pennsylvania Gazette*. Later on, he was appointed the official government printer for Pennsylvania, New Jersey, and Delaware, which gave him the steady business of printing paper money, state documents, laws, and treaties.

Finally, Franklin produced an international best seller. He published *Poor Richard's Almanack* for the twenty-five years between 1732–1757. This annual compendium of useful information and moral instruction sold ten thousand copies a year or the equivalent of fifteen million copies today—an astonishing record for a publication produced in a colonial backwater. Even more impressively, *The Way to Wealth*, his collection of more than one hundred of Poor Richard's sayings on "industry and frugality," was a hit in France. It first appeared in a Parisian edition in 1777 as *The Science of Good Richard, or The Easy Way to Pay Taxes*, and the luxury-loving French scooped it up for the thrifty price of four sous.[8]

Once relieved of the necessity of making money, Franklin was happy to be done with "the little cares and fatigues of business." He could have made a second or third fortune if he had taken out patents on his inventions. But he chose to keep these inventions in the public domain. He paid for public projects out of his own fortune.[9] He was generous to friends, family, and even strangers. He gave money to grandchildren, nieces, nephews, and especially to his perpetually straitened sister, Jane Mecom, to help them start businesses of their own. He left much of his fortune to philanthropic causes, including an endowment to provide start-up loans for worthy young married tradesmen.

If Franklin was not obsessed with making money, neither was he intent on hoarding it. He enjoyed spending what he had made. He built a big house. He bought a farm in New Jersey. He drove around in a fancy carriage. He boasted a well-stocked wine cellar. He sent his wife "crate upon crate of quality goods from London." He ate well. He relaxed his work regimen. Once lean, he grew fat. Once an early riser, he took to getting up at ten or eleven. Once a believer in vigorous daily exercise, he later found it hard to move a muscle.

His indolent habits drove the famously industrious John Adams absolutely crazy. During their mutual diplomatic service in France, Adams complained that Franklin rarely did any work. The man who, as Poor Richard, urged "Up, sluggard," was becoming a sluggard himself! He breakfasted late, spent his day entertaining visitors, never turned down an invitation to "dine abroad," and, after dinner, went to plays and then on to play chess with the ladies. In such "Agreable and important Occupations and Amusements," Adams fumed, he "spent his afternoons and evenings and came home at all hours from Nine to twelve O'clock at night."[10] (To be fair, Franklin was in his seventies, suffering from gout and kidney stones—and could be forgiven for taking it easy.)

Perhaps Adams did not fully appreciate, as Franklin did, that tardiness was an art form in France.[11] Or perhaps Adams, who admired Franklin for his public advocacy of "industry and frugality," was disappointed by the elder statesman's easy abandonment of these republican disciplines. Perhaps Adams, like many of Franklin's later critics, saw his lapse into laziness as hypocrisy. If so, he misread Franklin's notions of "industry and frugality." Franklin never thought of these linked practices as ends in themselves. Rather, he saw them as a means to an end. For Franklin, the practice of "industry and frugality" was the simple, natural road to freedom.

A PATHWAY TO ECONOMIC FREEDOM

Like other founders, Franklin was committed to the struggle for American independence. But his vision of freedom did not begin with political independence. It began with economic independence. Long before he joined the revolutionary cause, he was charting the path to economic independence for the vast population of "middling" Americans who were not born to wealth or privilege.

Franklin himself came from the middling ranks. He had none of the traditional advantages of aristocratic birth, upscale marriage, or inherited wealth as steppingstones to future distinction or success. His family was of modest means. His father made candles for a living. His parents could not afford to send him to school for more than two years. Like his fourteen older siblings, he had to learn a trade and make his own way in the world.[12]

Although Franklin's genius clearly accounted for much of his greatness, he never attributed his success to his natural gifts and talents. Indeed, he did not see himself as a special case. He believed that anyone who came from middling ranks could gain wealth by working hard, living simply, saving more than they spend, and diligently pursuing useful knowledge.

Franklin saw economic freedom as freedom from the servitude of debt. In eighteenth-century America, indebtedness was a widespread fact of life. Nearly everyone had to borrow money in order to make a living. Farmers needed credit in order to plant their crops. Merchants needed credit from wholesalers to stock their shelves. And, of course, consumers needed credit to buy merchants' goods. Merchants in New England, Pennsylvania, and Chesapeake colonies often sold as much as 80–90 percent of their goods on credit.[13]

Moreover, the colonies were locked into a highly interdependent system of commercial relationships that depended on credit. The upside was the expanding opportunities to trade and buy. The downside was greater exposure to the risks and penalties of overindebtedness. And in colonial America, the penalties for overindebtedness were incredibly harsh. Bankruptcy laws at the time allowed impatient creditors to demand instant payment in cash—a near impossibility in a cash-poor economy. Debtors who could not cough up the money on demand often went to prison, where they were thrown in with common criminals.

Even worse, insolvents were treated more severely than convicted felons. The state paid for the upkeep of convicts but not of insolvents. Debtors or their families had to pay for their own food, clothing, and rent. Oftentimes, mothers or wives had to beg or borrow money to provide for even the most minimal comforts for an imprisoned family member. In addition, a debtor's term of imprisonment was not fixed. Even the post-Revolutionary reform of the criminal codes did not deal with insolvents. They were the "only prisoners who did not know when or how or even if they would be freed."[14]

Franklin was not against the borrowing or lending of money. On the contrary, he firmly believed in the "prolific, generating" nature of money. As he often noted in *Advice to a Young Tradesman*, money put out in loans would yield more money in return: "Five shillings turned is six, turned again is seven and three-pence, and so on till it becomes an hundred pounds."[15] Nonetheless, he saw chronic indebtedness as a form of enslavement. Franklin, it should be remembered, had a deep, almost instinctive, hatred of servitude. As a young man, he rebelled against the stern strictures of Calvinism. He defied his father. He broke his apprenticeship to his brother. He challenged the Boston establishment. He fled his family in Boston for a life among strangers in Philadelphia.

For him, owing money was yet another limitation on human freedom. Indebtedness was like serving a term of indenture—it bound one over to another person for years. "When you run into debt," he wrote in *The Way to Wealth*, "you give another power over your liberty." And again: "Your creditor has authority to deprive you of your liberty by confining you in gaol for life, or to sell you for a servant if you should not be able to pay him." And yet again: "The Borrower is a Slave to the Lender, and the Debtor to the Creditor."[16]

He saw overindebtedness as morally debilitating as well as personally constraining. It could lead to lies, cheating, and fraud: "If you cannot pay at the Time, you will be ashamed to see your Creditor; you will be in Fear when you speak to him; you will make poor pitiful sneaking Excuses, and by Degrees come to lose your Veracity, and sink into base downright lying." Engaging in such behavior, the chronically insolvent also risked losing the respect of others, and loss of reputation could be irreparable. As Poor Richard said, "Glass, China, and Reputation are easily crack'd and never well-mended" (1750).

Reputation mattered in colonial society. In England, some four hundred titled and wealthy families made up the landed aristocracy. In colonial America, such strict class divisions did not exist. Nor did colonists have an ancient system of social rules that established one's place and rank in the society. There was no hereditary aristocracy, no titles, no peerage. Nor was it easy to know who could be trusted in an immigrant society where strangers arrived every day. In America, therefore, one's reputation, like one's livelihood, was not a fixed or inherited status. It had to be earned.

How, then, could one gain a reputation for trust and honesty? For Franklin, it required behaving in ways that inspired social confidence and public trust. People had to see evidence of trustworthiness in one's conduct. In commerce, that meant exhibiting a work ethic of "visible diligence"—getting up early, spending time productively, and avoiding the temptations of the alehouse. Such industrious behavior would give observers reason to believe that your business would not fold overnight, that you would pay your suppliers, and that you would be honest in your business dealings. "In order to secure my Credit and Character of A Tradesman," Franklin wrote in the *Autobiography*, "I took care not only to be in Reality Industrious and frugal, but to avoid all Appearances to the Contrary. I drest plainly; I was seen at no places of idle diversion; . . . and to show that I was not above my business, I sometimes brought home the paper I purchas'd at the stores thro' the streets on a wheelbarrow."[17]

Too, creditors would be more willing to extend loans to a hard worker than to a drinker or sluggard. As the historian T. H. Breen notes, in an insecure commercial environment, "appearances could determine a merchant's solvency. The kinds of values most often associated with the Protestant ethic—thrift, diligence, honesty and modesty—were forced on the colonial shopkeeper as a condition of doing business."[18]

In *Advice to a Young Tradesman*, Franklin also underscored the importance of appearances in securing credit: "The sound of your Hammer at Five in the Morning or Nine at Night, heard by a Creditor, makes him easy six months longer. But if he sees you at a Billiard Table, or hears your Voice at a Tavern, when you should be at Work, he sends for his Money the next Day. . . . It shews, besides that you are mindful of what you owe; it makes you appear a careful as well as an honest Man; and that still encreases your Credit."[19]

If Franklin saw "industry and frugality" as a commercial value, he believed equally that it was a household—and especially a wifely— virtue. Raised in the Puritan tradition, Franklin seldom thought of individuals as freestanding social or economic actors. He envisioned the household as the primary unit of society and marriage as the fundamental economic partnership. Thus, he focused on the role of wives as promoting industry and frugality in domestic life: "I and thousands more know very well that we could never thrive 'til we were married. What we get, the Women save."[20] And to his sister Jane on his son's choice of a bride, he commented, "If she does not bring a fortune, she will help to make one. Industry, frugality and prudent economy in a wife are . . . in their effects a fortune."[21]

Franklin did not leave the practice of thrift entirely up to wives, however. In many of his letters and essays, he addressed himself to husbands and fathers. In eighteenth-century America, apprentices were not allowed to marry because they were not yet prepared to become productive workers and independent householders. For men, therefore, marriage carried with it the responsibility for supporting a household. Franklin had stern advice for any young man who wanted to marry before he had the means to "undertake the expense of a family." This included his future son-in-law, Richard Bache. Franklin had heard rumors that Bache was a fortune hunter; worse, Bache had gotten deeply into debt, due to an early business failure. In a letter to Bache, Franklin made his disapproval abundantly clear: "I am obliged to you for the regard and preference you express for my child and wish you all prosperity; but unless you can convince her friends of the probability of your being able to maintain her properly, I hope you will not persist in a proceeding that may be attended with ruinous consequences to you both."[22] (Sally Franklin married Bache a month later.)

However, Franklin's notion of economic independence was not merely the negative freedom from overindebtedness. Economic independence gave one the freedom to do good and to serve others. For Franklin, the ultimate reward for industry and frugality was not more work or more money but more free time. This was the side of Franklin's thrift that John Adams failed to understand. Franklin believed that leisure and pleasure were the rewards for hard work and frugal living. If a man worked like a dog, he might eventually live like a gentleman.

At the same time, Franklin's conception of the life of a gentleman was dramatically different from the life of the eighteenth-century English gentleman. Born into wealth and property, the prototypical English gentleman had no real work to do and lots of time to waste. So he cultivated a life of idleness, spending time in fox hunting, card play-ing, dancing, womanizing, and traipsing around his estates. As Henry Fielding observed, "to the upper part of mankind, time is an enemy, and (as they themselves often confess) their chief labour is to kill it." Indeed, it was their social duty to do so.[23]

This kind of gentlemanly existence was entirely alien to Franklin. Much as he enjoyed a good time, he never espoused killing time. For Franklin, time, like money, was a resource. If the definition of a gen-tleman meant having leisure time, he thought, then that leisure time should be put to useful purposes. As Poor Richard put it, "A life of leisure and a life of laziness are two things" (1746).

THE PROPER USE OF WEALTH

Upon his retirement as a printer, Franklin looked forward to a life of leisure spent in "philosophical studies and amusements." But, as he recounted in the *Autobiography*, "The publick, now considering me a man of leisure, laid hold of me for their purposes, every part of our civil government, and almost at the same time, imposing some duty on me." Though the call to public service meant sacrifice of his own plan for retirement, there is no evidence that Franklin took on this duty begrudgingly or used it for self-serving ends. For gentlemen like him who were called to public service, he cheerfully proposed one simple rule: "Never ask, never refuse, nor ever resign."

Public service was just one way to put one's good fortune to use. A second way was to give away the fortune itself. Franklin did not believe in inherited wealth. As he saw it, riches passed on through the gen-erations bred habits of idleness, wastefulness, and self-destructiveness. Consequently, he contended that those who gained wealth should use their fortunes for the good of others rather than for themselves or their offspring. Moreover, he thought that "liberality," or what we might call "generosity," offered rewards to the giver as well: according to Poor Richard, "The Liberal are secure alone/For what they frankly give for ever is their own" (1750). And: "When you are good to others, you are best to yourself" (1748).

In his view of the proper uses of wealth, Franklin, writing as Poor Richard, often came close to professing a theology of good works: "What is serving God?," 'Tis doing Good to Man" (1747). In a letter written in 1753 to Joseph Huey, a "zealous Religionist," Franklin elaborated:

> When I am employed in serving others, I do not look upon my self as conferring Favours, but as paying Debts. . . . I can only show my Gratitude for those Mercies from God by a Readiness to help his other Children and my Brethren. For I do not think that Thanks, and Compliments, tho' repeated Weekly, can discharge our real obligations to each other, and much less those to our Creator.[24]

He added that he wished religious faith were more productive of good works—"I mean real good Works, Works of Kindness, Charity, Mercy, and Publick Spirit; not Holiday-Keeping, Sermon-Reading or hearing, performing Church Ceremonies, or making long Prayers, fill'd with Flateries and Compliments, despis'd even by wise Men, and much less capable of pleasing the Deity."[25]

In practice, Franklin's good works aimed at useful ends. He was not inclined to classical Christian acts of charity for the poor and needy. Rather, he belonged to the "teach-a-man-to-fish" school of philanthropy, or, to state it more precisely, he aimed to "teach future generations to fish." In his private giving, Franklin sought to create economic opportunities for worthy young householders. For example, as mentioned previously, he left a substantial fund in his will to provide loans for young, married tradesmen in Boston and Philadelphia. The recipients were required to pay back 5 percent of the principal each year, thus perpetuating the loan fund. By the mid-1820s, some two hundred and fifty Philadelphia craftsmen, from thirty different trades and profession, had taken advantage of Franklin's bequest to better themselves.[26]

THE THRIFT CANON

Franklin began his writing career at the age of fifteen and never again put down his pen. When he died at age eighty-four, he had just published a newspaper article arguing for an end to slavery. (Characteristically, the piece took the form of a hoax and appeared under the pseudonym, *Historicus*.) Over his lifetime, he produced a huge literature—at present filling thirty-eight volumes with still more to come. Yet from this prodigious output, only three works have endured over the centuries: *Poor Richard's Almanack*, *The Way to Wealth* (1757), and the *Autobiography* (1817). These three works—his "thrift canon"—established his popular reputation as the practitioner and exemplar of industry, frugality, and generosity.

Anyone expecting to find a systematic treatment of thrift in these works, however, will be disappointed. Franklin never attempted such a treatment. In the Enlightenment world, there were hedgehogs (thinkers who knew one big thing) and foxes (thinkers who knew many things). Benjamin Franklin was a fox. In Carl Van Doren's famous characterization, Franklin was a "harmonious human multitude," and his three thrift works contain, but do not exhaust, his thought on industry and frugality.

Nor do any of Franklin's three famous works resemble what might be called a treatise on thrift. Franklin was in the marketplace. He had to sell what he wrote. Consequently, he turned to popular literary forms, not learned treatises, to communicate his ideas.

In colonial America, the reading public favored nonfiction over fiction. In part, this preference was due to the lingering influence of Puritanism. Franklin's Puritan forebears saw fiction as threatening to religious piety and the sober contemplation of God's majesty. They tended to be less critical of nonfiction, particularly if it included moral instruction. But the popular preference for nonfiction was also driven by practical concerns. Colonial America was a self-help society, and people craved useful information of all kinds. Indeed, the eighteenth century saw an outpouring of such literature—marriage manuals, tradesmen's guides, bookkeeping and accounting books, codes of commercial conduct, and so forth.

As a young journeyman printer, Franklin had mastered virtually every popular form of nonfiction—the newspaper article, broadside, report, proposal, opinion piece, satire, letter to the editor, humor piece, and "true life" account. In 1732, with the publication of *Poor Richard's Almanack*, he hit upon the ideal literary vehicle. Next to the Bible, the almanac was the most popular and commonly read household publication. Pocket-sized and paper-bound, these annual guides usually appeared in October or November for the following year and set forth a month-by-month calendar of tide and weather forecasts, astrological predictions, medical nostrums, and other useful information.

But the *Poor Richard's Almanack* was not entirely nonfiction. In the inaugural issue, Franklin introduced the fictional character, Richard Saunders, as its putative editor and compiler. An amateur astrologist who described himself as "excessive poor," Poor Richard explains that he is going into the almanac business to appease his wife, Bridget, who wants him to quit his idle stargazing and make some money. In addition to providing useful information on weather, tides, and the sun's rising and setting, Poor Richard proposes to include "moral hints, wise sayings, and maxims of thrift, tending to impress the Benefits arising from Honesty, Sobriety, Industry and Frugality." After this litany, he might have added: but the greatest of these are "industry and frugality." For as Franklin later wrote in the *Autobiography*, Poor Richard's maxims were chiefly chosen to promote "industry and frugality as the means of procuring wealth and thereby securing virtue."[27]

Issue by issue, for two and a half decades, Poor Richard produced memorable sayings: "No man e'er was glorious, who was not laborious" (1734); "Eat to live, not live to eat" (1733); "Hope of gains lessens pain"; "He that waits on Fortune is never sure of Dinner"; "Look before, or you'll find yourself behind" (1735); "Keep thy shop, and thy shop will keep thee" (1735); "He that takes a wife, takes care" (1736); "He that buys by the penny, maintains not only himself, but other people"(1736); "God helps them that help themselves" (1736); "Creditors have better memories than debtors" (1736); "He that would have a short Lent/Let him borrow Money to be repaid at Easter" (1738); "Industry pays debt, while Despair Increaseth them" (1742); "Idleness is the greatest prodigality" (1743); "Rather go to bed supperless/than run in debt for a Breakfast" (1739).

In 1757, Franklin sat down to write a preface to the final edition of *Poor Richard*. At the time, he was languishing on a ship headed for London and facing a looming deadline without any of his notebooks or reference materials. Ever resourceful, he compiled from memory more than a hundred of Poor Richard's most popular sayings on industry and frugality and put them in the mouth of a new character, Father Abraham. The speech of Father Abraham became *The Way to Wealth*, the most widely reprinted of all Franklin's works. By the end of the century, it would appear in at least 145 editions, translated into French, German, Italian, Dutch, Gaelic, and Swedish—and later into Catalan, Chinese, Greek, Hungarian, Welsh, and Russian.[28]

In this famous fable, Father Abraham appears before a crowd gathered at a local auction, or *vendue*, as such sales were called at the time. *Vendues* were popular, but controversial, ways for colonial merchants to get rid of damaged or unsold stock. Consumers liked them because they could get luxury goods at bargain basement prices, but many merchants objected to them as unfair competition. Other critics saw *vendues* as a source of corrupting consumerism, creating appetites for frivolous luxury goods. Father Abraham belonged to this latter school. His speech is an appeal to the crowd to restrain their desire for things they do not need.

> Here you are all got together at this vendue of Fineries and Knicknacks. You call the Goods, but if you do not take Care, they will prove Evils to some of you. . . . Many a one, for the Sake of Finery on the Back, have gone with a hungry Belly, and half starved their Families; Silks and Sattins, Scarlet and Velvets, as Poor Richard says, put out the Kitchen Fire. These are not the Necessaries of Life; they can scarcely be called

Conveniencies, and yet only because they look pretty, how many want to have them.[29]

Father Abraham sputters on: "What Madness must it be to run into Debt for these Superfluities!"[30]

When Franklin put Poor Richard's sayings in the mouth of a biblical Abraham, he had his tongue firmly in his cheek. The patriarch's wise advice goes completely unheeded by the crowd. They listened, "approved the Doctrine, and immediately practiced the contrary, as if it were a common sermon." His satirical intent was even plainer when he called Father Abraham's speech a "sermon." Franklin hated sermonizing and other religious speechifying.

Yet Franklin was indebted to the sermon. In *Poor Richard* and *The Way to Wealth*, he borrowed from the pulpit tradition of parables, paradoxes, and cautionary stories. At the same time, though, he eliminated the religious message. His text was not scripture but the "world's treasury" of folk sayings. His goal was not salvation but self-improvement. And his rhetorical strategy was not designed to provoke fear and trembling but to get a good laugh. He cloaked his moral instruction in humor of every kind, ranging from satire, spoof, impersonation, joke, burlesque, quip, witticism, pun, and sheer nonsense. Ever the improviser and improver, Franklin added his own touches, often rewriting the sayings to make them crisper and funnier.

But behind the jokiness and even occasional impiety, Franklin had a serious purpose. He had a vision for a new kind of social order based on the virtues of the "middling" ranks. The widespread practice of Franklin's thrift was central to realizing this vision.

THRIFT FOR A MIDDLING SOCIETY

Franklin's long sojourn in France gave him a chance to compare American and European society from his perch on the other side of the Atlantic. Much as he savored the pleasures and refinements of Old World society, he was nonetheless disturbed by the gulf between rich and poor. (Thomas Jefferson and John Adams were similarly distressed by the sight of so many destitute people living on the streets of London and Paris.) He blamed the system of passing wealth, title, and privilege onto future generations for this division between the idle rich and the desperate poor.

Franklin saw such social divisions as vicious and demoralizing for both rich and poor. Neither class, he believed, was capable of behaving virtuously. Both lived for the pleasures of the moment—the rich because they had too much money and the poor because they had too little. "The poor have little, beggars none, the rich too much, enough not one," in the words of Poor Richard (1733). Both rich and poor were given to idleness and profligacy. Both were captive to their own greedy desires. For rich and poor alike, as Poor Richard observed, "The restless desire of getting is added to the cruel fear of losing." As Stacy Schiff writes, America "stood as a corrective to what Franklin described as the two most detrimental of European prejudices: the conviction that useful labor was disgraceful and that estates perpetuated families."[31]

Thus, people in the "middling ranks" offered the best hope for a virtuous society. Tradesmen, farmers, shopkeepers, printers, bricklayers, and the like were engaged in productive work, and productive work fostered the habit of industry. In Franklin's view, industry was not merely work in the sense of exertion in the performance of a task. Rather, industry was a particular disposition toward work. To be industrious was to manage one's time efficiently, to demonstrate diligence and steadiness in workaday routines, and to have faith that hard work and long hours would yield material rewards commensurate with effort.

Especially important was the productive use of time. As Poor Richard explained, "The Industrious know how to employ every Piece of Time to real Advantage in their different Professions: And he that is prodigal of his Hours is, in effect, a Squanderer of Money" (1751). To waste time was, in fact, far worse than losing money. "Money lost may be found," Poor Richard went on, "but the Treasure of Time once lost, can never be recovered" (1751). Again and again, Poor Richard insists on the advantages of conserving time by early rising: "The sleeping fox catches no Poultry, Up! Up!" (1743); "He that riseth late must trot all Day, and shall scarce overtake his Business at Night" (1742); "He would be beforehand in the World, must be beforehand with his Business" (1749). (As a young printer, Franklin was a "morning person," and no doubt his near obsession with early rising drew upon his own experience. Indeed, Franklin may be responsible for the sense of moral superiority among "morning people" even to this day.)

With Poor Richard's repeated injunctions on time-thrift, Franklin also drew an implicit distinction between the idleness of the leisured class and the busyness of the trading class. The highborn aristocrat slept late, dawdled over cards in the afternoon, and drank and caroused into the night. By contrast, the tradesman was up at dawn, opened his shop early, imbibed water instead of wine at lunch, and spent his evenings in the pursuit of useful knowledge.

Still, according to Franklin, the practice of industry alone was not enough to foster virtue. It had to be paired with the practice of frugality. The word comes from the Latin *fruge* for "fruit," and Franklin used *frugality* in the sense of careful stewardship of the fruits of one's labor. (He called his early earnings "first fruits.") Thus, if industry produced abundance, Franklin thought, frugality guided its use. As Poor Richard put it, "Industry's bounteous Hand may Plenty bring, But wanting Frugal Care, twill soon take away . . ." (1749).

By careful use and stewardship, Franklin wrote, small gains over time would accumulate and grow. "Weigh every small Expence, and nothing waste, Farthings long sav'd, amount to Pounds at last" (1749). Frugality also provided the chief means of extending wealth over time. Saving and conserving meant that one's children and grandchildren would be educated and prepared for earning their own living. Thus, riches would not be squandered in a single generation but would continue to multiply into future generations.

In short, Franklin's idea of frugality was expansive rather than constrictive. It was based on vision of abundance rather than scarcity, of fertility rather than sterility. It reflected Franklin's sense of the possibilities for a new kind of society. But, as he also made clear, this new society could only flourish in a spacious and bountiful land where one's work and savings would, in fact, bear fruit.

THE WAY TO WEALTH IN AMERICA, OR WHY SPOILED ARISTOCRATS SHOULD STAY IN EUROPE

Poor Richard's Almanack and *The Way to Wealth* were compilations of popular adages on thrift for an eighteenth-century American readership. Although both asserted the value of industry and frugality, neither work took pains to explain in detail how these linked values produced wealth. As it happens, however, Franklin did attempt such an explanation in another, less well-known, work. He wrote the piece entitled "Information to Those Who Would Remove to America" when he was in France in 1783. It was published in England and Ireland in that year and then, in the following two years, came out in French, Italian, and German translations.[32]

Like much of Franklin's writing, "Information" was not a theoretical treatment of his views. It was a journalistic response to a practical problem. During his eight years in France, Franklin was continually besieged with requests for money, favors, and help from people all over Europe who wanted to immigrate to America. Many of these petitioners were dreamers, bankrupts, adventurers, and property-less younger sons of noble lineage who wanted to get rich quick in the New World. Their heads were filled with "wild imaginations" and schemes: some thought that the Congress would pay for their passage and provide them with "land gratis, negroes to work for them, utensils of husbandry, and stocks of cattle"; others believed that they would be given high government and military offices by virtue of their aristocratic birth. Still others had the idea that "Americans are so ignorant of *belle-lettres*, fine arts, etc., that they would shower riches on those who possessed such talents."[33]

Such aspiring emigrants, Franklin later observed in his essay, "appear to have formed, through ignorance, mistaken ideas and expectations as to what is to be obtained through their removal to America." To dissuade the aristocratic riffraff from emigrating, or as he more tactfully put it, "to prevent inconvenient, expensive and fruitless voyages of improper persons," he set out to provide a more accurate picture of life and prospects in the New World.

In America, he explained, there are "few people as miserable as the poor in Europe and few that in Europe would be called rich . . . few great proprietors of the soil and few tenants . . . few rich enough to live idly upon their rents . . . or to pay the highest prices given in Europe for painting, statues, architecture, and other works of art that are more curious than useful." More pointedly, he continued, "Birth in Europe has value, but it is a commodity that cannot be carried to a worse market than that of America, where people do not inquire concerning a stranger: What is he? But "What can he do?"[34]

Thus, Franklin noted, his young nation was looking for people who knew how to make things and how to grow things: farmers, "laboring men," artisans, and apprentices with useful skills and the willingness to apply themselves to their trades. Most of all, newcomers must "work and be industrious to live." America, he wrote, is the land of labor.

But it was not simply the presence of a large population of laboring people that accounted for the crucial difference between the Old and New World, according to Franklin. It was the fact that America's natural wealth rewarded productive labor. His country's advantages included "vast forests, still void of inhabitants" and "hundreds of acres of fertile soil full of wood." Large tracts of empty land provided opportunities for young people to marry, have many children, and provide "ample fortunes" for their offspring. Indeed, in an earlier essay, *Observations Concerning the Increase of Mankind* (1751), Franklin argued that early marriages would contribute to a doubling of the population every twenty years.[35]

Such conditions were unique to America, Franklin believed. In Europe, the trades were overcrowded, land scarce, and opportunity limited. Poor people might toil their entire life and never realize the fruits of their labor. Further, European societies consumed too many useless things, creating want and misery for those whose livelihood depended on satisfying the taste for luxuries. In America, on the other hand, poor people could get ahead: "They begin first as servants or journeymen; and if they are sober, industrious and frugal, they soon become masters, establish themselves in business, marry, raise families and become respectable citizens. Moreover, everyone is welcome, because there is room enough for them all . . . and every one will enjoy security from the profits of his industry."[36]

Because of such advantages, Franklin believed, fruitfulness multiplied itself many times over: in the fertile yield of the soil, in the "swift progress of population," in the expansion of opportunities for useful work, in the accumulation of material wealth, in improved lives for offspring, and in the achievement of "cheerful leisure." A frugal life, in short, was a fruitful life with "comfortable provision for age and for children" for those who would remove to America.

THRIFT FOR A DEMOCRATIC SOCIETY

During his own lifetime, Franklin's reputation rested mainly on the great accomplishments of the second half of his life. He was known as Dr. Franklin, international scientist, statesman, and savant. His public portraits feature a bespectacled scholar surrounded by the symbols of his intellectual pursuits—inkwells, books, globes—and with a bolt of lighting illuminating his study.

But in the early decades of the nineteenth century, Franklin's image and reputation changed. He became the national (and international) exponent and exemplar of thrift. The *Autobiography*, which began to appear in excerpts in 1794 and then in a complete American edition in 1817, helped to create this new image.[37] Some editions also included samplings from Poor Richard's sayings and *The Way to Wealth*.

Written episodically over many years and still unfinished at the time of his death, the *Autobiography* stopped short of a full account of Franklin's life. The central focus was on his early years as a printer and successful tradesman. As a consequence, the figure that emerged from the *Autobiography* was "Ben Franklin," the enterprising young man with the wheelbarrow. His portraiture changed accordingly.

Woodcuts and illustrations portray him as a young man in a leather apron, tending his printing press, trundling his barrow through the streets of Philadelphia.

Franklin's story appealed to a democratizing nation. During the nineteenth century, as Franklin had predicted, the "middling" population of tradesmen, artisans, farmers, and mechanics increased. At the same time, those in the "middling ranks" were turning to self-improvement and self-education as the tradition of worker education through apprenticeships and craft organizations began to wane.[38]

Aspiring young men could identify with the story of the printer who "emerged from poverty and obscurity to a state of affluence and some degree of reputation in the world." The literary form of the *Autobiography*, as well as its content, made it highly relevant to nineteenth century workingmen. Cast as a letter of paternal advice to a son—a literary genre earlier popularized by such figures as Daniel Defoe and Lord Chesterfield—the *Autobiography* could be read not only as the story of an eminent man's life but also as a practical guide to everyman's life.

The *Autobiography* remained hugely influential throughout the nineteenth and much of the twentieth century. It inspired other ambitious young men to follow Franklin's example. Jared Sparks, the editor of Franklin's works and president of Harvard University, read the *Autobiography* as a young man and later remembered, "It was this book that first roused my mental energies. . . . It promoted me to resolutions, and gave me strength to adhere to them. . . . It taught me that circumstances have not a sovereign control over the mind."[39]

Through his writings and reputation, Franklin also became the hero of a working class. As early as Independence Day, 1795, the General Society of Mechanics and Tradesmen of New York, composed of both masters and journeymen, toasted the "memory of our late brother mechanic, Benjamin Franklin: "May his bright example convince mankind that in this land of freedom and equality, talents joined to frugality and virtue may justly aspire to the first offices of government."

Franklin's image as a workingman was particularly cherished by printers, who claimed him as their patron saint. In 1799, a group of printers founded the Franklin Typographical Society of Journeymen Printers. In 1822, another Franklin Typographical Society was established in Boston, and in 1844, a similar organization appeared in New York.[40] Throughout the century, printers held Franklin festivals to celebrate his birthday—and to proclaim, "Once a printer, always a printer, and never ashamed of the craft."[41]

Indeed, the printers' refrain reflected Franklin's larger influence in shaping the social identity and confidence of the "middling sort." With his life as a model, they were able to see themselves as the producers of goods and, through their productive enterprises, as the creators of a good life for themselves and their offspring. In their celebration of productive labor, as historian Gordon S. Wood observes, "These middling working people came to dominate nineteenth-century northern American culture and society to a degree not duplicated elsewhere in the Atlantic world."[42]

PART TWO

Thrift after Franklin
Institutions and Movements

Chapter 2

U.S. Mutual Savings Banks and the "Savings Bank Idea"

The Virtue of Thrift as an Institutional Value

Sorcha Brophy-Warren

"In their beginnings savings banks were merely voluntary associations of public-spirited and philanthropically inclined persons."[1]

LOFTY INTENTIONS

THE INSTITUTION MOST FREQUENTLY IDENTIFIED as the first modern savings bank was the "Savings and Friendly Society" organized by the Reverend Henry Duncan in 1810, in Ruthwell, Scotland. Distressed by the money "thrown away by young women on dress unsuitable to their state, and by young men at the ale house, for no other reason than that they have no safe place for laying up their surplus earnings," Duncan established the small bank to encourage his working class congregation to develop thrift.[2] Whether the Savings and Friendly Society was the first "true" savings bank is certainly debated, but many of the first incorporated savings banks in the United States cite the Ruthwell bank as their model.[3] Whatever the particular institution that served as the model, it was European voluntary organizations and "friendly societies" that provided the inspiration for their state-incorporated American counterparts.[4] These United States banks differed from

European institutions in that they were tied to the state through incorporation since the beginning.[5]

The first U.S. savings banks specifically designed to foster the practice of savings were *mutual* savings banks. The first incorporated U.S. mutual savings bank was the Provident Institution for Savings in Boston. Its December 1816 charter was the first government legislation in the world to safeguard savings banks.[6] Within a few years, mutual savings banks were started in New York, Pennsylvania, Connecticut, Rhode Island, and Maryland, and it was not long before the "movement" swept across all of New England and down through the eastern states.[7] Americans were already familiar with commercial banking, but these new savings institutions were envisioned with a different societal function—they were thought of as philanthropic endeavors, designed to uplift the poor and working classes by encouraging individuals to save. The exclusive function of these banks was to protect deposits, make limited secure investments, and provide depositors with interest. Unlike commercial banks, these new savings banks had no stockholders; the entirety of profits beyond the upkeep of the bank belonged to the depositors of the mutual savings bank. These savings banks prioritized secure investments over providing their depositors with high interest rates; they were not permitted to invest in "speculation, or money-making in a business sense."[8] The mutual savings bank did not have the authority to conduct the business of the commercial bank; it could not initially offer loans or allow customers to draw checks on the bank. Mutual savings bankers generated profits by investing in government securities and, later, in high-grade bonds, preferred stocks, and low-risk collateralized lending.[9] By the time that mutual savings banks had been around for a few generations, there existed a "mutual savings bank spirit"—a generally acknowledged commitment to compliance with state law, conservative investments, and remaining "true to savings bank traditions."[10] These banks relished the state-instituted limits that distinguished them from other types of banks. Because the banks' trustees thought of the institution as a philanthropic endeavor and because they had no financial stake in the bank, there was little temptation to test the limits of the law.

The savings bank was romanticized by its proponents as an institution with tremendous potential to teach virtue to society. It was glorified as wholly unselfish, and its relationship with its depositors was proclaimed to be one of dependability and security.[11] Rhetoric used by savings bankers to describe their establishments stressed the dissemblance of mutual savings banks to commercial banks and business enterprises.[12] Bankers committed to the institutions heralded the mutual savings bank for serving as a "unique exception to the rule, laid down by the economists, that the desire for personal profit is the one effective principle, for making business enterprise succeed."[13] "I like to think of savings banks, not in terms of dollars and cents, but in terms of widows and orphans cared for, in terms of poor and helpless people helped and guided," explained William E. Knox, the comptroller of the Bowery Savings Bank in New York City.[14]

Mutual savings banks arose during an era characterized by the great number of newly formed charitable organizations "by which the higher ranks can give aid to the lower."[15] These banks were driven by the same mission, though it was not "charity" per se in which these philanthropists were interested. Savings bank advocates throughout this period were careful to make the distinction between *philanthropic* and *charitable* organizations because it was on this distinction that the identity of the institution rested. Proponents of savings banks organized the institutions because they believed in their ability to educate the poor to help themselves, rather than rely on the assistance of others. To refer to the savings bank as a "charitable" establishment undermined this goal. Advocates of savings banks saw the institution as fulfilling a societal role morally superior to that of the charitable organization. The charitable patron was she who "with skirts held high, walk[s] once a week through the street with notebook in hand, and smoked glasses on her nose."[16] She gives alms generously to the poor, but this "indiscriminate relief" actually serves to train the poor "to be improvident, and to look for money as a reward of their thoughtlessness," thus "hold[ing] the poor man down instead of lifting him up."[17] The savings bank philanthropist, on the other hand, acts in the true interest of the poor because he offers to them the dignity that comes from financial stability and participation in the capitalist marketplace. As such, savings bank depositors were not the recipients of charity but shareholders. Any profit was something they had earned through their own industry. "Each depositor bears his share of the necessary expense of the bank, and the trustees no more consider their work charitable than is the work of citizens who, for example, serve on school boards."[18]

These trustees and boards of investment thought of the bank as a philanthropic rather than business opportunity. They were well-known "public-spirited men"; they managed the savings banks as unsalaried "acts of benevolence."[19] Their personal "success" (community standing, financial gain) was articulated as the result of hard work—the same sort of commitment that would ensure the success of the savings bank. They were heralded as morally upright and trustworthy and motivated by a desire to do good and improve the reputation of the bank. These officials were patriotic, stable, and progressive, and they believed the uplift of their depositors to be their primary responsibility.[20] William E. Knox said:

> Your savings bank trustee is your true altruist. He is actuated by a desire to serve his community in a practical way, and to the conduct of the business of the bank he brings the equipment of brains and energy that has given him his personal success. . . . He carries with him into his work a sense of his stewardship, a realization of his moral obligation, a knowledge that his neighbors and associates in the community have entrusted to his keeping, not only their savings, but their hopes for the future. With such a sense of his obligation strong upon him, is it any wonder that he is jealous of the good name of his bank that he uses every means to foster its interests, that he labors always with the welfare of the depositor, and that only, in view?[21]

Because these trustees received no fiscal compensation for their efforts, they were "absolutely disinterested in performing their tedious task."[22] As a result, it was argued, the risk of bank mismanagement was greatly reduced, and the motives of the bankers were aligned with the best interests of depositors.[23]

The language used to speak of the savings bank, its trustees, and the social campaign was incredibly lofty, as savings bankers saw much at stake in accurately communicating what was termed the "Savings Bank idea."[24] This complex "idea" was made up of principles about how to interact ethically with the material world, as well as convictions about social policy and the stakes of institutional communication and education. Often, it was this set of values rather than a physical institution that these bankers spoke of when they praised "the savings bank." These men saw their institutions as the ultimate demonstration of the validity of the thrift habit; through the savings bank, the depositor would see the rewards that the habit provided and continue to practice thrift.

The central thrust of the "savings bank idea" was a strong commitment to individualism, a cultural value that has manifested itself in myriad ways throughout U.S. history. Mutual savings banks (MSB) were instituted to encourage individuals to take initiative and attain financial independence through self-help. The language used by MSBs to encourage this self-motivated behavior demonstrates the enigmatic relationship between the collective and the individual that is at the heart of the American national consciousness. These banks appealed to both the self-interest of the individual and shared societal values in making a case for the importance of the institution. Savings banks arose in an era when "fraternalism" played a huge role in the collective identity of Americans. Throughout the nineteenth century, and well into the twentieth, it is estimated that 50 percent of U.S. people were members of fraternal organizations.[25] Savings banks appealed to this fraternal spirit in promoting the "mutual" concept. Savings banking was a cooperative social cause that "sister institution[s]" engaged in together, rather than a business wherein different corporations competed against one another.[26] The name itself suggested a collective endeavor—it was

the pooling of (small) funds that made investment possible and provided for mutual interests. Proclaimed American Bankers Association
officer William Kniffen in his history of savings banking,

> Here the widow with her mite or with her dowry; the legatee
> with his inheritance; the worker saving for a home; the youth
> struggling for an education; the saver laying aside for old age;
> the miser with his hoard, pool their savings, and it becomes a
> common fund with an uncommon power. . . .[27]

Despite the camaraderie between depositors alluded to in Kniffen's
statement, the mutual savings idea was communicated to potential
depositors as a decisively individual-oriented concept. In his exposition
on British friendly societies, historian J. Frome Wilkinson dismissed
the savings bank as an overly individualistic enterprise:

> Here the person who is desirous of making some provisions
> against the "ills that flesh is heir to" depends on his own
> resources—stands or falls alone; it is no matter to him how
> many other depositors make use of his Bank; it makes no dif-
> ference to him what provision others have made or not made.
> He puts his own savings in, and he draws his own savings out,
> and the amount of his deposit is a secret between himself and
> the Bank.[28]

Indeed, the mutual idea was based on the importance of the depositor's
"depend[ing] on his own resources." What was "mutual" was the equal
benefit that individual depositors received from the institution.[29] But it
was the individual who was rewarded for his or her own thriftiness.[30]

As with all cultural ideologies, individualism is entangled with other
societal values. In their best-selling diagnosis of the social ecology of
U.S. culture, *Habits of the Heart*, sociologist Robert Bellah and his
coauthors explore the history of individualism in America. Bellah and
colleagues argue that individualism has been sustained as a viable outlook in the United States only because of its connectedness to "more
generous moral understandings" like religious and civic values.[31] The

savings bank idea demonstrated this connectedness—advocates articulated that participation in the bank was both an opportunity to provide for one's physical needs and an opportunity to fulfill the shared moral responsibility to create a good society. Behind the savings bank idea was the conviction that saving provides access to lasting, rather than temporary, pleasure and that the act of self-denial itself was morally superior to extravagance. The busy ants who stored up enough food for the winter triumphed over the improvident grasshopper not only because they were better supplied when harsh weather arrived but also because they could find satisfaction in their self-sufficiency and independence. The grasshopper, on the other hand, was not only hungry but also disgraced by his laziness and his need to rely on the charity of others.[32] In the same way, the savings banks nurtured discipline, a virtue of both the American religious and civic traditions, in depositors.

The savings bank was intended as a didactic institution; it was thought that these banks would demonstrate to the poor and working classes the great rewards that a disciplined lifestyle of thrift would provide. The institutors of the Bank for Savings, the oldest bank in New York, stated their aim as to "promot[e] among [the laboring poor] a spirit of independence, economy and industry."[33] Proponents of thrift institutions asserted, "The way to encourage thrift was to hold out the certainty that the results of thrift and self-denial would be safely held against the time of need."[34] Because thrift was so rewarding, the practitioner would be motivated to further thriftiness.[35] Though the thrift advocated by savings banks was primarily fiscal, the institution endeavored to communicate that thrift was a lifestyle. It was a holistic ideology that meant "*administration* of a house; its stewardship; spending or saving, whether money or time, or anything else, to the best possible advantage."[36] Savings bank philanthropists intended to teach the public "broader thrift," an ideology that went far beyond the mere saving of money.[37] It was not only the saving of finances that the institution of the savings bank was believed to teach, but the practice of thrift in other areas of life.[38] J. H. Thiry, the founder of the U.S. school savings bank system, stated the connection between the skills taught in the bank and the virtues needed in life this way: "[A]ll virtues require self-control and husbanding of strength and resources, and these things invariably lead to thrift. The savings of time, of strength, of health, of intellectual force, of moral integrity, are all allied to the saving of money."[39] The savings bank, then, was the primary yardstick by which the thriftiness of a people might be measured. "Like the delicate instrument that records the slightest vibration of the earth's surface, the bank records the ebb and flow of humanity as measured in dollars and cents."[40]

This lifestyle, or "thrift habit," was believed to be a discipline developed through training. Concurrently, it was believed that the improvidence of the masses was a result of a lack of education in the virtue of savings. "If the history of the human derelicts that drift around our cities, like the flotsam and jetsam of the ocean, were unfolded, it would be found that their present condition is largely due to poor training," stated William Kniffen.[41] The thrift mentality of these nineteenth- and early twentieth-century bankers demonstrates very particular anthropological and religious commitments—ideas about human sin and potential were wedded to a presumed connection between education and wealth, poverty, and improvidence. Savings-bank advocates both affirmed that the thrift habit was "heaven born," or innate, and that man, if left to his own devices, was improvident.[42] Behind the idea that the thrift habit must be trained was a staunch belief that sinfulness was the natural state of man. Despite the innate presence of the thrift habit, it must be awakened.[43] The role of the savings bank was to orient individuals properly, training them to value lasting worth. It is only then "that there is a force sufficient to hold in check the spendthrift proclivities."[44]

When Alexis de Tocqueville visited the United States in the 1830s, he used the term *individualism* to identify the complex dynamic of impulses that motivated the people he observed—the quest for the better life and the value of independence and self-reliance as virtues unto themselves.[45] Tocqueville was astounded by "the longing to acquire well-being" that he observed in Americans of vastly different socioeconomic means; because democracy made ascent (and descent) on

the socioeconomic ladder a possibility for all, Americans were capti-
vated by the desire to attain and maintain wealth.[46] The commitments
that Tocqueville identified in American citizens have been a part of
the American consciousness for four hundred years; they are the ideas
that make up the "American Dream." The American Dream is perhaps
the most easily identified of all American cultural myths—and perhaps
the most pervasive.[47] Savings banks, as did other cultural institutions,
asserted that the better life was possible—and that individuals were
responsible for bringing this about through their own hard work and
self-denial.

The savings idea was essentially a concrete plan demonstrating how
self-help and self-denial could help individuals achieve the American
Dream. In an 1877 pamphlet titled, "How to buy a house: a story that
will interest you," the Excelsior Savings Bank told the tale of Charles
and Lottie Brown, a couple of modest means, who had discovered that
Charles's coworker had purchased a home. The Browns learned that
this coworker was able to purchase the home due to the prudence of his
wife, who had saved small amounts of money throughout their marriage. Mrs. Brown, inspired by the prudent wife's actions, deposited
three dollars into the savings bank. "Is that all?" responded Charles
when he heard of her deposit. "Why did you not wait until you had $5
or $10 before taking it to the bank?"

"Because *I have been waiting too long already*, and I am determined
in my resolution to save in amounts however small," she replied.[48]
Charles and Lottie Brown were, of course, rewarded at the end of the
tale. They saved up half of the $9,000 needed to purchase a home and
got a bank loan because of their good character. "Suffice it to say, Mr.
and Mrs. Brown continued their account with the Excelsior Savings
Bank, paid off the mortgage, and are now living in their own house
surrounded by a happy family and in the enjoyment of one of life's
greatest blessings—*Independence*."[49]

The story of the Brown family demonstrates the mode whereby the
savings bank affirmed the attainability of the American Dream. The
Browns were the archetypal everyman and everywoman—he made a

modest income, she was a homemaker. They were able to put only a few dollars in the bank each week, but by living frugally and being disciplined about saving, they achieved the "better life" of financial independence.

GUARDING THE SAVINGS IDEA

"We cannot correctly judge a bank unless we analyze its business—its name may be a misnomer."[50]

To the great dissatisfaction of mutual savings bankers, MSBs were not the only banking institutions that shaped American understanding of thrift and savings. True mutual savings banks were a product of the eastern (particularly New England) states, where the institution first developed.[51] MSBs were eventually established in nineteen states, but 95 percent of the total deposits in these banks can be attributed to only nine states—eight of which were in the Northeast.[52] The "savings banks" throughout the rest of the country were (and are) a mix of mutual savings banks, savings and loan associations, stock savings banks, and commercial banks that offered savings departments. That so much of America's savings was found in locations other than mutual savings banks demonstrates the challenge the savings bank faced in providing savings services that appealed to depositors' aspirations. The mutual savings bank concept developed in response to the needs and values of the nineteenth-century Northeast. These banks were staunchly conservative and both unwilling and legally incapable of offering increased services or interest rates at the risk of compromising security. As the geographic and economic landscape of the United States changed, this characteristically conservative approach did not provide for an expanding capitalist economy.

As the country grew and consumer expectations changed, the mutual savings bank model was incapable of providing for the banking needs of all Americans. As pioneers began to settle further and further west throughout the nineteenth century, banks became a necessity in previously unpopulated regions. These sparsely populated areas could not support multiple banks; they needed banking institutions that could provide multiple services. Because settlers to these areas were engaged in new business ventures and the building of homes, they were more likely to need personal and business loans. To meet these needs, savings and loan associations and stock savings banks began to spring up across the country.[53] The turn of the century brought an explosion of consumer goods and services. As a result of modern conveniences, Americans began increasingly to turn their consumer eye toward their banking commitments. Depositors looked for a bank "in keeping with the spirit of the times; for as we expect the great stores to supply all our wants from under one roof, so, in finance, one institution is able to do for a man anything he wants done."[54] As the market for bank depositors increased through westward migration and an influx of immigrants from abroad, mutual savings banks faced a new level of competition. Trust companies and national banks began to solicit savings deposits, which had previously been reserved almost exclusively for MSBs.[55] These commercial banks, as well as life insurance and savings and loan companies, reduced MSBs' revenue streams, detracting from savings deposits and slowing the growth of mutual savings banks.[56]

With this new competition for deposits, MSBs focused more and more attention on determining the institutional rights of the bank. Officials fought for the rights that they felt the mutual savings bank should have a monopoly on. "Savings bank men" concerned themselves with communicating to the public what a true savings bank was or was not. These bankers argued against institutions that "trespass[ed]" and "g[a]ve battle" to MSBs, tarnishing their name.[57] As mutual savings bankers ceded domain to competitors, they demanded that these rivals segregate their savings funds and invest this money differently from the money in their commercial departments, so as to protect the savings bank idea. The struggle of MSBs to maintain identity and protect their institutional ideals demonstrates the complexity of institutional communication in a free-market economy. As market forces made savings deposits more appealing to depositors and institutions with different priorities, they began taking on the role of the savings bank, subtly transforming the way that the savings bank idea was communicated to the public.

NURTURING SOCIETY THROUGH THRIFT

*"A people educated to practice the virtue of economy . . .
will prove to be a community where the laws are respected
and enforced."*[58]

Despite the competition for deposits that mutual savings banks faced after the turn of the century, they continued to flourish. By 1910, U.S. mutual savings banks numbered 637, with three billion dollars in deposits. Though after this point interest in establishing new MSBs waned, existing banks continued to thrive throughout the mid-twentieth century.[59] These banks remained successful because they invoked the social values of the day—self-help, self-governance, fraternalism, mutualism, and patriotism. These civic and religious values made up the American understanding of the good life. The challenge to save, put forth by the savings bank, was a moral one: by participating in the savings bank, the depositor engaged in the collective enterprise of creating the good society.

Though it is unreasonable to assume that Americans in the nineteenth and early twentieth centuries unquestioningly aligned themselves with the savings bank advocates' vision of a good society, these institutional spokespersons effused their message through vehicles of public learning—newspapers, education in public schools, thrift campaigns. As such, this message was a composite of the ways that individuals thought about their environment and conduct.[60] Savings banks encouraged individuals to think of themselves as citizens and relied on the values of the national consciousness to make the case for thrift. By invoking a characteristically American nationalistic identity, savings bank advocates connected their message to a set of shared societal values. Rhetoric about the economic and social stability provided by the institution of the U.S. savings bank served to "crystallize a sense of collective identity."[61] Bank advocates connected the thrift mentality to the

values of the American consciousness; they suggested that these institutions had the power to develop a nation universally identified with
economic stability and morally upright, peaceful citizens. Savings bank
advocates heralded the ability of the institution to "cure most of the ills
of the body politic." These banks would create better citizens because
they would demonstrate to depositors their stake in the economic and
political system and train their moral humors.[62]

The American experiment was explained as the perfect breeding
ground for savings banks to flourish and to train citizens in virtue.
Though Americans were not acknowledged as a thrifty people, the
American experiment provided them with the resources and opportunities needed to attain financial independence.[63] Migration throughout
the century provided a steady stream of potential depositors arriving in
pursuit of the better life that America promised. Savings banks, particularly in large cities, provided new immigrants with the opportunity to
participate in the process of American capitalism. In his 1911 address
before the American Bankers Association, William Knox boasted about
the cosmopolitan dream realized by the Bowery Savings Bank, the largest in New York City:

> If all our depositors should talk at once, each man in his own
> tongue, the confusion of speech at the Tower of Babel would
> be faithfully portrayed. But however they may differ in their
> origin and speech, from whatever race they spring, they have
> one common motive in this land of ours, and that is the pur-
> suit and capture of the elusive American dollar.[64]

As immigrants arrived at eastern port cities, the savings banks were
"helping to make good citizens" by increasing these newcomers' investment in American institutions.[65] Of the newly arrived immigrant, Knox
proclaimed, "He learns that it is his money that is building schools and
bridges, docks and streets, houses and water works, and so he comes
to take an intelligent interest in public affairs. He comes to look upon
the savings bank as a place where he may go for advice and counsel."[66]
On the role that the savings bank played in training new citizens, bank

treasurer Frederic Nichols concluded, "Such is the civilizing influence of America."[67]

As savings bank depositors participated in the bank, the MSB advocates argued, they came to understand better their community and the financial responsibility that citizenship entailed. The savings bank endeavored to teach depositors that participation in American society required one to be financially solvent and to avoid burdening the state with those things that one should provide for one's self and family. In this way, William Kniffen argued, thrift was "the problem of the nations."[68] The economic prosperity of the country was dependent on the relative thrift of its citizens. The money supplied by individuals to the mutual savings banks ushered the U.S. government through major crises—the banks invested in government bonds, American railroads, and utilities. To act as a functioning part of a capitalist society was a responsibility that individuals took on as they participated in the American experiment. To be an economic person was moral; to be a noneconomic, or "parasitic," person was amoral.[69] Savings banks provided "the non-producing class" with the opportunity to "become producers, thereby improving the community at large."[70]

It is noteworthy here to draw attention to a significant source of citizen training—the system of U.S. school savings banks that arose at the end of the nineteenth century. Because they are discussed in another essay, I did not include an in-depth exploration of the school savings banks here but mention them because of the important role that they played in training American youth in citizenship. School savings banks were instituted in U.S. public schools by Belgian immigrant J. H. Thiry in 1885. Thiry's savings education program was underscored by the belief that "children are the best agents of social reform."[71] To educate them in moral citizenship was to provide for the future, "transform[ing] the manners and customs of a people."[72] School savings bank curricula were explicit about the importance of thrift and savings to responsible citizenship. In her exposition on school savings banks, Sara Louise Oberholtzer wrote, "If the paupers and criminals, who are a drain on society and a menace to civilization, had been given instruction in moral and practical economy when young, few, if any, of them would have become what they are."[73] The savings bank education program was proclaimed to be an open door of limitless possibilities for the children who participated, regardless of their socioeconomic background. Through the program, they would develop thrifty habits and save for the future. Ideally, by the time they completed primary and secondary schooling, they would have saved the funds for further schooling or business endeavors. As a result, it was posited, these students were less likely to be dependent on society or engage in asocial behavior. In this way, teachers participated in the social vision of the savings bank—the creation of stable citizens whose futures were more secure.

Thrift was heralded as a policy strategy that would nurture governable citizens. Advocates of savings banks operated under the assumption that individuals would behave rationally if trained to do so (for the rise of rationality was necessary for social progress) and that the economic virtue of thrift aligned with this rationality. In *Democracy in America*, Tocqueville identified the tendency of Americans to speak of virtue in terms of utility—such was certainly true of the savings bank advocates throughout the century.[74] For them, the truthfulness of thrift was demonstrated through its applicability as social policy. It was in the best interest of all to behave thriftily because "society is safer where everyone in the community is interested in economic principles."[75] If citizens were able to see their stake in the nation's economy and realize that it was in their best interest to behave in the interest of their environment, they would be increasingly productive and peace loving. In an impassioned address before the Universal Scientific Congress of Provident Institutions in Paris in 1898, John P. Townsend, the first vice president of the Bowery Savings Bank in New York, asserted:

> It is a singular fact that in cities like New York, Boston and Philadelphia, where savings banks have been in operation the longest and where the number of depositors is greatest, the masses of the people are the most law abiding, and although

anarchists and socialists from abroad have lately come among the foreign born population, to incite to riot and resistance to law, the voice of public opinion has been almost unanimously against them, causing their arrest and indictment on the first breach of the peace, followed by trial and imprisonment, which has completely frustrated their attempts to destroy the power of the Government. While in places like Chicago and Milwaukee, having no savings banks, this class of people, with evil designs, have [sic] influenced "fellows of the baser sort" to riot, and together they committed murders. . . . It may not, therefore, be claiming too much to say that savings banks have demonstrated that accumulations in them of capital by the masses . . . influence the depositors to become more useful and peaceable citizens, for they correctly reason that the safety of their deposits and the certainly of dividends, depend primarily on the enforcement of law and the maintenance of order.[76]

The tendency of savings bank advocates to laud the bank's capacity to pacify echoes other twentieth-century economic and social models that prioritize "harmonic convergence." U.S. foreign policy scholar Walter Russell Mead used the term *harmonic convergence* to describe a Western vision of progress—a world wherein capitalism and democracy increase expectations for living conditions and generate collective well-being, causing the world to be increasingly peaceful.[77] This was the sort of "progress" that the savings banks claimed to bring about. Savings bank depositors, advocates contended, were most likely to act in a moderate, civil manner. Their counterparts, on the other hand, lacking the stabilizing moderation taught by the bank, were likely to participate in any number of radical, asocial movements—murder, riot, socialism, anarchy. Given the antiradical nature of the savings bank movement, it is not inaccurate to refer to it as a "temperance movement."[78] Thrift and savings were indeed disciplines, and it was the responsibility of individuals to develop these habits not only to provide for their own future but also to ensure that society continued to foster collective well-being.

SPREADING THE GOSPEL OF THRIFT

"[Jesus] didn't sit in his house and wait until the people came to him to be saved."[79]

The savings bank defined the concept of thrift for the public; it was through literature and campaigns sponsored by the banks and savings bank education in schools that Americans encountered the virtue of thrift. Advertising was the chief form of institutional communication. Advertising provides the clearest snapshot of the way that bankers perceived their relationship with the community and the responsibilities that they saw mandated by this relationship. The first generation of U.S. savings bankers employed a laissez-faire philosophy; they saw themselves as a willing resource for the communities where they were located but did not target potential depositors in a strategic manner. This is not to suggest that early savings banks did not pursue depositors at all—it was their mission to educate the previously unsaving poor about the importance of thrift. But because they thought of themselves as distinct from commercial enterprises, they avoided the traditional advertising tactics of businesses. In an 1880 New York court case, *Hun v. Cary*, the court determined that it was "not legitimate for the trustees of such a bank to seek depositors at the expense of present depositors. *It is their business to take deposits when offered.*"[80] By the turn of the twentieth century, this was no longer the case; in the face of the multiple industries competing for savings bank deposits and as a result of the influx of professionals from different industries into the savings banking business, mutual savings banks took advantage of financial advertising tactics to educate the public about the importance of saving—through their particular institution.[81] Their rationale was that, if saving was indeed a virtue and if the mutual savings banker knew his bank to be the best option for savings deposits in the community, he must assume stewardship over the savings habits of the community. "Of course, if a bank has no particularly attractive goods to sell it won't advertise," reasoned Raymond Frazier, the president of Washington Mutual Savings Bank of Seattle. "But if a bank is conscious of its ability to serve people, it will, if modern and progressive, employ the newspaper—that eminently friendly and unobtrusive salesman. . . ."[82]

In an address before the American Bankers Association in 1911, advertising advocate E. St. Elmo Lewis proclaimed the importance of the "savings idea," but it is not of conservative investing and judicious business practices that he spoke. Instead, Lewis described the responsibility that the banker had to increase the business of the bank: it was through the ensuing growth of the savings bank, he argued, that the thrift of a community was demonstrated. Lewis argued that it was the banker's responsibility to aggressively pursue and educate potential depositors. He urged savings bankers to think of their role as an obligation, rather than a privilege, and to adopt a proactive approach to increasing savings deposits. Lewis termed his approach the "philosophy of aggressive care"[83] or "aggressive conservation."[84] Because the banker knew the implications of saving better than the individual depositor and the dangers of the many financial institutions competing for a person's money, the banker had a moral responsibility to solicit depositors.

This responsibility was articulated with tremendous moral import; advertisers invoked religious imagery and terminology to drive home the significance of their mission. Lewis declared before the American Bankers Association,

> Let us not forget that while Christ was a meek and lowly spirit, he whipped the money changers out of the Temple, and that he preached a gospel; that he went up and down among the Jews and Gentiles, preaching a new life. He didn't sit in his house and wait until the people came to him to be saved. In fact, he enunciated the motto of the salesman who is king of the world.[85]

To describe Jesus Christ as an enterprising salesman is a somewhat fantastic (and possibly heretical) metaphor, but Lewis's statements provide a helpful frame for understanding the way that these savings bank advocates thought about the savings bank idea and the ideology of thrift. Thrift was, for these men, a comprehensive, orienting ideology; it provided solutions for combating societal problems and offered redemption, in the form of financial independence, to practitioners. Savings bank advocates were in the business of proselytization. "No one can sell a product, whether it be soap or service, unless he is something of a missionary," stated Mary Reeves, of the Philadelphia Saving Fund Society.[86] This was a truth of such significance that to believe it was to commit one's self to the spread of its message. "The gospel of thrift should be preached in the highways and byways until the last improvident soul is saved," proclaimed George E. Allen before the Savings Bank Section of the American Bankers Association in 1906.[87] Savings bankers perceived themselves to be in a fight against human nature, which led men to desire immediate gratification and left them victim to "get-rich-quick propositions, grafters, stock promoters."[88] Advertisements, then, were strategic plans laid to educate depositors about these dangers and provide the depositor with what he truly desires—"a friend, protector and guide."[89]

Savings bankers of the early twentieth century thought of advertising as an extensive endeavor. In *Beyond the Counter*, Mary Reeves advised savings bankers how best to promote savings in the community and increase the numbers of depositors utilizing the services of their branch. The "advertising" she recommended was not only the use of print media but also a comprehensive approach to encouraging thrift throughout the community, causing citizens to associate savings and thrift with their particular bank. Reeves detailed the importance of serving customers, developing school savings programs and savings clubs, targeting local employers for industrial savings plans (an incentive for employers because men who save make for satisfied, stable, less fanatical employees), and producing dramas and talks at playgrounds.[90] She recounted the story of a large urban savings bank in an area with a large Italian population. The bank effectively targeted these immigrants by hiring a well-known Italian woman fluent in multiple dialects to speak to various Italian organizations, community centers, and settlement houses about the importance of thrift. Reeves applauded this bank for capitalizing on the opportunity to draw in these "sturdy" immigrants.[91] These "community propaganda" outreaches, she explained, will increase the appeal of thrift to local residents and, if effectively associated with the name of the bank (Reeves recommended tactics like making sure that the bank's passbook was used for school, industrial, and club savings programs),[92] will bring depositors into the fold of the local savings bank.[93]

The process by which these savings banks endeavored to convince Americans that they were indeed "friend, protector and guide" involved significant accommodations of mainstream and commercial values. The twentieth-century savings banker began to think of savings in the community in terms of "retention," "buy-in," and "level[s] of participation" and to utilize modern psychology and advertising theory as a means of appealing to his target audience.[94] In "The Savings Idea and the People," Lewis provided a number of newspaper clippings that he believed were successful advertisements. The clips effectively entered "the public mind" by entertaining and appealing to emotion—they were narratives of successful upward mobility through savings and of the travesties of individuals whose lives were ruined because they were victimized by money-making scams and false investment opportunities.[95] Advertising methods involved significant ideological concessions—advertisers began to craft the message of the savings bank to appeal to the desires of potential depositors, rather than attempting to transform the dispositions of society to align with the savings bank idea. Reeves advised:

> The new psychology in bank advertising discourages an appeal to such unpleasant contingencies as sickness, accident, unemployment or other emergency. Having learned that the modern individual must have his serious considerations presented in sugar-coated form, the banker suggests that the depositor save for more immediate and interesting objectives such as Christmas or vacation.[96]

The above example demonstrates a departure from previous convictions about the indivisibility of the savings idea. Central to the ideology of thrift was the belief that the future is always a better investment than the present—savings bank advocates of fifty years prior would most likely have been unwilling to promote the thrift idea in terms of its capacity to provide for small-scale desires, while not attending to the long-term benefits of the practice of thrift. The advertising era of the twentieth century brought a paradigm shift in the approach to attracting depositors—because its advocates believed the savings bank idea was a gospel of such import (and arguably because savings bankers were facing new levels of competition for depositors), they were willing to make compromises to advance it.[97] In the above statement, Reeves advocated for such an appeal because she believed it was an effective means of appealing to the psychology of the potential depositor. Such tactics would get the savings bank depositor into the mindset that systematic savings would relieve one of financial anxiety, whether it be the less grave vacation or the long-term security, and this persuasion would then yield a depositor ready to be further educated in the virtue of savings.

The evolution of savings bank advertising demonstrates subtle changes in the audience targeted by the savings bank. These changes were caused by the growth of competition for savings bank deposits, as well as the tremendous population and geographic expansion of the nation during this period. Savings banks were established to provide a haven for the savings of the poor. As the institution proved successful and the nation expanded, the language of the savings bank idea became increasingly inclusive. Savings bankers began to speak of the establishment as having great potential not only for the indigent but also for the middle class. This change came at a time marked by the rise of American middle-class identity.[98] To be "middle class" was to share "American" values and a socioeconomic position similar to that of your neighbors. In response, the savings bank began to incorporate the importance of the relationship between the middle-class citizen and the savings institution into the vision of the savings bank idea.

The savings bank existed for hard-working citizens of moderate means. Savings banks printed pamphlets and advertisements, such as the one cited below, to communicate to middle-class citizens that the savings bank was their advocate and that they were all engaged in the same quest for the good life:

THE MAN WHO WINS

The man who wins is the average man,
Not Built in any particular plan,
Not blest with any particular luck,
Just steady and earnest and full of pluck –Barrett

Isn't this an inspiring thought? The men who win are the *average* men, like you and I, and the men we rub elbows with in the shop, the store, the factory and on the farm! *Just average men!* Men with a mission and a purpose! The *mission* to make for themselves an honorable place in the world in which they live; the purpose to fulfill the obligations of life.[99]

It is likely that the author of this advertisement, Mr. Rittenhouse, as the proprietor of a newspaper, spent little time at the factory or the farm, but affirming the middle-class experience was a means of affirming that the institution of the savings bank shared the vision of life and values of its depositors. Savings banks now represented themselves as "cornerstones" of the middle-class community, boasting that "the public looks upon them in about the way that it regards the family church, or school."[100] Mutual savings banks continued to employ rhetoric about the importance of security over increased interest rates but increasingly moved away from marketing the institution as the "Poor Man's Bank."[101] Language utilized by savings bank advocates was less likely to emphasize that the bank was a philanthropy instituted to stimulate savings by the poor. Instead, the bank was defended as an organization that prioritized the goals of the middle class. The institution must be revered and protected because it represented the "hard-earned accumulations by people of moderate means."[102]

Though the savings bank of the twentieth century began to move away from the label of the "Poor Man's Bank," its humble philanthropic origin was a significant part of the myth it continued to communicate to the public. The savings bank was a symbol of the American Dream—the institution began humbly but grew in keeping with the times. To understand its history was to understand the track of progress. Savings bank advocates called for the public to marvel over the modesty of the bank's beginnings: "In those days modern conveniences were practically unknown to New York," began a 1929 narrative of the Bowery Savings Bank in New York. "There were no telephones nor telegraph; no automobiles nor aeroplanes; no steam railroads, subways nor elevators; no typewriters, adding machines nor cash registers; no moving pictures nor radios; no running water. . . ."[103] Ninety years later, the city was privy to great modern developments—industry, technological advancements, a large public transportation system, the benefits of capitalism. The bank, as a symbol of this progress, was keeping pace with the needs of the booming metropolis. It had a magnificent physical structure, capable of serving the "great uptown currents of humanity . . . in this outstanding business center of the world."[104] The physical structure of banks like the Bowery served as public relations tools—they communicated to the public that they were strong, stable, and capable of meeting the needs of a broad base of depositors. This vision of progress did not neglect history because, despite the magnificent achievements of the modern age, savings bank depositors were "basically the same sort of people their ancestors were . . . with the same mental and emotional demands."[105] Like earlier generations, these citizens were described as desiring security, the ultimate reward of the savings bank idea.

MSBs THROUGHOUT THE TWENTIETH CENTURY AND THE FUTURE OF THE THRIFT INDUSTRY

Savings banks were not established as a countercultural movement; they arose in a society that valued fraternalism, self-help, and nationalism—all components of the "savings bank idea." The height of the savings bank movement coincided with the historical moment when the virtue of thrift was most palpably acknowledged as an American social value. It was the era of the National Thrift Week, savings education programs in public schools, and efforts on the part of the government to encourage thrift—all of which were heralded as intrinsic to developing a nation of good character. As the twentieth century progressed, competing social values and economic factors began to eclipse essential aspects of the thrift idea. Americans began to value different ways of relating to material possessions and understanding societal virtues. Concurrently, the economy began to shift in a manner that no longer supported the institution of the savings bank.

The end of the period is significant for the banking industry—the stock market crash of 1929 and the following Depression created a record number of bank failures and eventually prompted the emergency measures taken by Franklin D. Roosevelt in 1933—the mandatory bank holiday, the Banking Act of 1933, and the creation of the FDIC.[106] Despite the havoc the Depression wreaked on commercial banks, other thrift institutions, and the economy as a whole, the crisis had a much less apparent effect on mutual savings banks. In fact, as many financial institutions were foundering, MSBs experienced a net savings inflow.[107] The state laws that restricted them from investing in speculative assets continued to protect these banks throughout the mid-twentieth century.[108] And yet, the time period is significant for MSBs; the changes in the banking industry set in motion during this period dramatically altered the way that savings banks were forced to interact with the public and with other banking institutions.

Government regulation in the twentieth century brought about changes that caused the mutual savings bank to ill-resemble the savings bank so idealized by philanthropists of the previous century. Deposit insurance and government regulation enforced in the 1930s restored stability to the American banking system, but these measures also forced mutual savings banks to compete on the same terms as commercial institutions. Throughout the twentieth century, as the economic environment became increasingly competitive, banks were forced to think creatively about the services they provided depositors and investors. Previously, the services provided by different types of banks were clearly delineated. But as banking became an increasingly competitive business, individual banks had to respond with flexibility to meet many different consumer credit needs.[109] This shift greatly affected the mutual savings banks, whose conservative policies made them ill-equipped to compete with other banks.

By the 1970s, changes in the national economy began to turn the tide against mutual savings banks. Ascending interest rates and competition from other banks led to severe disintermediation, which ultimately overwhelmed many MSBs.[110] To protect these banks from insolvency, regulators introduced measures intended to allow them to provide higher interest rates and to compete with the money market mutual funds to which they were losing business. The introduction of these measures was radical because it signified that, in the words of Saul Klaman, then-president of the National Association of Mutual Savings Banks, "the philosophy of fixed deposit interest ceilings was shattered." No longer could MSBs expect to operate with a security-over-interest philosophy. Instead, they must "slug it out toe to toe with high flying money market instruments."[111] The lesson, as articulated by the FDIC was that "future success depends on the ability of these banks to adapt as the financial services industry continues to evolve."[112] No longer would the priorities of the mutual savings banks be protected by law; they must adopt the values of commercial institutions to remain solvent.

To represent the significant shift in the ideological identity of the U.S. savings bank as purely a result of market forces would be to underestimate the import of the complex connections between cultural values and historical circumstances. Ultimately, the changes in the banking industry that led to the downfall of U.S. mutual savings banks were rooted in societal values and the depositors' self-understanding. As individuals began to think about themselves and material goods differently, the virtue of thrift became less and less a part of the American consciousness. In its place rose different principles about self and fiscal morality. As this shift occurred, the institution of the U.S. mutual savings bank became increasingly less essential to the vision of a good society.[113] With the explosion of consumer options that increased throughout the twentieth century, Americans were barraged with messages encouraging them to think of themselves as consumers of goods and to define themselves through their consumption habits. Initially, this impacted banks because, as they were viewed through the eye of the consumer, they were evaluated by the number of services they provided, rather than only their vision for the community. Later, as consumerism began to eclipse other financial values, savings began to recede. With consumer options vying for Americans' loyalty along with the availability of credit and the rising cost of living, saving began to seem formidable. Concurrently, the individualism at the heart of the mutual savings bank idea was becoming disconnected from religious and civic commitments that supported the public ideology. As Americans became cognizant of the plurality of worldviews that composed the fabric of the "American" consciousness, the modes of acceptable civic communication changed.

The mutual savings bank era came to a close. The banking crises of the 1980s were resolved when a great many mutual savings banks were forced to submit to open bank mergers facilitated by the FDIC. These banks were swallowed up by commercial banks (and in a few cases, stronger mutual savings banks) or converted to stock.[114] As the savings bank changed over the twentieth century, the institutional voice in U.S. culture championing thrift became more and more faint. With their disappearance, the greatest institutional representation of thrift in this country has been lost—and with it, a cognizance of what the virtue of thrift even is.

This essay is not a lament for a golden age of American economic virtue. Yet, I do not take up the topic out of abstracted curiosity; I do so because I suspect that the thrift idea and the practice of saving have potential to improve our society. I do not advocate for a return to the particular fiscal morality espoused by savings bankers. As with any cultural value, the idea of thrift is bound up with other societal values and ideas. The savings bank idea is not above reproach—it is paternalistic, assumes gender biases, makes potentially harmful connections between poverty and immorality, and discourages revolutionary thought. Yet, savings and thrift are not unworthy of consideration in the present. It is true that context determines content—and in the case of thrift and savings, they are tied to outmoded social values. However, it is significant that thrift and savings are no longer an important part of the American consciousness. Today, the savings rate is at an all-time low, predatory lending has destroyed the hopes of countless Americans, and consumerism has gripped us as an all-encompassing dogma. Consumerism has become a holistic grid through which we make decisions about not only purchases but also relationships, identity, and meaning. In the face of these struggles, I believe that there are lessons to be learned in the fiscal values described in this essay—the value of planning for the future, self-denial, and living within one's means. It is in order to identify these elements that I have noted connections between cultural values and contexts.[115]

The savings bank carried legacies both good and bad. Certainly, many of the social values associated with the institution are no longer a part of the American vision of the good life. But in their place has not risen ambivalence about savings, money, and thrift. Americans still have strong beliefs about these topics, but they are beliefs that often go unexamined. How might we better understand societal ideologies on these topics? I suggest that a thorough examination of the ideologies of our institutions is not a bad place to start.

Chapter 3

Thrift for a New Century
Public Discussions about Thrift in the 1910s and 1920s

Sara Butler Nardo

THE 1910S AND 1920S brought a new visibility to thrift in the United States. During World War I, thrift emerged as the predominant civilian virtue—the subject of presidential speeches and government campaigns. Thrift was patriotism practically applied; it was the way the war was fought on the home front. The campaign for wartime thrift was aided by a preexisting self-conscious thrift movement, which, after the war, persevered in a peacetime thrift campaign before fading away in the Great Depression. While thrift had been a highly regarded virtue throughout the nineteenth century, the changing American economy of the early twentieth century brought with it new challenges for the partisans of thrift, who organized themselves into a thrift movement to address those challenges. The twentieth-century thrift movement contained several variations on the thrift ethic, but, in general, this genera-tion of thrift advocates saw their goal not as resurrecting a neglected virtue but rather as adapting thrift to address the new social circum-stances created by forces such as the rise of corporations, mass produc-tion, consumption, and advertising. Their vision was intended to be forward-looking and flexible, not reactionary and rigid.

During this twenty-year period, public discussion about the value of thrift accelerated, spearheaded by spokespersons from the banking, education, and activism spheres. These leaders coalesced around a commitment to propagate thrift, forming a movement identifiable both by a shared ideology and a more formalized network of organizations. The Young Men's Christian Association (YMCA) created a National Thrift Committee in 1913. The American Society for Thrift, founded by banker S. W. Straus, convened its first meeting in 1914. Shortly thereafter, and in large part because of the lobbying of the American Society for Thrift, the National Education Association (NEA) formed its own Committee on Thrift to investigate the possibilities of thrift education. Banks and bankers were key players throughout the course of the thrift movement, always on the lookout for new ways to encourage saving. The American Bankers' Association (ABA) established a "thrift department" in 1912,[1] which ran a public education campaign on thrift from 1913 to 1915, during which the association placed articles about thrift in hundreds of newspapers across the country and sponsored, with the New York City Department of Education, a lecture series on thrift at the Cooper Institute in New York City.[2] During this time, the ABA also began to take an interest in the growing school savings bank movement, forging connections with the thrift education work of the NEA.

NINETEENTH-CENTURY ROOTS

This twentieth-century thrift movement had deep roots in the philanthropy and moral reform efforts of the nineteenth century. Thrift was a defining virtue of the ascendant bourgeois class, whose accumulation of capital was, at least discursively, credited as the fruits of frugality. Thrift was the virtue that created the middle class; it enabled economic and social mobility. Naturally, members of that class turned to thrift as the solution for many of the lower classes' ills. Thrift was a key element of the philanthropy of "self-help," which was envisioned as replacing "charity," which was seen as simply a material gift of the rich to the poor. Charity, it was argued, could only ever ameliorate some of the effects of poverty, but self-help, it was hoped, would abolish "pauperism" itself. John Harsen Rhoades, president of the Greenwich Savings Bank and the Savings Bank Association of New York, described this philanthropic motivation in an 1899 speech:

> Let us remember that the savings bank in its essence and purity was founded as a means to lessen pauperism and as an incentive to thrift. Let us not forget that it rests upon foundations born of philanthropy. No selfishness, no greed, no profit to ourselves must be the motto which makes our administration of this great and solemn trust.[3]

Franklin Sherman, an early twentieth-century historian of the mutual savings bank movement explained the vision of nineteenth-century reformers thus: "This role [of the mutual savings bank] was not in the giving of charities—it was not for such a role that savings banks had been created; but in the urging upon the public the sort of vision which should make charities unnecessary: in urging forethought and thrift."[4]

If the solution was thrift, the problems of the poor, as seen by nineteenth-century thrift advocates, were a temptation toward speculation, get-rich-quick schemes, and gambling; the tendency to fritter away their small incomes on unnecessary things, especially drink; and a vulnerability to pawnbrokers and other predatory moneylenders. The "thrift institutions" created in the nineteenth century—mutual savings banks, building and loan associations, cooperative credit unions, and the like—were designed to address this rather narrow set of issues. Mary Wilcox Brown, general secretary of the Henry Watson Children's Aid Society in Baltimore, described these various institutions and their rationale in her 1899 volume *The Development of Thrift*: "The founding of [savings] banks has been the result of a belief that the poor need a place of deposit for their savings and that the result of having no depositary is to make them reckless in the expenditure of their earnings."[5] The presence of thrift institutions, it was believed, would produce thrifty behavior. While not quite achieving their founders' ambitious goals of putting an end to poverty once and for all, these thrift institutions were at least perceived as a threat by some who made their living off the distress of the poor. Brown reported:

> One of the important effects of the establishment of the provident loan societies has been that in each city which they have been organized the pawnbrokers have tried to protect themselves by lowering their rates of interest. The pawnbrokers so clearly realize the danger that threatens them in the establishment of such agencies, that they have in different states successfully fought the passing of laws to legalize provident loan companies.[6]

Thrift institutions blossomed throughout the nineteenth century. The first mutual savings bank was founded in 1816 in Philadelphia. Banks soon followed in Boston and New York. The first American building and loan association was created in 1831. These institutions grew throughout the nineteenth century; in 1883, deposits to mutual savings banks had passed one billion dollars, and there were about 2,900,000 account holders.[7] Despite this growth, as the nineteenth century drew to a close and the twentieth century opened, there was a growing sense of American thriftlessness among middle-class reformers and the leaders of thrift institutions like John Harsen Rhoades and Mary Wilcox Brown. At the same time, in the face of the organized labor movement, their rhetoric was increasingly off putting and alienating to the very people they hoped to inspire to thrift.

Changing circumstances required a new argument. In the twentieth century, a new generation of reformers organized a "thrift movement" to make a new case for thrift in the new century. Two of the most important issues the new thrift movement tried to address were the astonishing prosperity of the new era and the suspicion or outright hostility of the working classes to the thrift idea.

TWENTIETH-CENTURY CHALLENGES

Around the turn of the century, many economic theorists took note of a fundamental change in the American economy. Industrialization brought an unprecedented prosperity to the United States, transforming an economy of scarcity into one of abundance. Many hailed this as a sign of the progress of civilization, but thrift advocates saw cause for concern.

"Riches are a severe and searching test of character," Edmund Dane warned in *The Value of Thrift*.[8] Availability of new riches cast doubt in people's minds about the necessity of thrift, so thrift advocates of the twentieth century spent much of their time making the basic case for thrift's continued relevance. W. H. Carothers wrote:

> Living in the midst of abundance we have the greatest difficulty in seeing that the supply of natural wealth is limited and that the constant increase of population is destined to reduce the American standard of living unless we deal more sanely with our resources.[9]

Abundance only makes thrift *appear* obsolete, warned thrift advocates, which is why "it is in prosperous times that the temptation to use money somewhat recklessly is strongest."[10]

The new thrift advocates also faced skepticism from the very people they believed were most in need of their message—the working classes. As the nineteenth century progressed, the bourgeois thrift ethic was challenged by a labor-centered perspective that dismissed thrift as selfishness, the "virtue" of the exploitative capitalist. Many thrift advocates were stumped by this response, given the remarkable prosperity they saw at every turn, but one more sensitive and politically radical thrift advocate, lawyer Bolton Hall, explained the problem this way:

> The wage-earner, the clerk, the small professional and business man, and the small farmer have all been economically lowered in the social scale, in spite of the waves of prosperity. There is just one way to judge the material condition of the country and that is by the purchasing power of the average man.[11]

Wage-earners' purchasing power, argued Hall, was far from adequate—as "wages climb the stairs, the cost of living goes up in the elevators"[12]—and the labor movement encouraged the workingman to *spend* money on the argument that his consumption funded his fellow's wages. T. D. MacGregor, author of *The Book of Thrift*, complained about this argument:

> Some persons are trying industriously to spread abroad the foolish idea that is useless for a working man to attempt to save money. They argue that if he does save, his wages will be reduced proportionately; that if everybody saved, it would bring about a panic, and that the State ought to provide old-age pensions anyway.[13]

The labor movement's skepticism about thrift was also a response to sentiments actually expressed by thrift-pushing reformers. Earlier thrift advocates located the significance of thrift behavior in its ability to pacify citizens rather than simply its ability to increase financial stability. "The development of self-help will be found to kill the socialistic spirit," promised Mary Wilcox Brown in 1899.[14] Twenty years later, the thrift movement was still trying to repair the damage of insinuating that thrift was a way to control the masses. A conference on thrift held by the American Political Science Association stated the problem this way:

> One thing the American workingman will want to know before he will take the least interest in any movement designed to stimulate thrift is that it is not in intent or in tendency a scheme to make him more safe and sane, more content with his present lot, less disposed to organized and strike.[15]

These issues stimulated a reformulation of the thrift ethic. Not every thrift advocate addressed these issues exactly the same way, but several common themes emerged in the thrift literature of the twentieth century. None of these themes was completely new—they could all be found to one degree or another in nineteenth-century discussions of thrift—but some were given a new emphasis, while others were moved into the background. Other themes were given new life by being looked at from a new perspective. During this time, the thrift ethic, alongside economic thought in general, was broadened and eventually reoriented from a producer's perspective to a consumer's.

THE THRIFT ETHIC

Thrift advocates of the 1910s and 1920s understood thrift broadly. Whereas nineteenth-century moral reformers tended to see thrift as one of many necessary virtues they hoped to instill in the poorer classes, twentieth-century thrift advocates saw thrift as the cardinal virtue, its fruits being a moral and prosperous life. S. W. Straus, probably the most active and passionate national thrift advocate, a banker, and founder of the American Society for Thrift, explained: "Thrift is essential as the guiding principle of the individual because it imparts poise, moral stamina, courage, ambition, independence and efficiency."[16] Many treatises on thrift began with a brief etymology of the word *thrift*, tracing it back to *thrive* and emphasizing its broad application. Edmund Dane's treatment in *The Value of Thrift*, written for "young people," is typical: "To thrive means to do well. Thrift comes from thrive and means a way of so living as to make the best of ourselves; it means, in short, the art of doing well."[17] Thrift is no mere financial virtue, thrift advocates stressed, but a whole-life ethic, in Straus's words, "a state of mind."[18] It is not only applicable but essential to every arena of life: "[W]ith the individual, thrift means not only the saving of money, but it means the development of character, clean morals, wholesome living, education, progress, and the fulfillment of human destiny."[19]

Nevertheless, thrift advocates constantly had to battle the notion that, at best, thrift is a strictly economic virtue, and, at worst, it is vicious hoarding. "Thrift emphatically does not consist in hoarding money," wrote T. N. Carver, professor of economics at Harvard University, in 1920. On the contrary, he went on, "in these days that is one of the most thriftless things one can do with money."[20] Thrift advocates were notably defensive against the common notion that thrift was mere miserliness; "Let us understand always," wrote Straus, "that a miser is one thing, that a spendthrift is another, and that the thrifty man is as far removed from the one as he is from the other."[21] Some thrift advocates blamed this narrower, pejorative understanding of thrift on the well-meaning but simplistic work of earlier generations of reformers. Straus believed that charity workers had confused the working classes about thrift. In an article surveying the history of the thrift movement in Great Britain, he wrote that because of English charity work,

> the people gained confused ideas. Misconceptions were fostered. Thrift work, if not conducted along the lines of actual charity, was in many instances, encouraged in its most narrow sense. The broad, constructive principles of personal efficiency were ignored and the poor were taught to hoard their small earnings without thought of the underlying principle that thrift means the process of thriving, of upbuilding, of growing.[22]

Many thrift advocates defended the thrifty man from accusations of stinginess by pointing out that it is only those who have excess income—and presumably excess income produced by thrift—who are able to share their resources with others. "Stinginess is selfishness," wrote Dora Morrell Hughes, author of *Thrift in the Household*. "If you notice, you will find the givers among the thrifty. What they have not wasted, they share with others."[23] Rather than being its opposite, thrift is charity's prerequisite.

While economic frugality did lie at the heart of the thrift message, thrift movement leaders were careful to construct a broader message and frequently warned the grassroots leaders of the thrift movement away from an overemphasis on saving money, abstracted from the larger thrift ethic. In one of his many speeches, Straus described the mission of the thrift advocate: "We who have the interests of the great thrift movement in America at heart must realize that one of our chief problems is to teach our fellow men that merely putting money in a savings bank is not the sum total of thrift."[24] This theme can be found running through the writings of thrift advocates. This passage from a children's book on thrift is typical:

> Thrift, it happens, has rather been looked down upon because it has been thought to consist of putting money by, and joining mutual benefit and building and loan associations and nothing more. To join such associations is a very good step to take, yet if we were to fall in with just that narrow view of thrift we should only get part of the good it can do us.[25]

Members of the school savings movement were particularly solicitous about this issue. As one speaker at the 1934 meeting of the National Education Association put it:

> Saving money is not all there is to thrift. If we would accomplish the greatest good, the school bank must go hand in hand with the teachings of thrift. . . . It must be remembered that a vast amount of actual harm could be done the child if we went no further than to teach it to save money. Neither society nor the Nation would be grateful to us if we thus developed a spirit of miserliness and greed in the hearts and impressionable minds of these millions of children.[26]

And what were these broader "teachings of thrift" that moved it beyond the realm of mere economics? The key thrift principle—the virtue through which thrift bears fruit for the thrifty man—is self-control. "To be able to save means ability to control yourself."[27] Saving is not good because it allows one to accumulate wealth but because it teaches self-control and requires learning to delay gratification. Thrift advocates were fond of quoting Teddy Roosevelt: "Extravagance rots character, train youth away from it. The habit of saving money stiffens the will and heightens the energies."[28] In this understanding, thrift is synonymous with willpower and strength of character; it is "the power to save, which means self-restraint."[29] The action of Anna Steese Richardson's novel *Adventures in Thrift* is sparked by a young woman who, believing herself unable to manage a household on her fiancé's forty dollars a week salary, breaks off their engagement for fear of driving him into debt and ruin. She recounts their final argument to a married friend: "I tried to persuade Jimmy to let father loan him a few thousand, just for the good of his career. He accused me of trying to weaken his character."[30] Jimmy's fears were well founded, and he was wise to resist his fiancée's temptations to thriftlessness, at least according to Straus:

> In each instance there came a crucial day, a day of great decision, a day when every bit of will-power, moral stamina, and clearness of vision were needed. It was a day such as comes sooner or later into every human life. At such a time as this the thriftless man is quite apt to fail. His habits of thriftlessness have made him accustomed to yielding to impulses—day by day, year by year, these petty indulgences have vitiated his character.[31]

The thrifty man has learned to weigh his impulses before indulging them. He is able to look ahead to the future and judge his present situation by his likely future one, and he is, therefore, not at the mercy of his every passing urge. Thrift is the triumph of reason over desire, of will over whim. One thrift advocate explained:

> It is a good thing to put by pennies and dimes, and it is a good thing not merely because you then have them saved up, but because your putting them by shows that you have begun to think, and are no longer carried away by the first fancy that lays hold of you. You have put a check on yourself, and taken the first step towards the self-control which is the foundation of a firmly-built character.[32]

President Calvin Coolidge, in one of his most widely circulated sayings on thrift, connected this conception of thrift as the private virtue of self-mastery to the public virtue of self-government:

> The people of past ages did not fail to work, oftentimes they put forth great effort, but what they produced they at once

consumed. They did not get ahead. They made no progress. There came a time when they began to accumulate a surplus. From that hour civilization began to appear. The foundation of it all was thrift. On it was built character. It is the test of the power of self-control. Out of self-control by the individual grew the principle of self-government by the people. But the basis of it all is thrift.[33]

According to many of its proponents, thrift—the ability to resist present wants and lay aside surplus resources for future needs—was the spark of civilization: "Thrift is an active principle in social evolution and the growth of civilization is conditioned by its practice."[34] Thrift separates barbaric man, who obeys his every immediate impulse, from civilized man.

PRODUCER VERSUS CONSUMER THRIFT

The thrift movement emerged at a time when economic and social thought was undergoing an important paradigm shift; the producer-centered analysis of the nineteenth century was giving way to a consumer-centered analysis in the twentieth century. The effects of this shift can be seen in the differences between the thrift promoted in the nineteenth century and the thrift promoted in the 1910s and 1920s. While there is no clean break, generally speaking, there is a clear, if gradual, shift over the first quarter of the twentieth century. If nineteenth-century thrift was thrift from the producer's and small capitalist's perspective, then the early twentieth-century thrift was thrift from the consumer's and workingman's perspective. This can be seen perhaps most clearly in the changing goals of the thrifty life, the greater emphasis on wise spending as an element of thrift equal in importance to prudent saving, and a new take on the public dimensions of thrift.

Nineteenth-century reformers believed greater thrift was the key to alleviating poverty. And for the very virtuous and thrifty, a life of great prosperity and wealth was possible; the thrifty man becomes a capitalist and joins the middle class. Those themes certainly continued—the lives of successful businessmen were held up as modern fables of the power of thrift,[35] and the laborer was promised an escape from the working class if he would but practice thrift.[36] But a competing vision of the rewards of the thrifty life also emerged in the early twentieth century.

This new vision promised the thrifty man not individual prosperity and wealth but *independence*, particularly financial independence in old age or in case of illness or disability. Many treatises on thrift repeated the dour statistics about the percentage of men—88 percent—who, at the end of their working life, found themselves miserably dependent, at best, on their own children, or at worst, on public charity.[37] In the American Political Science Association's special publication *The New American Thrift*, Milton Harrison, executive manager of the Savings Banks Association of the State of New York, wrote:

> The evidence of thrift is independence; independence is secured through the saving of money, but the quality of that independence must not be disregarded. . . . High quality independence, therefore, presupposes the maintenance of a decent standard of living throughout the period of accumulation, and money saving must be consistent in order to reach real happiness during the unproductive days of life.[38]

Also indicative of this shift from prosperity and success to "freedom through thrift"[39] were the new thrift institutions that flourished in the twentieth century: "While England is a nation of stock buyers, France a nation of bond buyers, the United States is a nation of insurance policy holders."[40] If the nineteenth century had been the age of the founding of mutual savings banks, in the first few decades of the twentieth century dawned the age of insurance. "Life insurance is distancing all other savings institutions," reported one economist in 1920.[41] Life insurance was perfectly suited to the economic situation of the workingman. While the problem with savings banks had always been ensuring that the account holder actually made saving a regular habit, "life insurance causes policy holders to stick more steadfastly to their resolution to save than do other agencies for the inculcation of thrift."[42] The commitment made when purchasing a life insurance policy demanded the laying aside of surplus income at regular intervals, corresponding to the regular payment of wages. "Of the means to thrift," wrote Bolton Hall in 1916, "life insurance ranks first in importance. The fundamental principle of thrift is continuous effort. The payment of insurance premiums being semi-compulsory during life, it provides the most effective method of systematic saving and accumulation of capital."[43]

Another difference of emphasis in twentieth-century thrift was its greater emphasis on the importance of wise *spending*. "The thrifty man," according to T. N. Carver, "spends exactly as much money as the thriftless man," but he spends it wisely and thoughtfully.[44] Saving and spending were put on the same level, as two sides of the same thrifty coin. "Sometimes thrift is saving, going without," wrote Dora Morrell Hughes in her handbook for thrifty household management, and "sometimes thrift is spending—'there is a scattering that increaseth'— but always it is something for something."[45] Some thrift advocates went so far as to redefine saving in terms of spending. "Saving is simply deferred spending," wrote Edward Thorndike of Columbia Teachers College. He defined thrift as "all forms of delayed *versus* immediate use of purchasing power."[46] A popular phrase explained that the goal is "not saving to *get* money but saving to *use* money."[47] A leader of the thrift movement in Great Britain agreed: "Saving is urged as the practical method of providing the means for *wise spending* in the future."[48]

The stronger emphasis on spending in the thrift of the early twentieth century was often specifically addressed to women and their contributions to the household economy. "A family is supported in reality often as much by the unpaid useful work of the household as it is by the money brought in by the outside wage-earner," argued Benjamin Andrews of the Savings Division of the U.S. Treasury. "Men may be the chief money makers," wrote the U.S. commissioner of education in 1924, "but careful spending and therefore prudent saving will rest more with our women."[49] In 1920, 65 percent of savings banks account holders were women.[50]

> Looked at from this standpoint, the part women are called
> to play in life is as important or weighty as that of men, and
> in some respects even more so. As wives and mothers women
> have constantly to lay out money; and it is they who can turn
> the earnings of men to good or bad account.[51]

Of course, with this responsibility as "directors of spending"[52] came
plenty of criticism. "The American households as a whole have been
managed as if to use no more than was needed, to save the bit here
and there, were beneath their dignity," wrote the author of *Thrift in
the Household.*[53] American housewives were frequently exhorted to
follow the example of their French counterparts, who, it was universally agreed, were unmatched in their thrifty household management.
According to Bolton Hall, "With us, when the wolf comes to the door,
loves flies out at the window, but Madame would put the wolf in the
soup."[54]

Not all spending was deemed thrifty, of course. "Thrift does not
consist in refusing to spend money or buy things. It consists, under a
money economy, in spending money and buying things, but in spending money for things of a different kind from that which thriftlessness
buys."[55] If the miser refuses to spend at all and the spendthrift spends
without forethought, the thrifty man makes wise expenditures when
called for and only on things that will increase his own productive
capacities or those of the nation. Daniel Jordan, chancellor of Stanford
University, explained that spending "if it brings real returns in personal
development or in a better understanding of the world we live in, is
in accordance with the spirit of thrift."[56] Thrift advocates frequently
found themselves having to answer the argument that spending of any
sort is economically productive and always superior to saving because
it is spending that pays the workingman's wages. T. D. MacGregor put
it this way:

> They say that the spendthrift gives employment to others and
> that his money gets to the bank eventually, even if he deposits
> none of it there himself. That is all very true, but how much

better it is to have the money used constructively in ways which mean sobriety, industry, home-ownership, integrity, good citizenship, and education of children.[57]

Impulsive consumption on luxuries and other frivolities, said the thrift advocates, will actually cause harm. Hartley Withers, editor of *The Economist*, explained that "by spending money on luxuries [the thriftless man] causes the production of luxuries and so diverts capital, energy, and labor from the production of necessaries and so makes necessaries scarce and dear for the poor."[58] Some took a stronger approach. "It is necessarily a wicked thing for them to spend that which could be used to better ways," admonished Homer Seerley, the president of the Iowa State Teachers' College.[59]

On this question of waste, the morally charged rhetoric of the nineteenth century perhaps persisted most. "A true view of economic life requires that every expenditure be regarded as an act that involves a moral question, for an unnecessary and unwise expenditure is a misuse of the power of money."[60] For the thrift movement, waste was a great moral evil. "Thrift is a constructive force. Waste is its destructive opposite," wrote Dora Hughes.[61] H. L. Baldensperger, who had been an officer of the Army's Salvage Divison during World War I, argued that "we need to utilize our garbage pails as a barometer of the national thrift movement."[62]

Conspicuous consumption particularly was condemned by many thrift advocates. "Among current social and economic customs the practice of conspicuous waste for the gratification of the instinct of display and as a means of flaunting in the eyes of the onlookers superior economic status is open to attack on the grounds that waste is a sin against society," preached one professor of education.[63] "No person's wealth is enough to excuse waste, for waste is a sin," lectured another.[64] Thrift advocates spread the blame around. They reprimanded those who would live beyond their means and placed responsibility for resisting the impulse to consume conspicuously on the wealthy who set the trends. Edward Thorndike put it forcefully: "If the world as a whole is to be efficient, its mighty ones must distinguish sharply between expense for efficiency and expense for display, and leave the latter to peacocks, monkeys, the feeble-minded, and women who have to make themselves saleable."[65]

Also gravely immoral was the waste caused by expenditures on alcohol:

> The waste of strong drink, the making and consumption of alcoholic liquors has been the most wanton waste in our country, and in combating it we must cultivate thrift and that conservation of time and material that tends to upbuild and create plenty and prosperity.[66]

Thrift advocates often linked their disapproval of waste to a notion of efficiency, a timely topic in the wake of the publication of Frederick Winslow Taylor's book *Principles of Scientific Management* in 1911. "We must have individual efficiency, if we are to withstand the temptations that shall come with continued affluence," Straus said in a 1916 lecture.[67] "Efficiency is the prevention of waste, not of money alone, but of thought, time, and effort—the tools with which money is made," wrote T. D. MacGregor.[68] The language of efficiency also reflected some thrift advocates' application of thrift beyond the individual to business and industry. "The prosperity and well-being of Industry, then, depends upon thrift of time and effort," explained Edmund Dane.[69] The very health of the economy relied on the efficient use of time and energy and the elimination of waste. Even those skeptical of Taylorism and the "efficient" industrial workplace, like thrifty anarchist Bolton Hall, saw efficiency as an important part of thrift:

> Efficiency is not a mystery reserved for the elect. It is not a bugga-boo to be called "scientific management"; it is nothing but common sense applied to every-day affairs, doing things better, quicker, and more economically than at present; doing them the right way, the adept, the easy, the direct, and natural way, rather than in the wrong, the careless, the slovenly, and the roundabout way.[70]

PUBLIC THRIFT

If in the nineteenth century the individual and private aspects of thrift were emphasized, then in the twentieth century thrift advocates placed a greater emphasis on its social and public dimensions. "The exercise of thrift is a public service and a private virtue," argued Alvin Johnson, future editor of *The New Republic*.[71] "The bank depositor," wrote Bolton Hall, "aside from protecting himself and his family, contributes to the better morals and greater prosperity of his country—and that is good citizenthrift."[72] President Coolidge was not the only one to draw a connection between thrift and democracy—S. W. Straus was also firm on this point. "Thrift is the very essence of democracy itself," he wrote. "Thrift is upbuilding and constructive essentials without which no true republicanism can permanently endure."[73] The public aspects of thrift were most pronounced during World War I, when, according to Straus, "America began to realize for the first time in the history of our national existence the truth that thrift is patriotism."[74] Thrift was a way to fight the war on the home front with war gardens and Liberty Bonds; those who had been beating the thrift drum before the war felt vindicated. After the war was over, thrift would restore the wounded nations to their previous prosperity. President Harding expressed this common sentiment in 1923:

> I do not believe there is any other way to straighten out the tangle of financial and economic concerns into which the world has been precipitated by the war, than to produce a good deal more than we consume, which means, to save, and by our savings to re-establish the world's stores of working capital.[75]

Thrift could also protect democracy from other dangers, as some thrift advocates intimated that one public benefit of increased thrift would be the neutralization of the radical workingman. In 1915, MacGregor wrote, "Nor are the benefits of thrift to be measured wholly in terms of economics. The steadiness, the industry, the sobriety, the respect for property, which are fostered among thrifty and frugal people are political virtues that make for stability and permanence of government."[76]

Straus argued, "The thrifty worker is usually the efficient, regular worker. . . . He is the man whose interests are one with those of 'his' house."[77] George Palmer of the New York State League of Savings and Loan Associations assured one audience that "the home owner is never a bolshevist,"[78] and a savings bank president promised, "The man with the savings bank account is not going to be a revolutionary. He does not want the institution overthrown that holds his savings. . . . That man will stand for law and order and the existing order of things in an intelligent and constructive way."[79] Needless to say, such sentiments did nothing to mend relations between the thrift movement and the working classes and led one distressed thrift advocate to lament, "There is a great tangle of unhappy experience to be unraveled before you can say 'thrift' to a trade-conscious American workingman and not elicit a cold grin."[80]

But other thrift advocates, more attune to the sensitivities of the workingman, used this new emphasis on the social and public dynamic of thrift to introduce the notion that thrift was a virtue not just for individuals but for societies and governments, industry and institutions, as well. Advocates of some form of government social insurance or old-age pension tried to win supporters by depicting it as just another form of thrift. As one argued, "It is plain logic to suggest that thrift be safe-guarded by means of public, mutual, social insurance. . . . Such insurance is collective public thrift."[81] Some even went so far as to suggest that individual thrift belonged to an earlier era and was no longer relevant. Asked one thrift advocate,

> Is there after all such a thing as individual thrift? Is it not family thrift, group thrift, and community thrift? When we term a person "stingy" is it because he is individually thrifty, because he is spending in his own way and saving in his own way and not spending as it is down in the group?[82]

Thrift partisans of the early twentieth century believed that collective, not individual, thrift was the thrift of the future. "Modern society has left little for the initiative of the individual," argued H. L.

Baldensperger, who had been active in the wartime thrift movement, serving on the War Industries Board. "Group action is the basis of our modern communal life. Our thrift movements, heretofore, have depended upon individual initiative. In order to have our thrift movement conform with modern social conditions it is necessary to organize for communal action."[83]

Of course, these shifts in the thrift ethic followed not just changes in contemporary economic theory but also physical changes in the shape and structure of the American economy at the time. As early as 1907, Alvin Johnson argued that the advent of corporate capitalism was having a harmful impact on the thrift habits of the nation, as the rewards for thrift were decreased. "One of the effects of the tendency toward corporate forms of business organization is the destruction of one of the strongest motives for saving," he wrote.[84] He continued,

> In an industrial state where the high price of land has made the acquisition of landed property almost impossible for the man who starts without means, where the increasing size of the business unit reduces to a minimum the chances of the man of small means to create a business under his own control, there are also at work forces which cause expenses to approach very close to income. What wonder that the empty-handed laborer of to-day tends to remain a laborer, and that his hands remain empty.[85]

Johnson also explained the shift in emphasis from prosperity to independence as the goal of the thrifty life. Workers, he wrote, are less and less interested in becoming small capitalists; they believe they should be able to maintain a decent standard of living as workers. "It is no part of the workingman's view of progress that each individual should become the owner of a capital whose earnings may supplement those of his labor. No such supplementary income should, in the laborer's view, be necessary."[86] Yet some thrift advocates continued to promise the workingman that thrift would allow him to climb out of the working class, something that appeared less and less possible and also of decreasing interest to the workingman. As a result, Johnson warned, "middle-class schemes of cultivating thrift among the working classes will meet with increasing resistance."[87]

Most thrift advocates, however, were uninterested in Johnson's advice and were hardly aware of the effects of these structural changes on the exercise of thrift. While they agreed with Johnson that there was a remarkable lack of thrift among the American people—"none of us by the broadest possible conceit could think of ourselves as a thrifty people. . . . As a Nation we are extravagant, wasteful and careless of our resources as compared with the older nations of the world"[88]—the typical explanation for this blamed the particular national character of Americans. "They know how to make money," said the president of the California Bankers' Association, "but they do not know how to save it."[89] The United States was ranked thirteenth among nations based on the number of savings banks depositors per one thousand people, behind Switzerland, Denmark, Norway, Sweden, Belgium, France, Holland, Germany, England, Australia, Japan, and Italy.[90] Thrift advocates attributed the thriftlessness of the American character in large part to the remarkable bounty nature had lavished on the nation.

> America has been blessed with abundant and bountiful natural resources which have been easily obtained and sufficiently well distributed to allow the great majority of American people to live comfortably without undergoing the hardships suffered by those who live in old and impoverished countries. Moreover, the ease with which certain fortunate individuals have sometimes secured sudden wealth from our natural resources has caused a widespread spirit of speculation.[91]

The result of this exceptional abundance and good luck, according to the U.S. commissioner of education, was lack of thrift: "We have never been compelled to be a careful or thrifty people. We have found it possible to waste much of our wealth and still maintain a higher standard of living and enjoy more luxury than most other peoples."[92] S. W. Straus explained it with typical moral force:

Prior to the outbreak of the European War we were known as the most wasteful of all people. The phrase 'Thriftless American' was common everywhere. And, inconceivable though it now seems, no definite, systematic effort ever was made to divest public thought and public practice from these harmful habits. Nature, like a fond, generous parent, had heaped her gifts upon us, and we, with shameless prodigality, were wasting our golden heritage with utter disregard of our own welfare and unmindful of the awful effects which our thriftlessness might have on coming generations.[93]

While Johnson saw a decline in thrift as the economic structures changed, most thrift advocates did not look back to a golden age of thrift but looked forward to the day when America would finally join the ranks of the thrifty nations. The thrift movement was far more forward-looking and future-oriented than backward-looking and nostalgic.[94] J. H. Thiry, father of the U.S. school savings movement, argued that the "practical lessons of thrift and economy" would bring about a "progressive civilization":

We could succeed in bringing a kind of equalization among all the ranks of society and require that henceforth all men must possess equal strength of body and mind—all be equally industrious and saving; there would be no more weaklings, nor Samsons among us, not misers, no spendthrifts, every child meeting at the same school, opportunities equal, nobody too proud to stand aloof, nobody too humble to be shut out, moderation in the race for wealth, moderation in the amount desired, moderation in its expenditure.[95]

When World War I came, of course, many thrift advocates announced that it would spark the final maturation of our national character, prompting a new dawn of American thrift and resultant prosperity and social calm. The war, thrift advocates believed, would prove once and for all the nobility of "true thrift," which is not miserliness at all but "proper use . . . closely associated with effectiveness, loyalty, patriotism, victory."[96]

> Our pace in the future will probably be slackened. The nation will have mellowed. It will not be a case of indolence replacing fervor, but of fervor sensibly abated. The young child tumbles about and occasionally runs into things with his nose while gathering strength. But as he grows up he finds that unnecessary. When adults, we try to use our strength judiciously. We will leave it to wiser men to answer what the meaning of this life is. But surely we ought to endeavor to make it happy. Europe has long pursued a temp of life which was too tame for America. But we too have already begun to lay greater stress on cultural and intellectual satisfactions. The future America will be richer in human contentment. It will still be active. But it will use its energies not solely in a dizzy chase for wealth.[97]

THRIFT GOES TO WAR

When the United States entered World War I, thrift advocates were ready to seize the opportunity to promote thrift, having spent several years already forming societies and grassroots organizations, directing public education campaigns, and lobbying for thrift education in the public school system. Initially, thrift advocates seized on the war as a lesson in waste and thriftlessness. "The stupendous extravagance of the war, with its estimated cost of $50,000,000 a day, is awaking in us a realization of our own national and individual wastefulness," wrote one in 1915.[98] Prior to the entry of the United States into the war, its effects were already being felt among the American people:

> The purchases of the Allies had made serious drains upon the food supplies of the United States; there was fear of serious shortages; prices had advanced greatly; and in some cases there was profiteering, hoarding and speculation in foodstuffs.

Between April 6 and May 17 prices of seventeen selected food commodities increased 23 per cent.[99]

And for what? The destruction of lives and property in Europe. Thrift advocates portrayed war as the ultimate thriftlessness, something that the advance of thrift would prevent in the future. Once the United States entered the war, however, the forces of thrift enthusiastically threw themselves behind the war effort, and thrift became not a preventative tool but a weapon.

The war thrift movement had two primary goals: the conservation of goods on the home front so that materials could be given to the military and the raising of funds for the war efforts from the savings of civilians. In his speech before Congress declaring war, President Woodrow Wilson described the need for wartime thrift: "[This war] will involve the organization and mobilization of all the material resources of the country to supply the materials of war and serve the incidental needs of the Nation in the most abundant and yet the most economical and efficient way possible." His first address to the nation after the country had entered the war included an appeal to thrift:

> This is the time for America to correct her unpardonable fault of wastefulness and extravagance. Let every man and every woman assume the duty of careful, provident use and expenditure as a public duty, as a dictate of patriotism which no one can now expect ever to be excused or forgiven for ignoring.[100]

Initially, the government's efforts at promoting wartime thrift were coordinated by the Commercial Economy Board, a subsidiary of the Council on National Defense; its functions were absorbed by the War Industries Board in July 1917. Both the Commercial Economy Board and the War Industries Board "sought to secure by voluntary co-operation the conservation of food and material, and the elimination of waste."[101]

On May 17, 1917, President Wilson created the Food Administration. As head of the Food Administration, Herbert Hoover led the government's campaign for "food thrift." Initially, the campaign "was based entirely upon the principle of voluntary co-operation. By appeals to the patriotism of the farmer and housewife, it endeavored to secure increased production of food crops and the saving of food products by careful economics."[102] The Food Administration promoted the observance of wheatless and meatless days and encouraged the planting of war gardens—which, according to S. W. Straus, produced $850,000,000 worth of food over the course of the war.[103] In early December 1917, "a campaign to secure the signatures of every housewife in the country to a card pledging conservation in the choice and use of food was conducted."[104] The Fuel Administration, created in August 1917, also produced a great deal of thrift propaganda on uses such as "furnace management" and the "doctrine of a cool house."[105]

The U.S. Treasury Department directed its own thrift propaganda campaigns, as well as the campaign for the sale of Liberty Bonds and War Savings Stamps. "As the campaign proceeded, however," wrote a former assistant director at the Treasury Department, "the financial necessities of the government became more and more pressing and there was a gradual tendency to make the thrift campaign purely a selling campaign of war saving stamps."[106] And sell they did. A broader group of Americans became bond holders during the Great War than at any previous time.[107] The five Liberty Bond issues, with over sixty-five million subscriptions, brought in $24,072,257,500.[108] More than one billion dollars was raised by the sale of War Savings Stamps. "This vast accumulation of capital," noted one thrift advocate, "was gathered in small amounts and represented to a very great extent the savings of the people in the curtailment of small and needless expenditures."[109] The war effort even brought together the forces of thrift and the organized labor movement. Samuel Gompers endorsed the War Savings Stamps campaign, and not long after the war ended, the American Federation of Labor passed a resolution at its annual convention supporting the thrift movement's continued work in peacetime.[110]

THRIFT IN PEACETIME

If World War I brought a height in Americans' actual practiced thrift, the decade that followed brought the height of the thrift movement. The war had granted the thrift movement new legitimacy and, at least in the minds of some thrift advocates, had proved that thrift was a necessary virtue.

> During the war, every effort was made to conserve and save. Indeed, the war furnished an all-compelling motive for the practice of thrift and saving. Motives and objectives are as necessary in thrift education as in other life activities. The war had to be won and our fighting men at home and abroad had to be provided for.[111]

But the end of the war brought a new challenge—to encourage the continuation of thrifty habits developed during the war without the motivation provided by the war effort and amid the prosperity of the postwar era. Thrift advocates were distressed to discover the inclination of many Americans to splurge on the things they had done without during the war years rather than maintain their thrifty ways and hasten the repair of the war's destruction. "It has been exceedingly difficult to make headway against the natural tendency to fall back into the pre-war habits of extravagance deeply ingrained in American character through years of practice," reported George Zook, who had been with the Savings Division of the Treasury Department before joining the faculty at Penn State College.[112] The NEA's Committee on Thrift reported, "When the war ended, our people were well on the way toward establishing thrift habits in the school, in the home, and in business and professional life. But the close of the war brought a period of reaction."[113] With the goal of maintaining the levels of thrifty behavior that had been reached during the war, the thrift movement redoubled its efforts. Hoping to instill habits of thrift before the difficult-to-break habits of extravagance took hold, many members of the thrift movement intensified their efforts in what was probably the most successful arena of the thrift movement: school savings and thrift education.

SCHOOL SAVINGS BANKS AND
THRIFT EDUCATION

Like most other thrift activities, the groundwork for the school savings movement had been laid well before the Great War, beginning in 1885 when a Belgian immigrant, J. H. Thiry, became commissioner of the public schools in Long Island City, New York. One of his first acts as commissioner was to import the school savings bank, which had been spreading across Europe in one form or another for many years. The bank opened on March 16, 1885, with 450 pupils participating.[114] Thiry had extremely high hopes for the possibilities of the school savings bank. "It was his belief," wrote W. Epsey Albig, who authored a history of the school savings bank movement for the American Bankers Association in 1928, "that participation in school savings would habituate the child to practice the social law of self-government."[115] Thiry was soon promoting his system to anyone who would listen:

> The motive of school savings banks is an outcome of progressive civilization. Having stood the test of time and experience, they have proved to be a banner of progress, which ought to be carried forward in the world. Its ample folds are not to be furled until every child in the land will have been taught the practical lessons of thrift and economy in our public schools.[116]

One person who listened was Sara Louise Oberholtzer of Pennsylvania, a writer active in various women's organizations who, according to Albig, "had some years earlier developed a savings scheme for her own children and those of her neighbors."[117] Oberholtzer heard about Thiry's work in the winter of 1888 at a meeting of the American Economic Association, and she immediately began agitating for school savings banks in her home state. Just one year later, there were fifty school savings banks throughout Pennsylvania.[118]

Oberholtzer believed that school savings banks were natural allies to another of her causes—temperance. "Thrift is the handmaiden of temperance," she argued persuasively to Frances E. Willard, president of the National Women's Christian Temperance Union (N.W.C.T.U.), in

1889.[119] "That is a temperance movement, Mrs. Oberholtzer," Willard told her. "Bring it to the National W.C.T.U. It will help us, and we will help you." The National W.C.T.U. created a Department of School Savings and Thrift at its national meeting in Augusta, Georgia, in 1890 and appointed Oberholtzer superintendent.[120] From this position, she created and distributed pamphlets, developed a standardized school savings program, traveled the country speaking and assisting the implementation of school savings banks, and published a quarterly periodical, *Thrift Tidings*. In 1899, Mary Wilcox Brown reported, "The opening of a savings bank account in a school has a direct effect on the sales of the small candy shops in the neighborhood, and the owners of such shops are said to be the only enemies of the system."[121] By 1913, more than one hundred thousand copies of Oberholtzer's first circular, *How to Institute School Savings Banks*, had been distributed in the U.S. and Canada.[122] Oberholtzer remained the leading advocate of school savings banks for over thirty years, finally retiring from editing *Thrift Tidings* in 1923. In the final issue, she reported she was satisfied that the work could be better carried on by the other organizations, new and old, that had become involved in the movement: "*Thrift Tidings*, the humble carrier of the simple notes of the coming of school savings banks, is not especially needed now, because the national forces have heard and heeded."[123]

The main organization was the American Bankers Association, which took over collecting school savings bank statistics from Oberholtzer in 1915—although the war interfered with its ability to do the actual collection until 1919.[124] The ABA had been interested in school savings banks for several years. Oberholtzher had noted in a 1912 issue of *Thrift Tidings* that she had recently shared some of her school savings bank literature with the ABA.[125] But it appears that the passing of the torch from Oberholtzer and the N.W.C.T.U., who were squarely in the tradition of altruistic moral reform, to the commercial ABA troubled some. "It does not mark an attempt on the part of commercial interests to encroach on the schools," Albig explained in 1928. "The causes back of the introduction of manual training, domestic science and domestic art into the public schools were essentially the same as those which are making a place for school savings."[126] He expanded on this before a meeting of the NEA; since the family is no longer an "industrial unit" and, therefore, "the family as a teacher of thrift has passed, and since material prosperity now, more than ever before, is one of the factors in making life richer and more abundant, thrift should have a place in the curriculum of the modern school."[127]

The NEA itself had formed a Committee on Thrift at the urging of Straus's American Society for Thrift in 1915. The committee was charged with investigating the idea of thrift education; it reported back endorsing thrift education in 1917. The NEA sponsored annual student essay competitions on the subject of thrift, as well as annual teacher essay competitions on the subject of teaching thrift; in the 1917–18 school year, more than one hundred thousand students across the country submitted essays on thrift.[128] In 1921, a joint report issued by the NEA and U.S. Treasury Department suggested a standardized thrift curriculum and recommended "that henceforth [thrift] is not to be sought as a mere by-product of educational processes, but will take its place with the other standard subjects in the school as a great objective education."[129] In 1923, the cause of thrift education was also taken up by the National Congress of Mothers and Parent–Teacher Associations.[130] In 1924, the NEA convened a national meeting on thrift education that brought together educators and education professors from across the country and featured lectures from all sectors of the thrift movement.

State legislatures had also gotten involved. Massachusetts, thanks in part to its active mutual savings banks, was the first, in 1910, to mandate thrift education as a regular part of the public school curriculum. Minnesota and New York followed in 1915, and New Jersey, Ohio, Illinois, Nevada, Kentucky, and Oregon in 1921.[131] Although there were several competing school savings banks systems, the most common, which had been promoted by Sara Louise Oberholtzer, was the passbook system. Once a week, teachers would receive deposits from their students, keeping one set of records for the school and another set to be passed on to the bank with the deposit. Once a child had accumulated a set small amount, the banked granted him his own account and a passbook to keep the record of his deposits and withdrawals, which could be made through his teacher or at the bank itself. In some schools, students also served as "tellers," receiving their classmates' deposits instead of the teacher.[132]

In 1928, school savings banks existed in forty-six of the forty-eight states, with net savings of more than $9,500,000.[133] In the 1928–29 school year, with more than four million students participating (out of over twenty-five million enrolled in public schools) deposits totaled over $28,000,000 with a net savings of approximately $10,500,000.[134] Despite the apparently successful growth of the school savings bank movement, W. Espey Albig was concerned. Too many of the deposits were withdrawn at the end of the school year, suggesting that students were simply following curricular requirements rather than fully absorbing the lessons of thrift and saving. "Instead of the teaching being that of self-control, of thrift, and of income management, it is simply instruction in the mechanics of banking," he wrote in his book outlining the history of the school savings bank movement.[135] His annual report on the 1928–29 school year ended with a warning: "The one great plague afflicting school savings is that familiar to banks doing a savings business everywhere—that of too great withdrawals. If it is not conquered, there is grave danger that it may destroy the whole fabric of school savings."[136] His eleventh annual report, *Recession in Industry Affects School Savings Banking*, which also announced the news of Sara Louise Oberholtzer's death, contained reports from across the country that pupils' unemployed parents were raiding their children's school savings. Gone was the prosperity that had allowed children their own money to save and spend as they saw fit. While school savings banks and thrift education remained a part of the curriculum at many schools into the 1950s and even 1960s when that prosperity had returned, thrift education, as a national cause, never fully recovered from the Great Depression. Preoccupied by other, more pressing economic issues, this eleventh annual report on school savings banks was ABA's last.

NATIONAL THRIFT WEEK

The 1920s also marked the peak celebrations of National Thrift Week, a public education campaign sponsored primarily by the YMCA. The first Thrift Week was celebrated in 1916. Every year thereafter, it began on January 17, in honor of the birthday of Benjamin Franklin, "American apostle of thrift."[137] The celebrations of National Thrift Week were guided by several specific principles: Have a Bank Account; Invest Safely; Carry Life Insurance; Keep a Budget; Pay Bills Promptly; Own Your Home; and Share with Others.[138] Only a few years into the campaign, the YMCA had lined up a broad array of cosponsors from the Girl Scouts and Boy Scouts to the American Red Cross. Thrift week celebrations were held in cities and towns across the nation. In a testament to their popularity, President Coolidge's secretary, C. Bascom Slemp, rather wearily wrote in response to yet another request from some local thrift leaders, "Among the most frequent [requests for a comment from President Coolidge] are requests for statements to be used in thrift campaigns."[139] Banks were usually more than happy to work with the local YMCA to promote Thrift Week—especially Have a Bank Account Day—and merchants often ran special Thrift Week sales (wise spending, indeed).

In 1925, Adolph Lewisohn, chair of the YMCA's National Thrift Committee, boasted in his annual Thrift Week radio address, "Each observance of National Thrift Week . . . finds us saving more consistently and investing more wisely. It finds us more industriously applying our energies in the creation of wealth, spending more sensibly for necessities and comforts of life, and giving more liberally to worthy causes."[140] In 1927, the National Thrift Committee's newsletter and *National Thrift News* decreed, "The American people save about $30,000,000 a day. It has really become fashionable to be a saver."[141] That same issue announced the creation of "the Unit Plan," an initiative in honor of the tenth anniversary of National Thrift Week. No longer confined to one week in winter, the Unit Plan expanded the celebration and promotion of thrift year round, with each former daily theme being communicated instead throughout an entire month.[142]

THRIFT AND THE HOUSEWIFE

In 1926, the YMCA handed responsibility for Make a Budget Day over to the General Federation of Women's Clubs, which had already been an active cosponsor of National Thrift Week. After the war, women's clubs had taken a particular interest in promoting the use of family or household budgets "because many women are buying without a plan of their needs or any consideration of their income, therefore, half of our homes are inefficiently equipped and managed."[143] The American Home Economics Association had worked with the Bureau of Home Economics in the Department of Agriculture after the war to create "popular material on thrift."[144] Of course, women's organizations were involved in the thrift movement from the very beginning, often taking as their goal the teaching of thrifty household management. While American women had been addressed on this subject as long as there had been American women, the female thrift movement leaders of the early twentieth century had a strong sense that their movement was especially needed at that time. As society moved from an era of household production in an agrarian setting in favor of the cash economy of urban life, women leaders believed that "nobody thought to teach this new generation of women the value of money or how to spend it to best advantage." The American housewife was in need of new guidance to beat "the HC of L"—the high cost of living.[145] While there was room in this new housewife's thrift for some traditional practices—making meals with leftovers, taking care of clothes and furniture so they would last, producing some goods, where possible, in the form of a vegetable garden—equally if not more important was the art of thrifty consuming. "An empty garbage pail is the certain indication of two things: how to buy and how to use what one has bought."[146] Nowhere in the thrift movement was the newer emphasis on wise spending given more thought or practical applications than among its female members. "What we need under existing food conditions," explained Mrs. Moore, a character in Anna Steese Richardson's *Adventures in Thrift*, "is women educated as buyers, not cooks. It is no use to economize in the kitchen and waste in the market."[147]

Mrs. Moore belonged to a nonfictional organization that hoped to supply that very education, the National Housewives' League (NHL). The first step was for women to do their shopping, or "marketing" as it was called, in person; as T. D. MacGregor reported in 1915:

> Investigations in New York, Detroit, Baltimore, and other cities indicate that only one-third of our housekeepers do their own marketing. The other two-thirds, as a rule, entrust it to servants, children, and the telephone. It goes without saying that buying personally is the more economical way by far.[148]

The NHL hosted demonstrations by various merchants to explain how to get the most for one's money whether at the butcher, the department store, the grocery, or anywhere else. It also kept its members informed about the current market conditions of various items, so that housewives would know whether they were being unfairly charged for their apples or whether the price increase was due to a poor harvest.[149] The educated consumer was a thrifty consumer.

Other aspects of the household thrift movement were attempts at cooperative buying and direct exchange between producer and consumer. Particularly in urban areas, middlemen—brokers who added nothing of value to the foodstuffs they bought and sold—added significantly to the final cost of groceries. Whereas co-ops were successful at cutting out this expense in some places, they never enjoyed the popularity of those in Europe. Mrs. Moore's theory about the reason for this was the short-sightedness of her female fellows and also, as thrift advocates often said, the peculiar American character:

> [W]e woman seek economy in only one of two ways—an actual and considerable reduction in the price of goods sold, or the money we put in the savings bank. We lack the economic vision of the man, which sees money invested, paying a profit

six months or a year ahead. The feminine instinct for chasing so-called bargain sales blinds her to the bigger and safer saving which cooperation represents. Here in America cooperation is a form of fanaticism, not of every-day common sense.[150]

Her explanation is borne out by the protagonist of *Adventures in Thrift*, Mrs. Larry, who, returning from a visit to the Montclair Co-operative Store and Kitchen, sighs, "I can't rise to the heights of cooperation and the good of the greatest number and all that sort of thing."[151]

THRIFT AND CONSERVATION

While not a part of the thrift movement per se, many thrift advocates and conservationists were quick to point out the connections between their causes. "Conservation advocates the use of foresight, prudence, thrift, and intelligence in dealing with public matters, for the same reasons and in the same way that we each use foresight, prudence, thrift, and intelligence in dealing with our own private affairs," wrote one conservationist.[152] Thrift advocates and conservation advocates employed a similar vocabulary. They explained the "conservation idea" as "the idea of the wickedness of national waste and the value of public saving . . . the seeking to make the most of what we have."[153] Like advocates of financial thrift, conservationists described Americans as notably wasteful in their stewarding of resources. "We have almost unlimited resources in extent of territory, diversity of soil and climate and variety of production," wrote Arthur and James Chamberlain in a 1919 educational guide.[154] "Ours is a country of great extent, of tremendous possibilities, of beckoning opportunities. Herein lies the chief reason for our prodigality."[155]

Thrift advocates and conservationists were both highly aware of how the natural abundance of the United States had led Americans to take the bounty of nature for granted and shared a concern for the wasteful effects of industrial pollution.[156] Arno B. Cammerer, director of the National Park Service, proclaimed the National Park System, founded in 1916, to be "an outstanding example of National thrift."[157]

According to Herbert Smith of the newly created U.S. Forest Service, it is "the obligation of citizenship to see that the public resources of the country, on which depend the possibility of private thrift, of individual thrift, are protected through the practice of public thrift; that is, the conservation of our natural resources."[158]

Thrift advocates and conservationists also appear to have had to respond to similar criticisms or misunderstandings of their goals:

> The first great fact about conservation is that it stands for development. There has been a fundamental misconception that conservation means nothing but the husbanding of resources for future generations. There could be no more serious mistake. Conservation does mean provision for the future, but it means also and first of all the recognition of the right of the present generation to the fullest necessary use of all the resources with which this country is so abundantly blessed. Conservation demands the welfare of this generation first, and afterward the welfare of the generations to follow.[159]

These conservationists argued for the importance of public thrift by stressing the interdependence of all citizens in an industrialized society. Urban areas depended on the raw materials produced by rural communities, and rural communities depended on the finished commodities of the city. Waste of natural materials at any point was decried as a great injustice.[160]

REALITIES OF A NEW ERA

An older and more traditional aspect of the thrift movement was found in the continued growth of mutual savings banks and other "thrift institutions," especially building and loans associations, savings and loans associations, and insurance. By 1920, there were twenty-eight thousand savings banks across the nation; banks and building and loan associations were moving closer to their target audience, opening branches in plants and factories.[161] These thrift institutions had always understood themselves as philanthropic organizations both in the direct financial help they allowed and also in the cultivation of thrifty and provident habits. "The idea has always been to serve the wide classes of people who have no investing knowledge of their own, who are genuinely in need of a place to keep safely their money, and who above all are anxious that their money be kept intact," explained Franklin Sherman.[162] Although life insurance was perhaps the fastest growing of the "thrift institutions" at this time, building and loan associations and similar organizations primarily oriented toward assisting individuals in buying their own homes were not far behind. According to one thrift advocate,

> there have been many plans to force the habit of thrift upon persons otherwise careless of their savings, but it is doubtful if any other system excels that which a man voluntarily assumes when he decides to acquire ownership of his own home by means of monthly payments.[163]

The advantage of mortgages—and life insurance, for that matter— came in that the purchase, and the commitment to pay for it was made first. Saving first, while perhaps in some respects more thrifty, was also more likely not to be carried through. The threat of penalty if a regular payment was missed was thought to be a better motivator than the anticipation of eventually saving enough to make the desired purchase.

Of course, this same argument could be used for installment buying, a recent innovation looked upon with great skepticism by some members of the thrift movement. Other thrift advocates saw installment buying and the like as merely the next evolution of thrift:

> Those savings bankers who denounce installment selling as subversive of thrift must answer the question, what is thrift? Is it regular self-denial in order to protect oneself in emergencies? Or is it the sacrificing of pleasant things in the now for a more desirable end in the future? Is the time element important—must the reward of thrift be left to the future—is

it less virtuous to enjoy the fruit of self-denial first and do the self-denying afterward?[164]

Installment buying was just one of several novelties the thrift movement struggled to fit into its framework over the course of the 1920s. At the start of the decade, mutual savings bankers looked askance at the growing force of advertising. Savings banks that ran promotional campaigns often struck a defensive note in describing them. H. H. Wheaton of the Savings Bank Association of the State of New York said, "We are not interested in propaganda as such, nor are we interested in publicity as such. We do not care anything for advertising as such."[165] But by the end of the decade, savings bankers appear to have reconciled themselves fully to the new age of advertising, and hardly an issue of the *Savings Bank Journal* went by without an article addressing the topic.[166] For example, an advertising executive brought in to address a regional meeting of mutual savings banks gave this advice:

> There has been too much said, in advertising, about banks, and too little about how human aspirations may be achieved; too much self-repression preached instead of showing folks how to get what they want. The theme of more abundant living will find a far greater response from the masses than that of padlocked pockets. The best way to promote the savings idea is to encourage saving for spontaneous desires.[167]

Advertising was also portrayed as a way of capturing that desirable eighteen-to-thirty age demographic. In an article titled "Why Not Aid 'Spending Youth'?" Sophie Wenzel Ellis explained,

> Youth refuses to be preached to or at. Bank advertising directed to it will fail if it becomes too didactic. Accordingly, advertising that is constructive rather than destructive will gain its attention. It is not natural for a young person to look forward to the proverbial rainy day; he prefers having his attention called to the happiness and success that await him in the future.[168]

Of course, it was easier for the mutual savings banks to reconcile themselves to advertising when they felt the growing pressure of competition from other institutions, both "thrifty" and not. And by the second half of the 1920s, such pressure on the long self-congratulatory mutual savings banks was undeniable. The ninth national meeting of the National Conference of Mutual Savings Banks in the summer of 1929 was an opportunity for savings bankers to reflect on their situation. Thomas F. Wallace, president of the Farmers and Mechanics Bank of Minneapolis, had chaired the Survey Committee responsible for putting together a "Resume of Banking in the United States as It Exists at the Present Time and Its Past History, Together with Future Outlook and Possible Future Requirements." In his address to the meeting, he said this:

> In the days when mutual savings banks controlled the savings business, there was a clear distinction in functions between the mutual bank and financial institutions that did a general banking business. But today that distinction has vanished because commercial banking institutions, in addition to their general banking business, now supply practically all the personal financial needs of individuals and families. . . .[169]

"Whereas in 1911 more than 43 per cent of all savings deposits were in mutual savings banks," reported another speaker at the meeting, "they held only 30 per cent in 1928."[170]

Savings bankers were torn on how to address this problem. O. H. Henry, former superintendent of banking in New York, offered this advice to the ninth national meeting:

> Too many mutual savings banks are still under the influence of the founders and they have not realized that in our present day economics of mass-production and mass-distribution, spending may be considered by some persons as a greater virtue than saving. To too many savings banks the relative decline in the popularity of their institutions is a triumph of sin over virtue—like the decline in going to church. They cannot see

that it is not that thrift has gone out of fashion, but there is a new style in thrift. Why should we save for a rainy day when "it ain't gonna rain no more"?[171]

In addition to their "cobweb economics," Henry also castigated mutual savings banks for their elitism and condescension to the working classes. "Too many savings bankers made the mistake of expecting the poor but virtuous to 'know their place,' to realize forever that there was one investment law for the rich and another for the poor," he argued. But today, "the wage-earner is the new capitalist and he knows his money is as good as anybody's—and he is out to get his share of prosperity."[172]

Many savings bankers agreed with Henry's analysis and advocated modernizing the mutual savings bank to the level of a "progressive business." In particular, there was rising resentment of the legislative restrictions placed on mutual savings banks, something a few bankers had long opposed.[173] Others felt the steps advocated by the modernizers would destroy all that was unique about the mutual savings bank movement, particularly its mutuality and philanthropic character. But the number of savings bankers who maintained "cobweb economics" and a more traditional notion of thrift was shrinking.

The divisions among the mutual savings bank movement were echoed throughout the thrift movement. The tension between adapting to changed economic circumstances and being co-opted by those circumstances was always present and in need of negotiation. Ultimately, the fate of the thrift movement hinged less on the strategic and rhetorical choices of its leaders and more on the investment choices of those who ignored it. While certain thrift activities and many institutions built by the thrift movement continued on after the onset of the Great Depression, the movement itself, as a self-conscious entity, largely dissolved. As the thrift movement faded away, the practice of thrift—by necessity—made a big return, but even the thrifty suffered after 1929. The Great Depression spelled the end of the already anemic idea that individual thrift was enough to protect one from economic misfortune.

It also proved O. H. Henry's optimistic prediction of an end to "rainy days" to be an illusion.

THE SUCCESS OF A MOVEMENT IN RETROSPECT

Public discussion of thrift during the 1910s and 1920s rivaled any period in American history. Thrift was "in the air"—ordinary citizens were familiar with the vocabulary of thrift, largely because thrift movement crusaders spread the message through newspapers, speeches, education programs, and community organizations. Thrift advocates adapted the message of thrift to address the governing realities of the twentieth century—a new level of prosperity, a skeptical working class, and the rise of mass production, consumption, and advertising—all of which were changing the way Americans understood themselves. Thrift advocates, to the degree they were successful, impacted Americans' understanding of thrift by responding to the immediate concerns of the economy and the war. During this period, thrift was a fluid idea, reformatted in response to challenges identified by its advocates.

As influential as dialogue about thrift may have been during this period, little trace of its impact is apparent today. As the current U.S. savings rate hovers around zero, and the economy falters after years of abundant credit, how ought we to measure the success of the thrift movement?

Its value lies in the very debate about the relevance of thrift. Many of the conversations about the importance of thrift during the 1910s and 1920s foreshadow current questions about how to live ethically in the material world. One Colorado Springs newspaper skeptically editorialized in 1926: "It is one of the peculiarities of the movement to inculcate thrift into the American people that everybody agrees with the preachments, concedes the vast benefits to be obtained by their simple employment, and continues along in the old slipshod way."[174] Today, Americans seem to echo these sentiments. We proclaim the importance of thrift-oriented ideas like recycling, buying green, and reducing our carbon footprints, while also upholding priorities that are antithetical to the thrift message, such as convenience, disposability, and instant gratification.

Perhaps, as Henry argued then and some argue today, the defenders of installment buying and advertising were right, and thrift merely has been transformed to meet the needs of a changed economy. Indeed, some of the pessimistic accounts of allegedly enduring American thriftlessness are overdone. And yet, surely there comes a point beyond which thrift ceases to resemble the virtue advocated by these reformers. The thrift movement of the early twentieth century consciously argued over and struggled with where exactly that line fell. Today, we have the opportunity and the need to take up that question again.

Chapter 4

A Century of Thrift Shops

Alison Humes

"Oh, look, a thrift shop!" Muriel said. "My biggest weakness."
— *The Accidental Tourist* by Anne Tyler[1]

THRIFT SHOPS EMERGED in the United States a little more than a hundred years ago. From that time to the present, their social function, the values they represent, and the attitudes we hold about them have changed significantly. Tracing their history and our opinion of them shows how our cultural beliefs about thrift and generosity, about denial and indulgence, about altruism and acquisitiveness have changed. Indeed, our notions about thrift shops have always been enmeshed with our notions about philanthropy (or giving) and conservation (keeping). Over its still robust lifetime, the thrift shop (generally non-profit and connected with a charity) has modeled the American social ethic—the importance we give to diligent work and wise spending, to remediating waste, to helping others, to the pleasures of the material world, and to equal access for all. As other institutions and initiatives that promoted an explicit ethic of thrift have faded away (savings and loans, the Housekeepers' Alliance, thrift curricula and school savings banks, National Thrift Week), the thrift shop is still going strong.

My own relationship with thrift shops is longstanding; I have been a habitué for forty years. From an early age, I appreciated pretty things, and I learned to appreciate them even more if they were a bargain.

My appreciation was cultivated by the examples of my mother and grandmother, who tutored me in the ways of acquisition and thrift. I am also interested in the meaning of the things one acquires, what they signify to oneself and to others. I love luxury as well as thrift, and I love confounding expectations. I appreciate design and fashion, but they are not fetishes of mine. I like glamour, but I think it is a lot of work. I am constantly trying to save money, but I constantly have the urge to spend it as well. Overall, I can admit, I love to shop, but I hardly ever buy retail. The only way to do, and have, what I want is by being thrifty. And so, thrift shops—junk shops, second-hand stores, tag sales—have played a significant role in my life as a consumer, as have other kinds of discount shops. Being generous is my vanity, and I am occasionally extravagant. Like many of my generation, I like to mix it up.

ONLY AMERICANS BUY RETAIL

My grandmother Luba, the youngest daughter of a prosperous and devout Jewish merchant, was born in Riga, Latvia, between, I believe, 1900 and 1902 (she would not say). Tiny and willful, she believed in glamour, charm, and seduction—part of which was the exchange of presents and the pleasure that comes with them. She became a designer of dresses and linens, an entrepreneur. Beauty and lavishness were her calling cards, but though she might be flirtatious, she was nobody's fool. She left Russia in the 1920s for the Philippines and then, in March 1941, came to the United States on a business trip, accompanied by her nine-year-old daughter; as Word War II threatened to engulf the Philippines, she decided to stay put. An immigrant and a single parent, she was shrewd and hyperaware of the value of a dollar. The goal was always to get something better for less. She cultivated her trade relationships for favors, insider prices, and deals. In her view, the ability to behave like the princess she thought she should be required being a hard-nosed bargainer. She insisted on top service and value: people should work hard and be grateful for what they could get, and things should be made to last and then carefully used until they were beyond creative repair.

My mother, Anna Lou, recently told me what she referred to as "the famous story of the ham." She must have been around eleven when Luba sent her to buy a half-pound of ham. When Luba saw the ham, she thrust it under my mother's nose, saying, "You call this ham?" Anna Lou was to go back to the shop, pronto, and return it. The butcher was to replace it with good ham. My mother said she would rather die. Why couldn't they just forget it, or if need be, buy other ham elsewhere? A confrontation would be both embarrassing and humiliating. But my grandmother insisted: getting one's money's worth—practicing thrift—required vigilance and if need be, aggression. "Watch what you're given, and pay attention where your money goes. You can't afford to waste money to save someone's feelings, even your own."

The corollary was that thrift and saving money permitted the Über Luba, as she was dubbed by a waggish friend, to shower those she loved with treats of all kinds. In my family, treats often came in the form of food—being taken out to dinner for butterfly shrimp, being fed chocolate cake, receiving (among other things) pomegranates and persimmons for Christmas. Though personally thrifty, my grandmother could not bear to be considered mean. Plus, generosity was exciting and fun.

My grandmother paid sharp attention to the parsing of social status. She considered herself educated and her background privileged but realized that these distinctions might be lost on Americans, who she feared noted only her foreignness. She admired what she perceived as the breezy entitlement of the American upper middle classes, into which she wished to assimilate. (Think Katherine Hepburn to Jane Wyatt.) Unapologetically elitist, she scorned the uneducated, the unpolished, and anything that looked "cheap." An advocate of self-improvement through gracious living, she cared deeply about presentation and taste and championed the importance of quality and appearances. Her Europeanized view of the good life meant that everything should look like a Fabergé egg.

Her visits to thrift shops in New York City were certainly nothing to publicize, but she was thrilled by her "finds." She liked to fix things up so that they looked fancy and substantial—she "antiqued" furniture and sewed Alençon lace onto plain silk lampshades. One of her projects, and eventual gifts of which I am the beneficiary, was a small bedside lamp. Somewhere she found, along Ninth Avenue perhaps, a battered white painted metal lamp with a rather nice scalloped base. What, if anything, was on the base when she got it I do not know; in its place she glued a graceful Chinese lady in white porcelain with a lotus blossom on her shoulder—one of a pair. To top the bulb, she hand-stitched a shade out of softly gathered white cotton around which she sewed the inevitable lace in the color she called "ecru." The other lady she glued to a small round wood base painted gold. The two of them stand on my dresser, swaying in opposite directions and nodding at each other, just as they used to at her house, fifty years ago.

SPIRITUAL RESCUE

The concept of thrift shops emerged in the United States at about the same time that my grandmother was born in Latvia. Here, the Industrial Revolution was causing social upheaval in terms of the move to wage labor, urbanization, and the loss of the extended family, difficulties that increased with the U.S. economic depression of the 1890s. Cities developed slums filled with the unemployed, widows and orphans, and the elderly—many of whom had come to the cities and factories to work but who, nonetheless, could not support themselves. Thrift shops grew up in this atmosphere, before the advent of socialism and the increased responsibility of the state for public welfare.

Thrift shops grew primarily out of a desire to provide men with employment. Although they were built on charity—the generosity of the "haves" who gave their time and activism or used items to help the "have-nots"—and were nonprofit, what the original thrift shops provided was not charity but the opportunity to work. They also provided the working poor with an opportunity to purchase goods at accessible prices. Started by idealistic men with strong religious conviction, these programs provided a way for social reformers to model the values of thrift, education, and hard work for those downtrodden by poverty, alcoholism, or indolence. The philosophy was to care for others by promoting diligence and industry while making new use of what would otherwise be discarded—in line with the traditional and long-standing thrift ethic.

Thrift shops were spiritually inspired institutions; like savings banks, they were an expression of a belief in the rightness of helping the poor. Indeed, this is still true today: the Mennonite Central Committee runs numerous thrift shops around this country and in Canada to support its charity work, as does the Catholic Society of St. Vincent de Paul and many others. Today, thrift shops are also run to benefit health institutions, hospitals, rehabilitation facilities, local PTAs, and community programs.

The idea for Goodwill Industries, which runs one of the country's best-known chains of nonprofit thrift shops, with $1.63 billion in retail sales in 2005, came to Edgar James Helms, a Methodist minister, in Boston in 1902. Helms, who grew up in Iowa, was a strong supporter of the temperance movement, having written editorials and worked in local politics in support of Prohibition. At age thirty-two, with a background in journalism, politics, and the study of Methodist theology, he accepted a ministry at the Morgan Chapel in Boston's South End, at that time an immigrant slum. A year later, in 1986, to help supply his mission—which included the first church-sponsored day care center and residences for some of his struggling parishioners—he started to travel around rich neighborhoods of Boston, collecting donations of clothing and household goods. Then, in 1902, he devised a plan whereby he put his community to work, repairing and recycling these castoffs to sell at low cost. The scheme was a success: soon he was collecting goods with a horse and wagon and, by 1909, a truck.

His ambitions were grand—not to build an empire but to eliminate poverty. "We have courage and are unafraid," he wrote. "With the prayerful cooperation of millions of our bag contributors and of our workers, we will press on till the curse of poverty and exploitation is banished from mankind."[2] He believed that individuals could improve their lot when given the opportunity to do so. His motto was "a chance, not a charity."

At about the same time that Helms took up his mission, the Salvation Army set up its first "salvage brigade" and opened its first "industrial home" in New York City, forerunners of its rehabilitation facilities for the unemployed, homeless, or disabled. Since its early days, the army had maintained shelters for men, but the aim of these new institutions was to be self-supporting as well as to create meaningful work opportunities through collecting and repurposing discarded items. Salvation Army founder and evangelist William Booth had suggested such an idea, which he dubbed the Household Salvage Brigade, in his 1890 manifesto *In Darkest England*: "We shall not have far to seek before we discover in every town and in every country the corresponding element to our unemployed labourer. We have waste labour on the one hand; we have waste commodities on the other."[3] These brigades were to collect household waste, from food to bones and fat, to broken stoves and instruments, old shoes and boots, broken umbrellas, empty tins and bottles, newspapers and books, rags and paper. That which could not be immediately used would be the stuff on which the poor would be put to work, sorting, repairing, and repurposing. And so it had come to pass: although rags and paper were the main source of income for the industrial homes up through the 1920s, the idea of refurbishing used goods and selling them had found a footing.[4] The Salvation Army opened its first thrift store in 1897 in Chicago.[5] By 2004, as stated in its annual report, it had 1,526 thrift shops around the country, which support its current rehabilitation efforts, addiction-recovery programs.

The organizations that set up the original thrift shops and promoted thrift more generally were, like other social activist movements of the day, inspired by religious teachings about the importance of saving souls, and they attracted middle-class women who were looking for meaning outside the private sphere. Saving souls meant ministering to and helping the poor and, as a result, grappling with a prevalent belief that poverty was the result of moral turpitude and personal failure. As noted by social historian Louise Tilly, "One set of connections between middle- and working-class women on both local and national levels is that of respectability and domesticity. Working-class women were seen by middle-class opinion leaders as the key—if they themselves could be taught order and virtue—to male personal conduct."[6] The participation of women was central, for instance, to the second flowering of the temperance movement in the late nineteenth century. The Women's Christian Temperance Union, established in 1874, feared alcohol as the instigator of moral, financial, and physical failure in their men, and thus in their families and themselves. Women, who did not yet have any legal or political rights, saw temperance as a fight to protect the home. The thrift movement had a similar appeal.

The thrift ethic provided a potential remedy to poverty, one that women embraced as a solution that they could prescribe (as social workers) and implement themselves in their own families. In a paper that tells the interesting history of how poverty lines were established, Gordon M. Fisher, a former researcher at the Department of Health and Human Services, traces the evolution of social activists' thinking about charity: In the 1870s, charity organization workers "thought that the causes of poverty lay entirely within the individual. . . . They went to poor applicants for charity as 'friendly visitors,' investigating their cases but seeking mainly to regenerate them as individuals and get them to practice self-reliance rather than seeking the demoralization of material relief." Yet in coming face to face with the actual conditions of the poor, "shortly after 1900, [they] began to realize that much of the poverty they were investigating was due . . . to external social causes."[7] Many of these workers were women, as social work became a field in which women could develop independent professional careers. Indeed, Evangeline Booth became the commander of the Salvation Army in the U.S. in 1904. For thirty years, the outspoken daughter of founder William Booth led a major expansion of the army's social services, its fund-raising, influence, and property, until she became the organization's first woman general in 1934.

A PENNY SAVED

By the 1920s, as the consumer economy grew, belief in the power of the thrift ethic was in full swing. Presidents endorsed it. Warren Harding talked about the importance of saving money; and then, when Calvin Coolidge took the job, he received so many letters requesting his imprimatur on the importance of thrift as the route to progress that, in 1923, he wrote what became a form response. It stated, in part: "No man is so poor that he cannot begin to be thrifty. No man is so rich that he does not need to be thrifty. The margin between success and failure, between a respectable place in life and comparative oblivion, is very narrow. It is measured by a single word, THRIFT. The man who saves is the man who will win."[8] Banker and real estate mogul Simon William Straus preached the value of thrift in his 1920 book *History of the Thrift Movement in America.* Thrift, he argued, was about much more than saving money: the practice of this virtue early and often would mold character to survive practically any adversity. He advocated that schools teach the value of thrift in all things. "Thrift is essential as the guiding principle of the individual because it imparts poise, moral stamina, courage, ambition, independence and efficiency."[9] He exhorted the masses to improve their lot by bootstrapping and increasing their savings to help advance their family and society.

Although Straus acknowledged "it requires just as much moral stamina to conquer the temptations of opulence as it does to combat the onslaughts of calamitous circumstances," he sounded like a bit of a scold.[10] "Thrift is submission to discipline, self-imposed. Thrift is denying one's self, present pleasures for future gain. Thrift is the exercise of the will, the development of moral stamina, the steadfast refusal to yield to temptation." In his view, this was a challenge facing not just the poor but American society as a whole:

To-day we are recognized throughout the world, as the most thriftless nation among the great powers. We must get back to the ways of Benjamin Franklin. Want and waste, extravagance, debauchery, riotous living, artificial social and business practices must be eliminated; in a word, the nation must be remade, not only by talking thrift but by teaching thrift and practicing thrift.[11]

Of course, the purpose of this thrift was to build wealth and thus be better able to provide for others.

A VIRTUE OF THE DOMESTIC DOMAIN

Women were the soldiers on the front line in the war to advance thrift. Unsurprisingly, they were already well aware of the importance of practicing thrift at home. As Flora Rose and Martha Van Rensselaer wrote in 1919 in "A Program of Thrift for New York State," a home reading course put out by the Home Economics Department at Cornell University, "The best way to begin a thrift movement is by studying simple household problems." After all, the word *economy* comes from the Greek *oikos nomos,* or the law of the house. The household was still perceived as a center for the creation of wealth, though responsibility for its financial management had largely passed to women within it. Embedded as they were in the domestic sphere, women were already allocating resources in terms of running the household and making purchases and worrying about how to make it all work.

In 1923, Benjamin R. Andrews, a professor of home economics at Columbia University, published *Economics of the Household: Its Administration and Finance.* He understood the importance women played in the domestic economy, and he thought that the application of scientific principles to household management—home economics—could only improve the home's efficiency and its ability to create wealth (essentially, he admitted, the result of women's labor). Although "experience indicates the wisdom of relying exclusively upon the man as money-earner," Andrews accepted that some women want to work earning wages outside the home—not a problem as long as she did so "in the light of her responsibilities." However, he thought it worth pointing out that (a) "there is an opportunity for income-producing inside the home . . . which for all but exceptional women, is equal at least to that of outside wage-earning" and (b) "housekeeping and homemaking are too demanding a task . . . , too interesting in their variety and freedom, too productive of values by which the family benefits, to be dropped for the lure of eight-hours a day and the pay envelope."[12] Part of the challenge, it is clear, was not only reducing waste and helping her husband make his business profitable but also making sure that her family got as much value as possible for its money. Her success at these endeavors, she was instructed, depended on her skills at thrift.

Such cultural assumptions often fell hard on poor women: Gordon M. Fisher, in another discussion of poverty lines, writes, "if a (working-class) family with an income equal to the cost of a standard budget was unable to provide for itself an actual level of living as good as the theoretical standard . . . some argued that the family—and particularly the wife—was not a sufficiently 'efficient' spender or manager."[13] These attitudes reveal a continuing tendency in some quarters to understand poverty as a moral failure.

SORRY SECONDS

But twenty years and more into the twentieth century, the emphasis on thrift did not yet extend to purchasing goods second hand. One reason might be that many goods (clothing and linens, for instance) were still produced at home, "made from scratch" rather than bought as consumer items. Still, Andrews, for instance, commends donating to thrift shops, noting that extending the useful life of an item is socially responsible. It is interesting, however, that he never suggests shopping there:

> Articles of clothing, no longer of use to one family, can usually
> be passed on so as to give service elsewhere, either privately

or through a church or charitable organization or through the second-hand clothing trade. There is a social responsibility for such further utilization of clothing and every reason why the economic values represented by the partly worn garments should be recovered for the original owners if possible, or at least that they be utilized socially. There are in several cities clothing bureaus that solicit gifts of worn clothing and sell them at reasonable values, the proceeds going to charities, such as the Clothing Bureau and Everybody's Thrift Shop of New York, and such enterprises could be copied elsewhere.[14]

The stigma of poverty in the public mind still meant that those who were afflicted by it were fundamentally different from those who were not. Thrift shops were considered a service for the poor, which meant that, almost by definition, they were not a realistic solution for the middle class. Donations were commended, but society was still struggling to accept actually purchasing used items, particularly clothing. Anne Rittenhouse, in her 1924 book *The Well-Dressed Woman*, gives over three chapters to Jean Worth, son of the great designer Charles Worth. He associates buying second hand with showiness, as if that meant dressing above one's social station. He writes:

> Within the last few years, too, there have arisen establishments where second-hand frocks are sold, and to such places women flock who want to dress showily, heedless of the fact that their mothers and grandmothers would have spurned the mere suggestion of wearing cast-off clothing, as unworthy the contemplation of gentle-folk.
>
> Even the so-called smart woman is now not above selling her once-worn frocks, or of wearing at a public place, such as a fashionable resort or race-meeting, a gown that has been lent her free for the day to advertise a new "creation." This is wholly unworthy of a lady and cannot be too sincerely deplored.[15]

After Rittenhouse takes back the narrative, she acknowledges the difficulties confronting the social woman of little means. This woman often finds herself accepting clothes from her richer friends, even if it means being faced with the nightmare of imperfect alterations. "No, the path of a clothes beneficiary is not a pleasant one. Yet rugged as it is, it gives a woman a chance to appear correctly dressed in the society to which she is accredited."[16] She writes that it is hard for the rich woman to give away clothes to friends: "Rich women have often regretted that friendship and not judgment should govern the disposal of their clothes. An affluent woman rarely finds a friend who can wear her discarded clothes with brilliant effect, one who does not have to struggle frantically to make them pleasing, to whom they give joy without anxiety." The solution she proposes to the donor is that she give away her excess clothing while it is still fashionable, inviting friends to come take their pick while tea is served, her maids are present to help her friends, and she is absent—so as not "to embarrass her friends by her presence or advice." To the woman of little means, Rittenhouse suggests serious and early planning of fashion solutions to avoid the risk of rushed and unwise last-minute purchases.

TURNING TRASH INTO CASH

Even if thrift shops were not yet popular places to shop, by the late 1920s, charities and social activists started to realize that thrift shops could be profit centers, the source of funds to support various social services. The tagline of The Thrift Shop, which in one month during 1927 or 1928 raised four thousand dollars in Washington, DC, to benefit four children's health organizations, was "We turn your trash into cash." The chairpersons and board members were all women, forty-seven of them listed by name on the shop's letterhead stationery. In a letter to the membership, the chairperson requests that each board member donate ten articles a month; she reports also a new marketing scheme to spur sales, inviting prominent local women to help sell in the shop.

The Red Cross Chapter in Montclair, New Jersey, reported in the February 15, 1928, issue of the *Red Cross Courier* that for almost five years, it had run a thrift shop that

> sells partially used clothing, household goods, and other articles contributed by members of the community, distributes books and magazines to "shut-ins," students, and prisons, and arranges for the "rehabilitation" of toys to be given away at Christmas. . . . The profits on sales over and above all expenses are sufficient to support two scholarships and aid the visiting nurses' service.[17]

For the Salvation Army, too, the stores were becoming more important. In the 1920s, clothes started being separated out from rag piles to be hung on hangers for display. According to the army's thrift-shop managers, who "emphasized the sale of old pictures, lamps, vases, household items that were known as 'bric-a-brac,' and especially of furniture," these items were more expensive to collect, but they brought in significantly more money per sale than bulk rag and paper sales. By 1929, its thrift stores east of the Mississippi were enjoying more income than its paper sales and were covering half the annual budget.[18]

Thought started being given to merchandising, location, and salesmanship. By 1935, large Salvation Army thrift shops in New York and Philadelphia, which were making more than 75 percent of their income from store sales, were displaying nice items together in a particular area in an effort to attract antiques dealers and collectors. The first jobs that men in the program were assigned changed, too—from helping in the baling room and unloading trucks to sorting, repairing, and pricing.

Patronizing second-hand shops was still done at arm's length, socially speaking, although clearly someone was shopping there. In April 1931, the *Journal of Home Economics* included an item on using second-hand furniture for a first apartment or home. The article, submitted by two authors from Columbia University's Teachers College, discusses an exhibit at the Homemaking Center's annual meeting in Holyoke, Massachusetts, in which several rooms were furnished "for initial housekeeping" with refinished second-hand furniture at a cost of $100—"well within the reach of a very modest income"—as well as a student's project successfully rehabilitating the living space of a Harlem family almost entirely with second-hand items.[19] Shopping for second-hand items was acceptable for some but still not pitched as a thrift strategy for everyone.

By the 1950s, the Salvation Army stores were being redesigned to make shopping more convenient and appealing. In Petaluma, California, in 1957, Captain George Duplain came up with a new slogan for the more stylish store: "A place where good neighbors may shop with dignity." Gains continued to be made in revenue, with stores passing the million dollar mark in the 1960s. The biggest change was a consistent new sophistication in merchandising. The army produced a manual on rules for store operation that dealt with customer relations, inventory control, pricing policy, and display.[20]

THE TRANSGRESSIVE THRILL OF A BARGAIN

The thrift shop was developing a more nuanced personality. When Straus exhorted the nation to "get back to the ways of Benjamin Franklin," he did not grapple with the fact that Mr. Franklin—in his later years, at least—had little taste for eliminating "waste, extravagance, debauchery, riotous living, artificial social and business practices." Benjamin Franklin, source of many pithy aphorisms about life, appreciated that, in the wrong hands, thrift could be a bore, a vice as much as a virtue. Franklin did not make a fetish of thrift, but he did love irreverence. His sophistication was such that he could appreciate that, like all ideals, thrift is in the eye of the beholder. From one point of view, thrift shops were mean places where downtrodden people could make limited choices from the leavings of others; an emerging alternative was that thrift shops were mysterious places that allowed people to subvert the system, subvert meaning about what things were worth, where something could be made out of nothing or undeserved treasure could be found.

The promotion of thrift and the value of saving made great inroads in society in the first half of the twentieth century. My grandmother Luba, a total capitalist, was constantly on her guard to be frugal; meanwhile, she did her best to have everything look glamorous and abundant and to lavish treats on her grandchildren. She saved everything. Fear of scarcity played in her mind; savings and thrift were ways of propitiating the abyss. And she loved finding a bargain.

According to my mother, Luba perused thrift and second-hand shops for a number of things, from bed jackets to dishes. She kept an eye out for a particular kind of terrycloth slippers that she favored—popular at the time, unused pairs made their way frequently enough to thrift shops. When she bought clothing or linens, she paid close attention to the quality of the fabric and examined the seams—double-stitched showed that a garment was well made. Even when buying retail, thrift was important. As my mother was growing up in New York City, my grandmother would take her to Saks or Bloomingdales to buy clothes. My mother remembers one winter coat that was on sale, really warm, very good quality, and to my mother's mind, appallingly ugly. My grandmother purchased it one size too big so that my mother would be able to wear it for more than one season. Then she took her out to dinner.

Luba loved to find furniture that been left on the street for the Sanitation Department to dispose of. So as not to be seen recuperating discards, she would hail a taxi on the avenue close by and tell the driver that she had a chair to take for repair but could not carry it herself. Then they would stop outside her "house," pick up the chair, and take it to a furniture repair man she knew on Amsterdam Avenue. She found her antique bedroom set at an apartment estate sale. If someone asked about the chair or the chest, she thought it socially preferable to say that she had bought it at auction. Buying something from somebody's apartment was the bottom of the shoppers' social order, even if a little better than rescuing furniture from the street. Getting something that cost little but looked as though it cost a lot provided a thrill: not only was the object pleasing but it allowed her to play in very much the way that horrified Jean Worth. Years later, in the same way, the local thrift shop provided old ball gowns for my sisters and me to play dress up.

SECOND-GENERATION THRIFT

My grandmother passed her hawk eyes on to her daughter, my mother, who distinguished herself from her mother by having no interest in glamour or appearances whatsoever but who, nonetheless, likes to acquire things that are unique and undervalued and to give presents. My mother, Anna Lou, has lots of possessions and very high standards—cotton must be 100 percent, frying pans should be cast iron, chocolate can only be dark, furniture should be wood, pillows can only be down, jewelry should be old, and silver can only be silver. She is an Olympics-caliber thrift shopper—a connoisseur not only of thrift shops but also of garage and yard sales, junk shops, second-hand stores, factory outlets, discounters, and dollar stores. If she has to buy something not available in one of these establishments, getting a deal is still paramount. In extremis, she will frequent an outlet. She likes to buy only things that are on sale, are discounted, or used.

As a shopper, my mother disdains anything that is expensive or disposable. In her view, people who buy retail are either rich or fools and most likely both. She does not give a fig about what others think of her consumption habits, even though her children and friends have given pet names to some of her more outlandish items—"the wimple," for instance, was a hat/headdress she wore against the cold. The white hat promoting Coca-Cola that she unselfconsciously wore practically daily one summer to the Wadawanuck Yacht Club in Stonington, Connecticut, was so non-U as to defy parody. A former bank vice president, she is proud that most of her extensive wardrobe and possessions have been found at thrift shops or their equivalent. Finding something that has been used but is "perfectly good" is as worthy a pursuit as any other kind of productivity. Even better is finding treasure—Art Deco silverware, say—mixed in with the dusty jumble in a junk shop and rescuing it at low cost to grace a daughter's dining table. Whereas my grandmother's presents always came in elaborate packages festooned with ribbons, lace, and baubles, my mother's presents often are presented in the paper bag she was given at the shop.

My mother, militantly generous in her own way, also sees thrift in moral terms. She installed a swimming pool to delight her son-in-law and grandchildren, but she had the heater taken out because she feels that a heated pool is profligate. She is appalled that her grandchildren do not really pay attention to which clothes are dirty and which are clean but just throw them all in the wash, resulting in wasted water. When I suggested that the children do their own laundry, she objected because they would use the dryer and waste electricity rather than hang their things carefully out to dry. Also, I suspect, properly spoiled grandchildren should not have to do their own laundry when at grandma's house. She does not see any real purpose in paper towels or store-bought garbage bags. To her, these are luxuries so useless that they do not even deliver pleasure—in other words, true waste. Even though her family is the object of her generosity, she does not trust any of us to be thrifty. Even as she worries that I am wasting money left and right, she offers me cashmere sweaters ("only 25 cents!" she crows), brings me two chandeliers (so I can choose the one I like best), and pays close attention to the lists of perishable electronics that her grandchildren feel are "les musts," as the Cartier people say.

THRIFT GOES MAINSTREAM

In the second half of the twentieth century, against a backdrop of growing consumption, increased immigration, and loosening social strictures, thrift shops became a more acceptable and familiar location for domestic activity. Thrift shops became places where one could acquire quantity (for instance, costumes for the school play), learn how to evaluate the quality of goods, and find items of value that had been overlooked. They began to be frequented by the middle class.

After World War II, the quantity of things available to Americans increased exponentially. More and more finished goods were purchased on the market rather than built and crafted at home. Choices, even for those of low socioeconomic status, became abundant. Low-priced goods made overseas were being imported, and people started to find that possessing lots of stuff did not free them from the desire to accumulate more. As mass-produced goods proliferated, the status of "new" grew. To take in the new, at some point one had to get rid of the old, even if it was not used up. There was more and more that could be donated to the thrift shop, and the variety and quality of goods one could find there increased just as well. The willingness of thrift shops to come and collect the stuff one wanted to get rid of was a huge service— a convenience presciently promoted by the Salvation Army as early the 1930s, under Evangeline Booth's command.

The discovery that one could find items of high quality in thrift shops was powerful enough that this information was passed back to lower-class women, who had inherited the idea that these were dubious places to shop. For instance, in an article that Rosemary Specian published in 1969 in the *Journal of Home Economics,* about training women on public assistance in Philadelphia for jobs as homemaker aides, she describes an assignment the women were given in comparative shopping. The students were to purchase items of children's clothing at a diverse array of shops, including large department stores, neighborhood shops, and discount and thrift shops:

> Each group returned with children's clothing they had purchased and compared prices, color, quality, and construction. Several of the women in the class took these garments home for their children to wear during the ten-week class period. A record of wearing times, washings, and mending or repairing was kept. . . . The students were surprised to find that the clothes from the most expensive stores did not always wear well and that neighborhood stores did not always provide the best buy. Although they were not too pleased with the idea of shopping in a secondhand or thrift shop, in the final evaluation it was

obvious to them that the thrift shop selections were the best buys of the group.[21]

THE HIPPIE ECONOMY

Thrift shops benefited hugely not only from the popular rejection of conformity, materialism, and standardization in the 1960s but also from broadening notions of what constituted good taste. In his history of the Salvation Army, *Somebody's Brother*, E. H. McKinley acknowledges that in those years "the Army gladly cashed in on the public demand for nostalgic and bizarre clothing."[22] And, indeed, when I was about fifteen, wearing second-hand fur coats became very popular in my set. None of us, of course, could afford to buy a new fur coat, and even thinking about doing so seemed ludicrous and stuffy. But the style of the day among the girls my age was hip-hugger bellbottom jeans, frayed at the hem, over well-worn Frye boots, and all covered in the cloak of an old fur. These we obtained from grandmothers' and mothers' closets or from thrift shops. I remember going to a shop in the East Village, in an unfinished, undecorated warehouse space on the second floor of a shabby quasi-commercial building, and finding racks of old fur coats, with worn patches and even in some cases rips. Of course, we wanted to find ones that had the fewest rips and were in the best shape, but since the designs of all these coats from the postwar years were capacious, it was more important to find ones that offered a semblance of fit, so you could move without being swamped by material.

These were beloved but not honored items; we would wear them sitting on the floor in the corridors of our high school or lie wrapped up in them in the meadows around Central Park's Bethesda Fountain or, when they had become too hot or unwieldy, leave them in heaps in the nearest available corner. Besides being warm, part of the pleasure they imparted was at once the luxury of the fur with all its expensive high-society allusions and the fact that they were very cheap to acquire and often in bad shape, so they did not need to be taken care of like some really valuable item. But then, as the fashion spread, used fur coats started becoming too expensive, even second hand, and so we gave them up as dated and also as a false projection of femininity. As one girlfriend shockingly remarked, "Women who wear fur coats don't know how to use their own fur to keep warm."

By the mid-1970s, when I was in college, "vintage" shops became popular, particularly in areas traversed by college students. The clothes in these places were inexpensive—used leather jackets, old jeans and party dresses, housedresses from the 1940s, and stilettos from the early sixties. There were also more expensive pieces—really well-preserved and cared-for cottons and linens that had been undergarments or night-clothes when people routinely wore many more layers of clothing than we did. I remember many beloved items that to this day remind me of how I felt at the time and who I thought I was—one short-sleeved dress with a full skirt, bias cut, that fell beneath the knee, found in Cambridge, Massachusetts, in, probably, 1971. It was made of a shiny, soft, somewhat frayed, white polyester, with swirling patterns of bluish flowers, in the style of a 1940s suit dress. Though it was really a little too big for me, I nonetheless wore it throughout the summer for years. At the same shop, I also got a hefty brown suede bomber jacket lined with red wool, padded and frayed at the cuffs and the collar (also too big), that made me feel as invincible as Snoopy, the World War I flying ace. The line between dressing and playing dress-up was happily fuzzy. I have been invited to only one explicit garden party in my life, and it was in those years, but I knew exactly what to wear: an old chemise of muslin and lace, over a full slip, which I cleverly held together with a lilac grosgrain ribbon. Whoever wore it originally may have thought of it as underwear, but to me it screamed "garden party."

Vintage shops were really edited versions of the stuff available in thrift shops, and as fashions dated, style avatars returned to the source to revive other forgotten garments. In *Spree: A Cultural History of Shopping*, Pamela Klaffke identifies Woody Allen's Annie Hall (1977) as the first character to bring thrift-shop style to the national stage, followed in the 1980s by Madonna and her edgier bustier-anchored look, and then, in the early 1990s, by grunge god Kurt Cobain and his consort Courtney Love's styling of the kinderwhore.[23]

THRIFT 2.0

Shopping in thrift shops continues to suggest thrift, originality, and chic. No longer just stopgaps for the financially challenged, thrift shops have become the terrain of the savvy shopper. It is no longer shameful to buy secondhand. Even the *New York Times* agrees: on the "Personal Business" page of the June 24, 2006, edition, the headline of a full-page article declares, "Savings Outweigh Any Stigma at Upscale Consignment Shops."[24]

According to the National Association of Resale and Thrift Shops—which promotes resale as "recycling"—there are more than twenty thousand resale, thrift, and consignment shops (profit and nonprofit) operating in the United States today. While overall U.S. retail sales grew 24 percent from 1997 to 2002 (to $3.1 trillion), the Census Bureau reports that, over the same five-year period, used-merchandise stores grew by 29 percent to $7.8 billion in sales. In 2002, the bureau listed 18,207 used-merchandise establishments, with a combined total of 117,776 paid employees and an annual payroll of $1.7 billion.[25] These numbers suggest that, from the consumer's point of view, the stigma of buying secondhand is fading.

For many, the message that "used" (let's say, "pre-owned") delivers is no longer "shabby" but "open-minded," socially flexible, and "good value." "Shabby chic" has become a style category of its own. Our feelings about the value of old things have changed somewhat: something does not have to be a rare antique or a family heirloom to have a history on which meaning accrues. Even short of becoming serious collectors, people unaccountably develop affection for certain objects or classes of objects—old books or tools or china—that increase their value. Look at what has happened to Fiestaware and kitchen furniture from the 1950s.

Today's thrift shoppers may have a multitude of motives: a desire to express individuality, a lack of interest or concern in matters of class, a wish to acquire designer labels for less and to appear of higher class than one can afford, an unwillingness to be counted among those co-opted by corporate capitalism and power branding, the ability to spot treasure overlooked by others, and a willingness to get by with less. Accordingly, thrift shopping is promoted in various forms and venues from the mainstream magazine *Real Simple* to the web site *The Dollar Stretcher* (www.stretcher.com/menu/first.cfm) to the pseudoreligious Reverend Billy, who preaches for "local economies and real—not mediated through products—experience" through his Church of Stop Shopping (www.revbilly.com).

Some are using the thrift-shop idea as a way of building communities around the ideal of sustainable living and in counterpoint to a culture perceived as wasteful, insatiable, superficial, and uncaring. Wanting to "stay true to the charitable spirit of thrifting," Thethriftshopper.com is a web site for thrifters looking to help nonprofit causes as they shop. Its founders and designers, Michael and Cookie Gold, have compiled a searchable database of 8,400-plus charity-driven thrift shops around the country. Michael thinks the list will top out at ten thousand shops, perhaps even twelve thousand. The Golds distinguish between charity-driven thrift shops and resale or consignment shops, listing only the former because they want to promote nonprofit thrift shops, not-for-profit businesses that may seem to be charities. "[D]onors . . . are misled by the fact that the business has the word *thrift* in [its] name. Now anyone who wants to support a charity by shopping or donating can use our directory and be sure that their [*sic*] monies and donations do indeed support those charities."

Buying secondhand fits nicely with current ideals about environmental conservation. Thrift shops actively appeal to those interested in recycling, who see thrifting as an antidote to wasteful consumption and overflowing landfills. One page of the Salvation Army's Canadian web site is headed "Recycling since 1890."[26] Some individuals are bypassing the idea of purchasing altogether with clothing swap events, such as ThriftOn and Swap-O-Rama Rama, which are organized and publicized via the Internet and hosted at different locales in cities across the country.[27] Often considered a community service, these efforts are motivated by a desire both to recycle and to move away from our highly consumerized contemporary culture. (Of course, in a footnote of postmodern irony, mass-market clothing manufacturers like Urban Outfitters, Abercrombie, and Aeropostale are getting hip to the trend and are designing and selling clothing that aims to look like thrift-shop finds—vintage T-shirts, team jackets, etc.)[28]

THRIFT IS GOOD BUSINESS

Over time, the goals of the many charities running thrift shops shifted from their original purpose of lifting up the poor in their own communities by providing employment to making money to support their mission. Suzanne Horne, in her book *Charity Shops: Retailing, Consumption & Society,* analyzes English thrift shops—she calls them "charity shops"—as having four main functions:

> to provide a method of raising unallocated funds that can be used for any purpose . . . to provide a social service, offering cheap goods to those customers who cannot afford to shop at commercial retail outlets . . . to raise awareness of its particular charitable cause . . . [and] the recycling of goods, or the "green" function. . . .

She writes that "as the economic potential of the shops became evident, commercialization and profit making became a main reason for selling goods. Most charities go into retailing in order to make money, which will in turn enable them to carry out their individual primary purpose. . . ."[29]

With the potential of becoming more profitable, thrift shops upped their profile by moving to better locations that could attract more shoppers with more money. (This is not a new idea. Indeed, the Salvation Army store management noted the importance of this as early as the

1930s.[30]) Housing Works—a group of New York City charity shops that raise money for people with AIDS—has a stylish edge, stores in popular neighborhoods, attractive window displays, and an auction site on the Web. Its various enterprises in New York City—thrift shops, a secondhand bookstore and café, a catering business—are stylish and sophisticated, designed to be profitable businesses that fund the organization's efforts as well as provide meaningful work for clients of its services. Thrift is not an explicit part of its values, which it publishes and which involve not passing judgment on others, direct action, and human rights. Housing Works' shops choose the secondhand objects they sell for quality and style. Much thought goes into the arrangement and chic of objects displayed in the shop windows, which are auctioned online—for instance, a barely worn light-camel-colored pair of Bruno Magli open-toe, pebbled sling backs, lined in gold leather in my size, minimum bid $35, was auctioned off on September 5. Of course, they will not go for that, I think. I bid $60 online and am surprised to get them for $38.50. (Housing Works, in an indication of its seriousness, suggested I donate the difference.) They will make a good Christmas present for one of my sisters.

The Internet has taken on an increasingly important role in the thrift-shop marketplace, allowing charities as well as others to sell secondhand goods to the highest bidder. Goodwill Industries claims to have started the first nonprofit Internet auction site, in 1999. The site, shopgoodwill.com, allows the organization to offer its donated goods to a much larger public. Similar to the way that thrift shops were able to play a role in a neighborhood almost a century ago by encouraging community and bringing people together to share, swap, or recycle goods, Craigslist.org has multiple community-based message boards where individuals can barter, buy, or get free goods and services, recycle objects, find work, and help one another. The idea of the thrift shop has evolved into eBay and the like, where bargain seekers with a credit card can anonymously join the mass-market hunt for both the cheap and the precious. (Pierre Omidyar, founder of eBay, the pioneering and hugely successful world-as-thrift-shop community, became a millionaire many times over. Simon Straus would find in his story the perfect example of the thrift ethic: inspired to create a worldwide local network, community, and market, Omidyar created enormous wealth and now has retired to be a philanthropist, setting up the Omidyar Network—as has his engineering partner, Jeff Skoll, who runs the Skoll Foundation.)

TOO MUCH OF A MUCHNESS

The problem with my thrift-shopping habits is that they are out-moded—reflexive instead of effective. I do not need more stuff. For example, I have a trunk full of fabrics—all shapes, sizes—that I keep for the curtains, upholstery, and repairs I intend to make someday, along with a sewing machine that I use about once every three years. The reality of my life is that sitting down to the family sewing is at this point pure extravagance. Time is the most costly commodity: it is far more efficient to pick up a pair of jeans for one of my kids from practically anywhere than to sit down and sew up a pair. And, frankly, watching a TV show with my son is of greater value to me. Despite my awareness of this, I continually ponder more potential projects and finds. This habit may be part of the reason my mother does not really trust me to be thrifty.

My thrift and saving are expressions of sentimentality toward the past and uneasiness about the future. For example, I keep not only my own sewing box, given to me by a friend of my grandmother's when I was about twelve, but also my grandmother's own sewing box. Both these objects hold a history of personal thrift, although neither is frequently useful. They are like keepsake boxes that reassure me from time to time that not everything has changed. Inside are buttons, zippers, ribbons, bobbins, spools of thread, remnants, snaps, pins, pieces of string, the odd unattached key, skeins of wool, a yard of lace, some emery boards, bobby pins: I am prepared for any kind of couture emergency. I do not think I fear scarcity as my grandmother did, but I fear not being prepared. Mostly I hate the idea of not having them.

In addition to all the stuff I have, there is a seemingly infinite abundance of more available, for sale at any price point. If I want to save money on clothing, I am not limited to the thrift shop. I can get designer items at sample sales or designer knockoffs at department stores, Isaac Mizrahi at Target, or Karl Lagerfeld at H&M. In New York City, the cost of fashions worn by women on a bus is very similar to the pricing of airplane seats—you might have bought your handbag retail when it just came out, the woman in front of you may have purchased it overseas at a discount, the woman across the aisle may have picked it up for a song at Daffy's (which brands itself as offering "bargains for millionaires"), and the students up front got theirs from street vendors hawking copies in the West 30s. Our notions of value have changed. Clothing, furniture, stuff can be forever, or it can be disposable. In my New York City neighborhood, which is largely made up of immigrant families from the Caribbean and Central America, there are dollar stores that sell a lot of household merchandise off brand (from shampoo to notebooks to phone jacks) and department stores that sell overage or seconds from big-name labels (for instance, Diesel or Sevens jeans at twenty-five dollars a pair). The young ladies at 157th and Broadway are just as fashionable as their peers in Soho.

What I end up buying is a mix—sandals at an outlet for $19.99, a Norma Kamali gown at a designer's sample sale for $500 (and then tailoring for $150), a pair of tennis shorts at a thrift shop for $1.50, a well-crafted sofa for $3,000 (50 percent discount for a floor sample), old wood bookcases for $25 each from Craigslist.org. There is such variety to play with that my spending is not restricted to a particular aesthetic or class. The current "look" is playing an ever-greater role in all of our lives, yet I am constantly calculating how to get whatever I want to buy for less.[31] And insofar as I am able to create wealth in my household while engaging with others, I try to get rid of the stuff spilling out of closets and corners—outgrown toys, clothes, sports equipment, furniture made redundant by moving, curtains that have been replaced, kitchen equipment never really used (ice cream and popcorn makers), insufficiently appreciated gifts—by selling what I can, giving some as presents, and donating to thrift shops. The last resort is putting stuff out with the trash, although, frankly, I sometimes suspect that that would be the most sensible thing to do.

Thrift and luxury are entirely intertwined, for one cannot exist without the other. In any circumstance, people routinely make judgments on where to scrimp (or if not scrimp, get value for one's dollar) and where to indulge, whether on the level of deciding to have a turkey for a Sunday dinner or of making sure you are not being overcharged by the five-star restaurant. As managers of their families and households, women are continuously making these choices—which purchases can wait, who has a birthday coming up, who needs shoes—constantly balancing necessity and pleasure.

But the tendency to see thrift and luxury as opposites still endures. Generally, we are likely to be more critical of others' choices than we are of our own. In *The Economics of the Household,* Benjamin Andrews acknowledges this human frailty:

> Indeed it would be well if we gave up entirely our present concept of luxury, which is largely an envious criticism of others who have things which we do not possess. We might better check each his own spending in terms of individual welfare and the results of our spending on social welfare. In the smallest income family there is some margin of spending for tobacco, drink, unwise selection of food, clothing, and other commodities, poorly chosen recreative and cultural goods, that bring to the family less of satisfactions that it might secure on a better regulated scheme of spending.[32]

While it is true that everyone sometimes makes poor choices, making a place for the giving and receiving of pleasure is also, after all, what the practice of thrift allows one to do.

THE LUXE AND VOLUPTÉ OF THRIFT SHOPPING

Finally, in this age and culture of surfeit, luxury today is about time, not stuff. Because successful thrift shopping requires browsing, thrift shops require time. So for me, thrift shopping at its best is a leisure activity to do with women I love. Unless you are in search of a very basic item—t-shirts, say—you do not go to a thrift shop with specific expectations. In that way, thrift shopping is very different from the home economics principle of making a list and buying only what you need. You do not go to a thrift shop for the service because, unless you have a personal relationship with the store personnel, there is not any. You go with the idea of browsing, spending time, and being open to finding anything from the practical to the frivolous.

Although thrift shops were originally organized by men who aimed to help their downtrodden fellows, the keeping of thrift shops (excepting the big chains) has turned easily over to women, who support the hundreds of small shops around the country. Their patronage not only as shoppers but also as volunteers and employees benefits various charities. In many small towns, these independent thrift shops are a gathering place for women in the community.

I visited one, near White River Junction, in Vermont: I do not remember its name and the town currently has at least six. It was on the main square. As a couple of local elderly female clerks tended the cash register, folded donated linens, and chatted companionably, I browsed the racks and shelves. My finds: a red-straw boater, a leather change wallet I have never used, old kid gloves (for my mother, who repurposes them for gardening), and a pair of L. L. Bean thick, khaki trousers.

Because thrift shops are not conducive to directed shopping, they can be frustrating to the goal-oriented. Perhaps this is one of the reasons you do not often see men hanging out there. Indeed, none of the men I have ever known has suggested stopping in at a thrift shop. Occasionally, one has accompanied me when we have been looking for, say, a dresser or a dining room table. Not that they do not exist, but not one man I have ever known personally has ever been caught up in the spell of undirected wandering and looking over what the shop has in store.

Thrift shops are great places to explore possibilities not only of thrift but also of generosity, gift giving, and pleasure. They are places to practice the arts of discretionary spending, unique in the invitation they offer to indulge one's acquisitive desires and feel virtuous at the same time. One of the things my mother really loves about thrift shops is knowing that, when she walks in, if she finds something she really wants, chances are she will be able to afford it.

In his book *A Theory of Shopping*, Daniel Miller, who studies material culture and, in this case, the shopping habits of women in North London, posits that a woman's routine shopping behavior is one way she expresses the importance of her relationships. Shopping is a ritual of devotion to her family, behavior by which she tends the relationships that matter to her. In her purchases, she creates who she thinks these people are and who she wants them to be, considering what she gauges to be necessities and treats for her loved ones as well as how she can make economies. Thrift is central to how she chooses to spend her money, when to scrimp, when to spend.

Recently, while I was spending a summer weekend at my mother's house, she took me on a tour of local thrift shops—to assess the wares, as it were. Our first stop was the COMO, the thrift shop in her Connecticut town. The COMO, which started as a local community center in 1946, supports a variety of local programs, among them a preschool, low-cost meals for the elderly, and recreation and pottery classes. Its thrift shop is a place where you can find all manner of old stuff, from furniture to coffee pots, the odd dish, sunglasses more or less from the 1980s (my mother buys all her sunglasses here because, as she points out, they always get lost), and lots of clothes for suburban women and children. We cruised for awhile but did not find too much. We picked over the china offerings—I considered some old plates, which I rejected when my mother told me they were junk. I got a plastic wall plate and a brown suede box. I passed up a cat carrier as too heavy and unwieldy and later regretted it when I needed to take our family kitty to the vet in a picnic basket.

We moved on to the Mystic Women's Club Thrift Shop, which is a smaller store staffed by volunteers. They were having a three-dollar-bag sale—all the clothes you could fit in a brown grocery bag for three dollars. There was a skirt I liked, but it was too small; I settled for two pairs of shorts—not enough to fill the bag—and a phone answering machine, never used, $7.99. I told my mother to forget the pants she wanted to buy my fifteen-year-old son. First of all, they did not fall into the fairly rigorous category of what he considers jeans; and, second, the label revealed that they were originally marketed to women—the kiss of death for any garment's hope of joining his wardrobe.

What this relaxed and easy Saturday was all about was not really getting stuff cheap or even the stuff itself, although I am wearing the shorts and using the phone machine. The satisfactions of our thrift-shopping experience were perhaps the values of thrift itself—spending time with my mother, talking through possibilities of profit and loss, recycling used things, thinking about others, knitting an experience together in support of our joint enterprise of family and community. This was mother–daughter quality time, the quality being in our creating meaning together and for each other, exploring our shared and separate tastes, values, and judgments, feeling out where the boundaries are. Although we can practice thrift at thrift shops, for me and mine, they also offer the thrill of profligacy, the luxury of browsing, and a connection to where we came from and where we still want to be.

Chapter 5

In Savings We Trust
Credit Unions and Thrift

Clifford N. Rosenthal

*A credit union is not an ordinary financial concern, seeking
to enrich its members at the expense of the general public.
Neither is it a loan company, seeking to make a profit at the
expense of the unfortunate. . . . The Credit Union is nothing
of the kind; it is an expression in the field of economics of a
high social ideal.*

—Alphonse Desjardins[1]

ORIGINS OF THE CREDIT UNION MOVEMENT IN THE UNITED STATES

THE CREDIT UNION MOVEMENT in the United States was born in the
first decade of the twentieth century. It did not arise from a groundswell
of popular sentiment nor as an offshoot of a broader social movement.
Neither was it quintessentially American in its origin. Cooperative
finance generally traces its roots to the middle decades of the nineteenth century in Germany where rural and urban poverty spurred
Friedrich Wilhelm Raiffeisen, Hermann Schulze-Delitzsch, and others
to develop organizations to provide mutual credit. In North America,
credit unions began to emerge in the very first years of the twentieth century, through the work of Alphonse and Dorimene Desjardins in Levis,
Quebec: They joined with their neighbors, raised $26.40 at a meeting,

and in December 1900 founded a *caisse populaire*.[2] Interestingly, one of their first initiatives was to establish a children's "penny savings" program that eventually moved into the schools.

The success of this early *caisse populaire* soon attracted attention south of the Canadian border in Manchester, New Hampshire, where many French-Canadian immigrants had settled. In 1908, with the encouragement of Monsignor Hevey of St. Mary's Church, La Caisse Populaire Ste. Marie—"St. Mary's Bank"—was formed for its parishioners. It was called a "bank" (a word that remains in its name today) because there was no law, state or federal, that provided for the creation of a credit union. In 2008, St. Mary's Bank—the only credit union in the United States that has *bank* in its name—celebrated its hundredth year as a thriving, community-oriented institution. Its original home in a three-story house has now become America's Credit Union Museum.

The key figure in the spread of the credit union movement in the United States was a capitalist and philanthropist whose name became known to millions of Americans for another kind of thrift: Edward Filene, best known for Filene's Bargain Basement. He became familiar with cooperative finance during a visit to India and later became acquainted with Desjardins' work. He saw the problem of usury first hand: As his workers left the gates of his enterprise in Boston with their pay in hand, moneylenders descended upon them for their usurious share.

Filene was convinced there had to be a better way. He proceeded to bankroll a decades-long crusade to establish credit unions around the country. Roy F. Bergengren was his chief organizer, traveling around the country to seed the credit union idea among groups of working people and lobbying for state laws to enable the creation of this new financial entity. Only in 1934 was a federal law passed and signed, providing another means to establish credit unions.

THE GREAT DEPRESSION AND ITS LEGACY: SHAPING VALUES ABOUT THRIFT

In the depths of the Great Depression, when the Federal Credit Union Act was signed into law, my parents were adolescents, facing a future that promised nothing but economic insecurity. Like those of the rest of their generation, their early experiences marked them for life. Thrift was not a philosophy, not a set of moral precepts; it was a necessity, the survival path through hard times.

Despite my parents' frugal ways, ironically, it was not their habit of thrift that set them on the path that eventually brought our family into the middle class decades later. My immigrant grandfather, who ran a small neighborhood grocery in inner-city Newark, New Jersey, won two hundred dollars playing the numbers. (Do not try this at home!) With that windfall, he was able to pay my mother's tuition for secretarial school. The skills she learned started her on a fifty-year career as a legal secretary. Her income, supplementing my father's modest wage as a postal clerk, enabled our family to live a life without luxury but without want.

None of that would have been possible, however, without financial discipline. One of my earliest memories of money was seeing the set of small metal boxes, in faux-wood grain, into which my mother sorted money for the various household needs. Another, less pleasant memory: the arguments I heard about money—not that it was squandered on drink or extravagances—but simply that there was scarcely enough to go around. Hearing this, I offered to give up my 25-cent weekly allowance. (It was not accepted.)

I remember, too, the school-based saving programs—the cardboard folders with slots for coins of different denominations, which we could fill and eventually deposit in the local savings bank. I rarely meet a person of my generation who does not have similar fond memories of that practice—long abandoned but now making something of a revival.

I have no doubt that my early experiences and the values I absorbed shaped my life's trajectory. For nearly forty years, I have worked in various ways to help people, especially those in low-income and minority communities, save money. I spent the better part of a decade working with and without pay as a food co-op organizer, trying to build systems through which low-income people could economize on their groceries and free up money for their other survival needs. In 1979, my lifework found me. The migrant farm worker organization I worked for established a credit union, and I became its first president.

I was hooked immediately by the elegant simplicity of the credit union concept: people joining together to pool their savings and make loans to each other. "Not for profit, not for charity, but for service"— that motto and mission statement clearly defines credit unions in the financial marketplace. For me, credit unions were the perfect marriage of my ingrained family values about thrift and my commitment to social justice forged in the 1960s. Credit unions were a pathway to dignity for low-income people, institutions for self-help at the family and community levels. Credit unions could help their members escape the vicious cycle of poverty. With their business model, credit unions could help sustain low-income communities even when public sector help was diminishing or absent.

Even in the most challenging circumstances, you will find many individuals who, like me, are "addicted" to credit unions. It is rarely the pay or status that keeps them engaged; rather, credit unions resonate with their core values in the most satisfying way: not for profit, not for charity, but for service.

THE "RELIGION" OF CREDIT UNIONS

Missionary zeal marked many of the leaders and organizers of the credit union movement in the first half of the twentieth century. Credit union field workers traveled tirelessly, brought people together, educated them about the benefits of pooling their funds, and helped them formally charter credit unions. They were people like Dora Maxwell and Louise Herring, whose names are honored to this day in the credit union movement with awards named after them. Their work was always demanding, sometimes dangerous (especially during times when use of the word *union* could engender hostility or violence in some quarters). But little capital was needed to form a credit union, and the technical requirements were (in the early years) not formidable: as few as seven people with a "common bond"—of employment, geography, or membership in an association—could pool a few dollars and apply for a charter. Lawyers were not required; credit unions were a movement of, by, and for lay people, typically workers of modest wages. Louise Herring was able to claim credit for organizing some five hundred credit unions over the years—a number that would be utterly impossible today because regulatory procedures have become far more complicated and financial entry barriers much higher.[3]

Economics generally keeps people out of the commercial banking system. But in the United States, race long played a role in excluding people from the financial system—especially but not only in the segregated South. The late James Gilliam recalled the formation of the St. Luke Credit Union in rural North Carolina in 1944. "We'd meet every Wednesday night in a one-room schoolhouse with a stove. And we'd put in a quarter or a dollar. Out of that . . . we started a credit union."[4] Under the leadership of Mr. Gilliam, the credit union served the African-American community for more than sixty years, growing to become a multimillion dollar institution. It helped countless members buy farms, add indoor plumbing, start small businesses, and more when banks refused to lend to African Americans trying to gain a foothold in the economic system.

In the African-American community, churches played an especially important role. Faith-based credit unions have a distinguished lineage, going back to the very origins of the credit union movement, in the work of Alphonse Desjardins in Quebec and the parish-based St. Mary's Bank in Manchester, New Hampshire. In June 1952, members of the Second Mt. Sinai Baptist Church in Cleveland, Ohio, formed a credit union for their congregation.[5] To become a member, one had to purchase a "share account" with at least five dollars. Many of the members could not afford that, so they brought in 25 cents each Sunday after church until they reached that goal. Rita Haynes, who later would rise to the top ranks of the community development credit union movement, began serving as a volunteer secretary of the board of directors in 1958. The credit union operated for decades through space lent to it by the church, growing gradually. As local banks were leaving the community, the credit union expanded its vision: it renamed itself the Faith Community United Credit Union, acquired a donated branch facility, opened its doors to the community, and doubled its membership in a year. A ten-million-dollar institution today, led by CEO Rita Haynes, it has been a tireless innovator in pioneering savings and lending products. It was one of the first credit unions in the United States to introduce Individual Development Accounts (IDAs) to incentivize savings through matched contributions, and its Grace Loans—an alternative to high-priced "payday" loans—have been a huge success financially and in member service, winning national recognition.[6]

MODERNIZATION AND GROWTH: SOMETHING IS GAINED, AND SOMETHING IS LOST

Up to 1970, credit unions were essentially "pure" cooperatives, owned entirely by their members, whose deposits were called *shares* (as they are, for the most part, today). This terminology reflected the risk borne by members for the financial health of their institution: if the credit union became insolvent, they stood to lose their entire stake. (In contrast to shares held in stock corporations, however, the upside of ownership was limited because credit unions are not-for-profit cooperatives with restricted investment powers.)

In 1970, the credit union world began to change dramatically.[7] Legislation was passed extending federal deposit insurance to credit unions, similar to that enjoyed by banks. An independent federal regulatory agency, the National Credit Union Administration, was established. Some in the credit union movement considered these changes a "deal with the devil." On the one hand, members henceforth would enjoy security for their savings. But the autonomy, the collective responsibility, the complete ownership by and accountability to members would be compromised. Government supervision and regulation, some felt, would inevitably transform and increasingly burden credit unions.

Still, the case for deposit or share insurance was compelling. If all other banking and thrift institutions enjoyed deposit insurance, how could credit unions hope to attract savings from their members and survive? Faced with the choice between savings backed by "the full faith and credit of the U.S. government" and savings backed solely by the prudent financial management of their fellow members—most of whom were not bankers by trade—most credit union members sooner or later would have abandoned their institution for other financial institutions.

Once credit union members received the assurance that their savings were backed by federal insurance, just as were deposits in banks and thrifts, the credit union movement expanded dramatically. In 1977, credit unions gained the power to offer "share drafts"—checking accounts. This was especially important because it enhanced the ability of consumers to save and transact at a single institution. Over the course of the 1970s, the number of members of federal credit unions more than doubled (approximately 12 million to 24.5 million), while assets in federal credit unions nearly quintupled ($8.9 billion to $40 billion).[8]

SAVINGS: THE MESSAGE AND THE MEDIUM

The concept of thrift was integral to the credit union movement from its very beginnings.

For decades, credit unions preached the gospel of thrift with a slogan and a symbol. "Pay yourself first," credit union managers urged their members; no matter what you make, put a little aside in a savings account. The message was simple and positive: savings was not a form of self-denial but rather was something you did for yourself. Although less prevalent than it once was, the slogan is still used today by many popular financial advisors.

Graphically, credit unions promoted themselves through the image of a small, cheerful, mustachioed man in an overcoat carrying an umbrella onto which rain was falling, bearing labels such as "hard times, sickness, financial distress." The message resonated for generations of Americans: save for a rainy day! Credit unions were there to help ordinary, prudent people with life's emergencies. The imagery of "the little guy" is now a historic relic, having gradually disappeared after the 1960s. But the precept of building an "emergency fund" to buffer against unwelcome life changes, like job layoffs and medical bills, is no less relevant today and is often the first advice given by financial planners.

The key to successful savings for individuals—and a key to the success of the credit union movement—is that savings must be regular, systematic, and, preferably, automatic. The majority of credit unions in the United States (unlike some other countries) grew out of workplaces—factories, government, or other enterprises. Members were encouraged to sign up with their employers for payroll deduction, a weekly or biweekly allocation from their paychecks that would go directly into their credit union accounts. It is the best, most painless example of "paying yourself first"; the money never reaches your hands, and you are not tempted to spend it. Similarly today, advocates for increased retirement savings are urging that participation in 401(k) and similar plans be offered on an "opt-out" rather than "opt-in" basis—that is, savings deductions should be automatic unless an individual explicitly chooses not to participate.

SAVINGS AND THE POOR

"It's all very well to urge people to save," some might argue, "but what about the people without a regular paycheck, the poor? Is it realistic to expect that they will save?" To the contrary, credit unions would argue that *everyone,* even the poor, can, should, and actually do save, even if in small amounts.

On September 23, 1995, Oseola McCarty was awarded the Presidential Citizens Medal. In June 1996, she became Honorary Doctor of Humane Letters, Harvard University, one of many national and international awards she received in her lifetime.[9]

Oseola McCarty was a laundress. For seventy-five years, she washed and ironed clothes for the people of Hattiesburg, Mississippi, initially for as little as $1.50 a bundle. In 1995, at the age of eighty-seven, recognizing "I'm old and I'm not going to live always," she made some decisions about where her life savings should go: 10 percent to her church, some to her relatives, and 60 percent to the University of Southern Mississippi. She noted, "They used to not let colored people go out there, but now they do, and I think they should have it."[10]

Ms. McCarty came to the savings habit very early in life, saving money as a child to help take care of her grandmother for whose sake she left school in the sixth grade. Eventually, as she began earning a little more on her laundry work, "I put it in savings. I never would take any of it out. I just put it in. It just accumulated."[11]

Oseola McCarty, African-American washerwoman with a sixth-grade education, gave $150,000 to endow a scholarship "with priority consideration given to those deserving African-American students enrolling at the University of Southern Mississippi."[12]

The message is clear: the poor can and do save. It is true in the Untied States, and it is true even in the third world. For decades, international aid organizations have promoted microenterprise funds to provide loans to the poor. But after years of working primarily through government agencies, more and more donor organizations have concluded that microenterprise funds *must* encourage savings among their clients, if these funds are to be independent and sustainable.

IN THEIR OWN WORDS:
HOW SAVINGS CHANGES LIVES

In the United States, community development credit unions (CDCUs)— credit unions that specialize in serving low-income communities—have grown gradually for decades by pooling the savings of low-income people, whose accounts typically are too small to interest banks. In most CDCUs, the majority of member-depositors have accounts of only a few hundred dollars or less. But even small amounts of savings can make a profound difference in people's lives.

What do savings mean for people of modest means? In 1989–1990, the National Federation of Community Development Credit Unions conducted an intensive study of a credit union that we had helped organize during the period 1984 to 1986 in a low-income, inner-city Manhattan neighborhood.[13] In the course of this study, we analyzed the complete lending history of the credit union in its earliest years and used this opportunity to interview some of the credit union's members. The interviews provided rich material for an understanding of how financial services—lending, savings, and transactions—actually are perceived by low-income consumers.

Savings and borrowing are generally viewed as opposite activities. But our interviews suggested that it is more appropriate to view them as linked on a spectrum. Take the case of "Arturo" (all names have been changed), who earned $24,000 a year and borrowed $2,000 from the Lower East Side People's Federal Credit Union to improve the co-op apartment he had bought more than a decade previously. He had taken other loans, as well—not because he was overly dependent on credit but because he believes in borrowing as a method of forced savings. In each case, he deposited the proceeds of his loan into his savings account at the credit union and then made monthly payments on his loans from his salary. "This is the only way I see to save money," he said.[14]

"Emilio" had a similar approach. He had borrowed $1,000 from the credit union to purchase furniture and was able to lower the cost of goods significantly because "I had the money in hand." Emilio did not spend all the proceeds; he kept a portion of his loan as an emergency reserve. "If my mother is sick and calls for help on the weekend when the credit union is closed, I have to be able to help."

Whatever stereotypes might indicate, many low-income consumers are credit averse. As "Annette" put it, "I like to pay for what I buy.

For example, I just bought a sofa after saving for seven months. I put away $100 a month for seven months so that I did not have to owe anybody."

INNOVATIONS IN SAVINGS

Over the last decade, the savings rate in the United States has steadily declined, reaching negative numbers by the year 2006. This has troubling implications both within the country and for the country's position in the world. Financial regulators at the highest level have joined forces with consumer advocates and financial institutions to promote financial education and thrift. The Consumer Federation of America was the leader in developing one prominent family of initiatives, the America Saves campaign, which has spurred various regional and sectoral offshoots, such as Cleveland Saves, Hispanic Saves, and Military Saves.

Credit unions have played a prominent role in many of these social marketing campaigns and have shown themselves to be creative and entrepreneurial in promoting savings. One of the most successful initiatives, Savings Challenge '07, was conducted by the largest CDCU in the country, GECU of El Paso, a $1.4 billion, 281,000-member financial cooperative that serves a largely Latino population on the Texas border with Cd. Juarez, Mexico. Inspired by television "reality shows," GECU started a year-long competition offering $10,000 cash awards to two families, one in the English-speaking category, one in the Spanish-speaking category, who managed to come closest to their savings and debt-reduction goals. More than one hundred families applied, and six member families competed. Their progress, tracked on two local stations, generated huge media interest: nearly 1.5 million viewer "hits" on the stations' web sites.[15]

One winner was Gloria Aguilar, a widowed single parent, ten years from retirement, caring for an elderly mother and a twenty-year-old daughter with a disability who needs vocational training. "The reason I wanted to participate in GECU's *Savings Challenge '07* came after

I took a long hard look at my finances," she said. "The truth is I've always lived paycheck to paycheck and managed to stay afloat with credit cards." After a year, she was almost able to eliminate her $24,000 in credit card and medical debt. For the first time, she was able to set short-term and long-term goals, to pay tuition for her daughter, and to sleep at night.

The Savings Challenge spurred others in the community to open accounts and increase their own savings as well.

More broadly, the idea of providing incentives to promote savings has played a prominent role in the development of new antipoverty strategies. In his book *Assets and the Poor,* Professor Michael Sherraden of Washington University (St. Louis) argued that the cycle of poverty was perpetuated not only by inadequate income but also by the lack of owned assets that grow in value.[13] He introduced the concept of Individual Development Accounts (IDAs)—incentivized savings accounts for the poor—that provided a matching contribution for each dollar saved by a participant, subject to certain limits and particular purposes (generally, home ownership, small business, and postsecondary education).

Community development credit unions, which had long demonstrated that the poor could and would save, eagerly adopted IDAs. The National Federation of CDCUs cosponsored the first national IDA conference, presented by the Corporation for Enterprise Development (CFED) in Chicago in 1995. The federation subsequently raised foundation and other funding to provide CDCUs with the match needed to leverage public and private support (generally three dollars for every one dollar). Credit unions have long participated in the largest federal initiative to support IDAs, the Assets for Independence (AFI) program funded at twenty-five-million dollars annually by the Department of Health and Human Services.

THE CREDIT UNION MOVEMENT TODAY

As of June 2007, the credit union movement in the United States comprised 8,410 separately chartered institutions, with total membership of 88,251,444 and assets of more than $757 billion.[16] The trend, as elsewhere in the financial sector, is toward consolidation—fewer but larger institutions. In 1969, the number of credit unions peaked at more than twenty-three thousand independent, separately chartered credit unions,[17] and in recent years, approximately three hundred credit unions annually have merged. There are many small credit unions—the median size is about $13.1 million,[18] far smaller than the typical bank—but there are more than 125 with at least a billion in assets. Navy Federal Credit Union is the largest, with $35 billion and more than three million members.[19] Some credit unions serve tightly defined groups, or "fields of membership"; others are much more expansive, embracing entire communities or hundreds of separate employee groups. All credit unions, regardless of size or type, are nonprofit cooperatives, exempt from federal taxation.

Credit unions have a small share of the nation's savings: approximately 7.34 percent as of March 31, 2008.[20] But their role is disproportionate to their market share. Banks have waged a thirty-year struggle, in Congress and in the courts, to curtail credit union powers and stop their expansion. This opposition, presented as a call for a "level playing field" in which credit unions would pay taxes, is largely motivated by the fact that credit unions on average pay slightly more on deposits than banks and charge lower fees and interest rates on loans.[21]

THE BUILDING BLOCKS OF HEALTHY COMMUNITIES: INDIVIDUAL AND SOCIAL VALUES

Why are we in the credit union movement—and especially, CDCUs, which work every day among low-income and disadvantaged communities—so passionate about savings? Saving money is sensible, rational, logical, prudent—all those things. But more powerfully, savings promote human dignity. Savings help us to become and remain independent and self-sufficient in the face of life's vicissitudes.

What is true for the individual is also true for communities. This is the vision that gave birth to and sustains the community development credit union movement. CDCUs are dedicated to the principle that, by capturing and aggregating the savings hidden in low-income communities, it is possible to build strong, self-sustaining, not-for-profit financial institutions. CDCUs are based on a belief in community self-help: although there is much that the public sector must provide for the common good and the sustenance of "the least among us," the poor must have an ownership stake in our society, a vehicle through which they are not merely recipients but economic actors who can control their own resources. By empowering individuals and communities, credit unions are vital, vibrant contributors to civil society and democracy.

In 1980, I joined the National Federation of Community Development Credit Unions, the charitable association that represents and serves low-income credit unions. Two years thereafter, we lost all of our funding, which came virtually entirely from the federal government, and, with it, our paid staff. For many months, until we were able to rebuild gradually, we operated from my house, and I ran the remnants of the organization without pay. Our prospects were dim.

But is it a coincidence that *credo*—Latin for "I believe"—is at the very root of the credit union movement? Attending the annual national conferences of the federation's membership during those difficult years, I was struck repeatedly by the observation of the late James Gilliam of St. Luke Credit Union in Windsor, North Carolina: "It feels like a revival meeting!" A loyal core of true believers kept the community development credit union flame burning. Over the last quarter century, the federation has rallied increasing numbers of credit unions serving low-income communities. Today, our 225 member CDCUs from Vermont to Hawaii, from Harlem to the reservations of Arizona, represent more than four billion dollars in aggregate assets—savings owned and cooperatively managed by low-income communities themselves. But more than money, CDCUs represent hope for families, for neighborhoods, and for our country.

EPILOGUE

Since writing this essay and as of December 5, 2008, the United States has plunged into a recession evoking comparisons to the Great Depression. Huge financial institutions in the country have been merged or liquidated; others have dramatically changed their financial structure. Amid the widespread economic devastation, many credit unions have escaped damages, attracting additional savings deposits from their members and providing loans even when access to credit has dried up elsewhere. Now, more than ever, credit unions exemplify the critical importance of institutions that address basic human financial needs—a safe place to save and a place to borrow at reasonable cost. As our nation labors to reconstruct a sustainable financial system, credit unions are an indispensable part of the solution.

PART THREE

For a New Thrift
Meeting the Twenty-First Century Challenge

Chapter 6

Confronting the American Debt Culture[1]

Barbara Dafoe Whitehead

FRANK CAPRA'S 1946 FILM *It's a Wonderful Life* is the American Film Institute's pick for the number one most inspirational American movie of all time. Set in the fictional upstate New York town of Bedford Falls, the story's grand narrative is about the wondrous gift of human life, but its less lofty plot line is hardly less grand. It is about the travails of George Bailey and Bailey's Building & Loan, an institution that, Capra makes clear by contrast with the evil fat cat banker Mr. Potter, is an inseparable part of a stable, prosperous, and, above all, virtuous community. At the film's climax, George Bailey's Bedford Falls neighbors and customers merge into a single society, grateful and generous and all pulling together in the face of adversity.

In an America just emerging from the cauldron of the Great Depression and World War II, no one needed to point out to viewers what a building and loan was or why it meant so much to many small and mid-sized American communities. Everyone understood that thrift was socially constructive, for through the accumulation of individual savings, everyone benefited from rising prosperity, better education, and hope for a brighter future. What war bonds had been for national security, thrift and home-building institutions were for family security. The social capital created through thrift institutions limited social

145

polarization and marginalized the depredations of greed, so the real small towns of America never decayed into Pottervilles. This was not just sentimental bunkum from Hollywood; in 1946, this was as real as a social fact could be.

It's a Wonderful Life still makes for great entertainment, but a hint of sadness pervades the film today in a way it did not sixty, or even thirty, years ago. That is because the American culture of thrift, epitomized by no less beloved a founder than Benjamin Franklin himself, is at best on institutional life support. Somehow, we as a society have managed to undermine a precious social virtue and enthrone what amounts to industrial-scale loan sharking. In doing so we have undermined a source of America's real wealth and put its global leadership at risk, as recent shocks to the U.S. economy ought to make clear. What has happened to America's thrift institutions? How did it happen, and what can we do to recover before it is too late?

THEN AND NOW

The United States is experiencing a sharply growing polarization in access to institutional opportunities to save and build wealth. For most of the twentieth century, nearly all Americans had access to grass-roots institutions that helped them build a nest egg. These institutions included local retail banks, mutual savings banks, credit unions, savers' clubs, school savings bond programs, building and loan associations, savings and loans, and labor union-sponsored savings plans. Some institutions, such as credit unions, building and loans, and labor union plans, grew out of a cooperative, nonprofit banking tradition expressly created for the "small saver." But even local retail banks offered passbook savings accounts and children's savings programs for families of modest means. Together, these institutions constituted a broadly democratic "prothrift" sector of the financial service industry.

In addition to providing opportunities to save, prothrift institutions also limited the amount of debt consumers could carry. Banks had strict rules for consumer lending. Americans who wanted to buy a house had to accumulate savings, apply to a local bank, document their credit worthiness, undergo the scrutiny of the lending institution, and usually make a 20 percent down payment. Lending institutions were likewise constrained by government rules. Federal and state regulations set limits on the interest and fees lenders could impose. And some forms of thriftlessness were outlawed entirely. Lotteries were illegal in all states, usury laws prohibited predatory interest rates, and casino gambling was allowed in just a few venues like Las Vegas and Atlantic City. To be sure, some Americans still borrowed from loan sharks, pawned their wedding rings, or gambled away the family farm. But such behavior was disreputable, desperate, and beyond the pale of responsible institutions as far as the vast majority of Americans were concerned.

Any American under the age of forty today can gain knowledge of this reality only by reading about it in books, for it can no longer be experienced directly. A thrift sector still exists, but it has ceased to be broadly democratic in its reach. The institutions that encourage thrift have moved uptown, catering to upper-income Americans with an ever expanding array of tax-advantaged opportunities to invest and build wealth. The "small saver" has been left behind as prey to new, highly profitable financial institutions: subprime credit card issuers and mortgage brokers, rent-to-own merchants, payday lenders, auto title lenders, tax refund lenders, private student-loan companies, franchise tax preparers, check cashing outlets, and the state lottery. Once existing on society's margins, these institutions now constitute a large and aggressively expanding antithrift sector that is dragging hundreds of thousands of American consumers into profligacy and overindebtedness. America now has a two-tier financial institutional system—one catering to the "investor class," the other to the "lottery class."

The investor class, with ample access to institutions that foster wealth-building discipline, are served by a bevy of insurance agents, tax lawyers, stockbrokers, tax accountants, deferred-compensation experts, and investment bankers. They are likely to work in organizations with 401(k) plans, profit-sharing, Keogh plans, deferred income compensation and retirement savings programs. The lottery class, on the other hand, works in jobs that offer few prothrift benefits. As of 2004, seventy million of America's 153 million wage earners worked for employers without a retirement plan, for example.[2] And rather than being courted by investment firms, they are targets of modern day, made-to-look-respectable loan sharks. Tens of millions of working Americans who might join the class of savers and investors under more favorable circumstances are being recruited into a burgeoning population of debtors and bettors.

DEBT AND ITS DISCONTENTS

The ability to borrow is a good thing—or ought to be. Credit helps consumers buy houses, get educations, start businesses, and acquire goods that may boost their job prospects and future income. As economists like to point out, consumer credit helps smooth out spending over a lifetime, allowing people to borrow in their lower-earning years in order to build assets and investments for the future.

But consumer credit is a double-edged blade: it can lead to greater opportunity and freedom, but, if promoted deceptively and used recklessly, it can lead to disaster, as the subprime mortgage failure has so painfully revealed. Even before the subprime debacle, however, many Americans were struggling with a growing debt burden. According to the Federal Reserve's measure of burdensome debt, in 2004, the typical family spent more than 18 percent of its income on debt payments, the largest share since the institution started collecting these data. Moreover, the proportion of families with debt service payments exceeding 40 percent of their income rose to 12.2 percent in 2004. Consumer loan delinquencies also rose during this period.

Some of this debt is natural in the sense that middle-income and young families—who make up the largest share of households in the heavy debt service category—are at the stage in life where they are rearing children and buying big-ticket items like houses, cars and computers. Many families have also been hit hard by stagnating wages and the rising costs of health care, food, and energy, leading them to rely on credit not to build assets but to make ends meet.

Some are not making it, however. Late fees and missed payments on credit cards have risen sharply, costing American consumers $17.1 billion in fees in 2006. About one in every seven American families reports that, at some point in their lives, they experienced debt problems serious enough to have caused them to file for bankruptcy or to use a credit consolidator. More than one out of three say their financial situation was "out of control" at some point in their lives. Even those able to manage high household debt are increasingly operating at the razor's edge of solvency, with little cushion to cover an unexpected expense such as a major car repair or a medical emergency.

Why are so many Americans struggling with high levels of debt? Some blame individual greed and recklessness, and human frailty and irresponsible choices are clearly part of the story. Others point to a culture of rampant, corporate-driven consumerism, buttressed by marketing techniques so sophisticated as to exceed the imagination of George Orwell himself on his better days. If you can find someone who honestly denies that this is part of the problem, sell him a bridge before it is too late. But soaring levels of household debt are also tied to another, often overlooked, source: recent changes in America's institutional/ regulatory landscape.

That this is so is made clear by both statistical evidence and common sense. As to the former, many other countries in the world are similarly embedded in a corporate market economy, and yet, as Figure 1 on page 155 shows, no other advanced country confronts a debt debacle comparable to that of the United States. The only independent variable that can readily explain the data is the different institutional/regulatory environments in the different countries. As to common sense, it is evident that, in money matters, as in most things that matter, authoritative institutions play a role in guiding individual choices and in setting cultural norms. Few people understand the full range of forces affecting them or have time to acquire the knowledge and self-discipline necessary to make informed decisions. That is where authoritative institutions come in. They establish the norms, conventions, and values that vest individual decision making with broader social wisdom and knowledge. But not all institutional setups are created equal. Some inculcate norms and values that foster unwise choices or contribute to unjust outcomes. Such is the case in today's American debt culture. Newly powerful and aggressive antithrift institutions are promoting behaviors and attitudes that have undermined our nation's traditional culture of thrift.

THE PLASTIC TRAP

Perhaps the most pervasive of these new antithrifts is the credit card industry. Plastic has become an American way of life. There are now more than a *billion* cards in the hands of U.S. consumers, and more than three-quarters of American households have at least one of them. The average age of credit card holders is getting younger, too. Many teenagers get their first card in high school, and most college students have at least one—indeed, a whopping 56 percent of final year college students carry four or more cards.

It is little wonder that credit cards are so popular, for they are convenient, fast, and easy to use. It is not the credit card itself that is the problem; it is that, in the wake of the financial deregulation of the 1980s, the credit card industry was the first antithrift sector to discover the huge but untapped profitability of the subprime market. In so doing, it upended the conservative philosophy that had guided consumer lending in the United States for a century. Instead of limiting the small loan market to prime customers who were likely to pay off the entire debt in thirty days, the industry went after subprime customers who were likely to pay only the low minimum balance and to incur the additional costs of late fees, overlimit fees, and other penalties on a regular basis.

The credit card industry was also the first to develop practices and products that ensured long-term consumer dependency on expensive credit. Low teaser interest rates that converted to double-digit rates, extra transaction fees and penalties, the securitization of debt, and abrogated relationships between the originating lender and borrower were not innovations of the subprime mortgage business. These practices were pioneered by the credit card industry.

During the 1990s, the credit card industry promoted its expansion into subprime markets under the banner of the "democratization" of credit. The industry was "reaching out" to the unserved and underserved, so that Americans who once had to make do with the cash in a weekly pay packet could now use plastic to make their everyday purchases. The democratization of credit, however, led to the widespread propagation of debt. Between 1989 and 2001, credit card debt almost tripled, from $238 billion to $692 billion. By fall of 2007, the amount of revolving consumer credit had reached $937.5 billion, a 7 percent increase over the previous year.

In the generally flush 1990s, many families were able to manage higher credit card debt without undue distress, but in today's more troubled times, families who once kept on top of their credit card balances—even if it meant paying only the minimum on several cards—are now toppling into delinquencies and defaults. Nearly half of all credit card holders have missed payments in the last year. With declining home values and tighter credit, fewer homeowners can draw on the equity in their homes to maintain their standard of living or to consolidate credit card debt. More households struggle simply to live from paycheck to paycheck, with no cash reserves or unused credit to keep them from economic freefall.

PAYDAY LENDERS

For families on the financial edge, however, there is another place to turn to for "fast cash"—the local payday lender. Payday lenders serve up "fast cash" and "free money" to fifteen million people every month. The industry solicits wage earners with incomes generally ranging between $18,000 and $25,000, people who generally live from paycheck to paycheck and sometimes run out of money before their next payday. To qualify for a loan, most borrowers typically have only to produce a recent pay stub, current bank statement, blank personal check, driver's license or other government ID card, and proof of current address. (While this is more evidence than some credit-challenged borrowers had to produce to get a $500,000 subprime mortgage, it is hardly enough to establish genuine creditworthiness.)

According to a recent *Wall Street Journal* investigation, payday lenders are now intensively soliciting elderly and disabled recipients of government benefits. The reason is a change in the regulatory environment. For years, Social Security recipients received their government checks in the mail and cashed them at a neighborhood store or local bank. By the late 1990s, however, the federal government began requiring electronic deposits of benefit checks into an established banking account, unless recipients chose to opt out. This saved money for the government, but it turned into an unexpected boon for the payday lenders. With the advent of direct deposit, many lenders could make predatory loans as an "advance" on the next month's benefits check. Since Social Security, veterans, and disabled benefit checks arrive every month for as long as the recipient is living, they represent a highly secure form of collateral. Making a loan on future Social Security checks bears about as much risk to a lender as spotting Warren Buffett twenty bucks.

Storefront payday lenders are commonplace in thousands of towns throughout America, and they work hard to cultivate a reassuring image of normalcy. Their clean, well-lit shops fit comfortably into the franchise landscape, with all the amenities of a McDonalds or Burger King. Like fast food, payday loans can be ordered up and ready to go in a matter of minutes. At a local Check 'n' Go in the typically Midwestern Muncie, Indiana, a sign on the door reads: "Getting a loan is as easy as 1-2-3: l. Just Write Us a Personal Check. 2. Get the Cash You Need Instantly. 3. We Hold Your Check until Your Next Payday. . . . It's Quick, Easy and Confidential."

Unlike fast food, however, fast cash is not cheap. It typically costs the borrower the equivalent of a 300–400 annual percentage rate. Payday loans contain another financially unhealthy feature, as well: they are structured so that it is hard for the borrower to repay in the requisite two weeks. Instead, many consumers end up with little choice but to pay special fees to "roll over" the original loan into the next payday, a practice that can lead to chronic dependency on expensive credit. Indeed, the profitability of the payday business depends heavily on getting borrowers into multiple rollovers: about 56 percent of payday lending revenue is generated by customers who take out thirteen or more loans per year.

Payday lending has been able to thrive because of lax state usury laws. In 1965, every state in the union had a usury limit on consumer loans; today, seven states have completely deregulated interest rates within their borders. At least thirty-five states allow lenders to charge the equivalent of more than 300 annual percentage rate on a typical payday loan. There are also significant regional differences in usury caps. The northeastern states have been the most aggressive in limiting the pricing of consumer loans, while the Rocky Mountain West (Arizona, Colorado, Idaho, Montana, New Mexico, Utah, and Wyoming) has been the most permissive. It is there that the median annual percentage rate of state usury limits increased from 36 percent in 1965 to 521 percent in 2007.

So far, twelve states, plus the District of Columbia, have essentially banned payday lending by placing interest rate caps on small loans. Likewise, Congress has imposed a 36 percent cap on payday loans to young, low-income military families—a popular target for the predatory payday industry. And the FDIC has encouraged banks under its purview to market small-loan products to the general population with interest rates of 36 percent or less. Other, more narrowly focused efforts to discourage payday lending, such as limiting the number of outstanding loans per consumer, restricting the number of rollovers, or introducing extended repayment plans, have been less effective in eliminating the payday debt trap.

STATE LOTTERIES

Payday lenders are not the only antithrift outfits to set up shop in post-1980s America. After being shuttered for seventy years in every state in the union, the lottery has now become an all-American institution. In the past year, more than half of the nation's adults have played one of the nation's forty-three state lotteries, and about 20 percent of all Americans are frequent players. In 2006, state lotteries raked in fifty-seven billion dollars, representing a roughly 500 percent increase in per capita spending on the lottery since 1973. No other government agency makes itself such a regular presence in Americans' daily lives. Lottery tickets are sold at about two hundred thousand mini-marts, bodegas, newsstands, bars, bus stations, check cashing outlets, mall kiosks, liquor stores, supermarkets, and self-serve gas stations nationwide. Lottery ads pop up on buses, subways, and billboards. Live drawings take place during the nightly news.

State lotteries do not simply make their products available. They have a mission to "grow" their market. Lotteries work hard to hold on to current players, entice new players into the game, and increase the frequency of play. Their business plans set the goal of making regular betting a part of individuals' daily or weekly rituals, and their methods seek to habituate players to the game: the suspense of scraping the latex square on the instant ticket to reveal the number underneath, the excitement of watching numbered balls drop down a chute in televised nightly drawings, the emotional rush over getting a small payout, and the addictive cycle of trying to beat the lottery "house" with just one more try. And, of course, they go out of their way to market the big winners, to make it seem as though winning big is vastly more frequent an occurrence than it really is.

As a source of public revenue, state lotteries are highly regressive. As Figure 1 shows, players with lower incomes tend to spend *more* on the lottery than those with higher incomes. Even more to the point, people with lower incomes spend a larger *share* of their incomes on the lottery: a household with an income under $12,400 spends 5 percent of

Figure 1:   Annual Lottery Spending by Household Income

2006 Dollars	
Under $12,400	$645
$12,400-30,999	$626
$31,000-61,999	$575
$62,000-123,999	$373
$124,000 and up	$419

Data are from the National Bureau of Economic Research.

its gross income, but a household with an income of $124,000 spends about one-third of one percent of its gross income.

Furthermore, lottery players at the lower-income range suffer a larger antithrift effect: they give up the opportunity to save the proportionately larger share of dollars spent on the lottery and to realize any return on that money. Presumably, if a low-income household can spend $645 dollars a year on the lottery, it can save and invest the same $645. The Tax Foundation estimates that, if that household were to invest the same amount in stocks every year for forty years, it could expect to have $87,191 (in 2006 dollars.)

Although the lottery extracts its revenues disproportionately from the less privileged, it distributes funds to causes with broad public support across all income groups, such as education. Lotteries rarely dedicate revenue to chronically underfunded programs for halfway houses, prisoner release services, homeless shelters, services to the disabled, domestic violence prevention and drug abuse treatment. In some states, lotteries have even funded projects that favor the more privileged. For example, a 1991 study of the Florida lottery found that lottery-funded expenditures for K–12 education disproportionately benefit those at higher incomes, and a University of Georgia survey showed that black respondents were significantly less likely to have someone in the household who received a HOPE scholarship, the lottery-funded program for college-bound students. Even more tellingly, in Massachusetts, where lottery revenues are distributed in local aid to the 321 cities and towns across the state, communities with the strongest lottery sales do not receive commensurate levels of local aid. Residents in the old industrial city of Lynn spend eighty-five million dollars a year on tickets and games, but the city receives just fifteen million dollars a year in lottery-financed local aid—a net loss of seventy million dollars.

SHAPING A DEBT CULTURE

Few people enjoy being over their heads in debt. It is usually a stressful and unhappy experience, straining family and work relationships, leaving a blot on one's social reputation, and limiting one's freedom to achieve life goals. Under ordinary circumstances, people try to avoid what earlier generations called "financial embarrassment." In past decades, too, the social geography of the financial world reinforced psychological inhibitions against carrying too much debt. Reputable lenders were located in the commercial heart of town, disreputable ones on the shadowy fringes. Bank architecture conveyed solidity, while loan shark architecture reflected seediness. And a moral language that unabashedly labeled usurious lenders as "loan sharks" and "payroll leeches" set these businesses apart from the respectable mainstream. This combination of personal aversion to debt, the social stigma of overindebtedness, and the grubby image of predatory money lenders provided extralegal checks on the temptation to live beyond one's means.

The antithrift industry has worked relentlessly to destroy these traditional inhibitions and stigmas. One strategy has been to improve the image of their businesses—hence, the familiar franchise architecture of the suburban strip mall for payday lenders. Another approach is to treat overindebtedness as commonplace. Payday lenders cast themselves as friendly professionals who offer "finance solutions for all situations." Indeed, they have expunged the words *debt* or *loan* from their advertising. One payday lending web site brazenly calls its product a "cash advance savings account." What's more, their marketing pitches proclaim that they have solutions for your problems. They pretend to care about you. Indeed, they are "there for you as often as you need them"—in other words, as often as you need to roll over your existing loan.

Whatever the specific antithrift business—whether payroll advances, credit card purchases, or lottery tickets—they all offer instant gratification. They promise "fast cash," "fast service," and "fast solutions" to money problems. To deliver on that promise, they structure their services in such a way as to separate maximally the time of the loan or purchase from the time of payment. This makes it easier for the consumer to get the money or goods immediately without having to think hard about the high cost of the credit—or, in the case of the lottery, the infinitesimal odds of a major payoff.

Further, to foster the trust of the borrowing public, some antithrift institutions link their business interests to those of highly credible institutions. The credit card industry, for example, makes deals with colleges and universities to use their campuses to market expensive credit cards to students. College students who accept cards from on-campus marketers are likely to be more indebted than those who obtain cards through other means, yet they are also likely to believe that the card issuers are more reputable because they have been screened by the college.

Like other value-shaping institutions, the antithrift industry takes seriously the task of initiating the young into a debt culture. Lottery officials now see eighteen-to-twenty-five-year-olds as the demographic group with the greatest future potential for increasing lottery play and revenues, especially with the expansion of online gambling. The Texas Lottery, one of the few state lotteries required to provide detailed demographic breakdowns of its consumers, looks to be well on the way to cracking that youthful market. According to its 2006 report, eighteen-to-twenty-four-year-old players spend a median of fifty dollars per month on lottery play, the highest level among all age groups.

The credit card industry, meanwhile, is intent on making the acquisition of a teenager's first credit card a rite of passage into a cashless consumer culture. Some card companies market their cards as money management tools, although most financial experts believe that kids are better off if they learn to save first and then use cash. Clearly, young credit card users often fail to appreciate how much things cost, fail to grasp the concept of a sales tax, and, perhaps most important, fail to experience the *tristesse* of an empty wallet following a spending spree. Nonetheless, to appeal to college students credit card issuers often dangle the lure of prizes and points: Chase +1SM Student MasterCard offers the limited edition Facebook t-shirt, plus "Karma Points" for purchases of music, movies, and electronics; Citi mtvUTM Platinum Select Visa Card delivers extra "ThankYou Points" for "every dollar spent on restaurants, bookstores, record stores, movie theaters, MTV events, and airline tickets" as well as 250 to 2,000 "ThankYou Points" twice a year for maintaining a good grade point average. Even Pavlov would be aghast.

TWO MODELS OF REFORM

This is not the first time that America has faced a tide of antithrift. A century ago, loan sharks reaped huge profits making small loans at usurious interest rates. The most notorious practice was salary lending, a business that offered short-term, high-interest loans to wage earners as an "advance" on future wages. Salary lenders had been around since the Civil War, but the business expanded rapidly in an urbanizing America. By the early twentieth century, nearly every major American city had a cluster of salary lenders, some part of large, multistate chains. According to an estimate made in 1911, one out of five wage earners in cities with more than thirty thousand people took out a salary loan in a year.

Two conditions spurred this phenomenal growth. The first was the growing market for consumer loans. As the population of the nation's industrial wage earners grew, so too did the need for cash to stretch their meager wages from payday to payday. Unlike farmers and small business owners, wage earners were entirely dependent on the dollars in their pay packet to meet their family's needs. As one contemporary writer, Robert Kelso, put it: "The wage has not the certainty of food produced on the farm. . . . The workingman's dollar has a way of depending on world finance to tell it how much food it will buy."

Nor could strapped wage earners turn to local banks. Most commercial banks did not make small personal loans because it took just as much paperwork and investigation to establish the creditworthiness of an individual as it did for a business. Furthermore, existing state usury laws capped the amount of interest that could be charged on a personal loan at between 4 and 12 percent annually, with 6 percent being typical. Under such restrictive caps, bankers contended that they could not cover the additional costs of making small consumer loans and still turn a profit.

Salary lenders, on the other hand, faced few such obstacles. They needed little capital to start their business. Once established, they earned healthy profits from high-volume lending, frequent loan roll-overs, and usurious interest rates—plus late fees, protest fees, application fees, collection fees, and other add-ons. Some of the big chains integrated the lending and collection businesses, thus generating another stream of revenue. Of course, all this was technically illegal, but the prospect of huge profits far outweighed the small risk of being caught and punished. Besides, enforcement was difficult because lenders disguised usurious rates in fees and service charges, required borrowers to sign blank or partially completed contracts, and failed to give receipts for payments. And even in those infrequent cases when a lender was convicted of usury, the penalties were generally civil and mild, ranging from forfeiting the amount of usurious interest charged to suffering the loss of the principal plus interest.

But this was the Progressive era, and a handful of reformers set out to combat the "loan-sharking evil." They wanted to satisfy the growing need for consumer credit and shut down the loan sharks all at once. To do so, they followed two very different strategies.

One strategy was to make the small loan business more profitable for banks and other legal lending institutions. The reformers agreed with the bankers: restrictive usury laws kept commercial lenders out of the consumer credit business and fed the growth of the illegal loan sharking businesses. By raising the interest rate caps, reformers hoped to create an incentive for banks to drive the loan sharks out of the consumer lending business. The eventual legislation, the Uniform Small Loan Act, raised the interest cap to 42 percent per year and prohibited fees or other add-on charges. It also required licensing and oversight by state agencies and provided consumer protections for the borrower (the lender was required to disclose fully the terms of loans and provide receipts of all payments).

A second strategy was to create a prothrift institution for working people: the credit union. Like usury law reform, the credit union sought to solve the loan sharking problem by providing an alternative source of consumer credit to workers. Rather than trying to incentivize consumer lending for commercial banks, however, the credit union movement sought to institutionalize cooperative savings among wage earners themselves. The credit union was not intended as a competitor or imitator of the commercial lenders or even as a charitable "remedial" lender. Instead, it offered something new: a local, nonprofit, democratically run entity whose first purpose was to provide its members with the incentives and opportunities to save and then, when necessary, to borrow from each other.

Although these two Progressive-era strategies grew out of very different assumptions and approaches, they complemented one another in quelling the spread of predatory lenders for most of the twentieth century. The reform of usury laws, however, had a longer-term and wholly unintended consequence. As Christopher Peterson, a leading expert on usury law, explains: the higher interest allowed under the small loan laws diluted long-standing moral strictures against usurious lending. Legal principle and practice shifted from imposing strict limits on interest rates to introducing flexible and variable caps. Once that happened, it became much more difficult to resist further deregulation. From the middle twentieth century on, Peterson writes, "each state began to chart its own course," creating all kinds of exceptions and loopholes for consumer lending. Especially during the 1980s, amid deregulation and inflation, political pressure to weaken or eliminate usury laws grew in the states. This climate, in turn, created a hospitable legal environment for the resurgence of a legal successor to the salary lending business—now called, of course, payday lending.

The irony is hard to miss. The Progressive-era reform of usury laws, aimed at combating the first wave of predatory lenders in the twentieth century, helped to open the door to the second great wave of predatory lenders in the twenty-first. Compared to usury law reform, the credit union has turned out to be a more durable solution. For nearly a century, the credit union has served the small saver and investor; today, more than 8,100 credit unions provide savings accounts, low-cost credit, financial education, and investments for more than eighty-six million Americans.

The credit union model has been successful for at least four reasons. First, it began as a social movement and was fueled by the energy, commitment, and sense of mission that is common to social movements. Second, it united two ideals: democratic economic cooperation and thrift, broadly understood as the wise use of resources for productive purposes. Third, it adopted an organizational model that applied a prothrift solution (cooperative savings) to a contemporary problem (predatory interest rates on consumer loans). Fourth, it was organized to fit the habits and routines of its members' daily lives. People did not come to the credit union; it came to the people.

TWO GOALS

These experiences and our current predicament recommend two goals: to renew thrift as an American value and to create broadly democratic, prothrift institutions as alternatives to the current crop of antithrifts. Ultimately, these changes can only be achieved in the context of a broad-based social movement. We need, in short, a national thrift initiative with a broad-based social sponsorship whose purpose would be to share ideas, incubate strategies, and identify creative ways to promote thrift.

Based on American history and (what is left of) our common sense, we can identify candidate objectives.

1. Reestablish a Public Education Campaign

During World War II, Americans saved at extraordinarily high rates—about 25 percent on average. This impressive display of thrift and sacrifice was driven primarily by the war, but it also had a more proximate source: the U.S. government, partnering with the leaders of civil society, actively stressed the importance of saving for the war effort while also providing a specific new savings tool in the form of war bonds. Perhaps the time is right to reestablish a prothrift public education campaign. Similar campaigns to reduce drunk driving and smoking and to encourage seatbelt wearing appear to have had a demonstrable impact on people's behavior in recent years. Why not thrift?

2. Challenge "Consumer Spending" as a Main Solution to Economic Problems

Whether it is a national security crisis like 9/11 or worrisome economic news, our leaders in recent years seem increasingly determined to insist on the catchall economic salve of prodigious consumer spending. But this is, at best, partial and misleading advice in a society marked by dangerously high levels of debt and dangerously low levels of saving. Perhaps it is time to balance the message of more spending with a message of more saving and wealth building.

3. Create a Thrift Savings Plan Available to All Americans

Since 1986, the U.S. government's Thrift Savings Plan (TSP) has permitted federal employees to build wealth and save for retirement by systematically placing a portion of their earnings into diversified stock and bond index funds. These funds are managed by an independent board, with oversight from the public and private sectors. The expense ratios on TSP funds are low (0.06 percent), making them cheaper than similar commercially run funds. Currently, the TSP boasts 3.7 million participants, manages assets of approximately $225 billion, and is widely viewed across the political spectrum as a major success. Federal policymakers and others should consider offering this same wealth building opportunity to all working Americans.

4. Build New Thrift Institutions

New, community-based thrift institutions can stand as attractive alternatives to payday lenders and other antithrift institutions. If we are serious about confronting the debt culture, building these new institutions is our most urgent task. They must possess three core traits: functionally, they must offer opportunities and incentives to save and offer credit at affordable costs for prudent purposes; structurally, they must be broadly democratic, organized as not-for-profit cooperative or mutual organizations; physically, they must be accessible to low-income Americans.

5. Repurpose the Lottery

State lotteries are the most egregiously antithrift state-run institutions in America. Because lotteries typically enjoy broad support by politicians and the public, it would be hard, if not impossible, to outlaw these operations at present. But it is possible to repurpose the lottery, at least in part, as a thrift-promoting institution. In every state lottery outlet in the United States, a customer should be able to purchase "savings" tickets as well as lottery tickets. In this way, a comprehensive public apparatus devoted to encouraging everyone to become a bettor would simultaneously become an apparatus devoted to encouraging everyone to become a saver. It ought to be an easy sell: "Every ticket wins!" because, in fact, every single savings ticket would improve the financial well-being of the purchaser.

There are many other such ideas out there, and nearly all deserve exploration because a society in which ever more of us are over our heads in debt—a society in which a place like Bedford Falls seems no longer to exist, except in our fading collective memory—is unlikely to remain a thriving society for very long.

There is reason for hope. After all, our forebears a century ago met head on many of the same challenges we face today; if they could succeed, there is no reason we cannot do so as well. Their success helped reinforce the virtues that made America great, and their foresight helped make it greater still. They left America and the world a better place. We should aspire to do no less.

Chapter 7

Crafting Policies to Encourage Thrift in Contemporary America

Alex Roberts

As the preceding essays in this volume have argued, there is a deepening economic and institutional cleavage in the contemporary United States. On one side of the divide is the American mainstream. It consists of commercial banks and wealth management companies, financial advisors and 401(k)s, and the citizens who use these institutions to save and build wealth. On the other side of the divide is something quite different: predatory subprime and payday lenders, check-cashing outlets, state-run lotteries, and a group of Americans who save little.

This essay takes up a simple question: what can policymakers do to help those caught up in the debt culture join the mainstream?

To answer that question, I begin by taking a quick look at the aforementioned American mainstream. Has the average American family been able to thrive in recent years? If so, how? What has helped them to succeed? Based in part on this analysis, I then offer an explanation for why so many other Americans have been saving too little and falling behind. I argue that the specific nature of our saving problem should inspire us to rethink current policy and to launch a new initiative promoting thrift in the United States.

WEALTH BUILDING IN MAINSTREAM AMERICA

One metric commonly used to track wealth accumulation in the United States is the personal saving rate. It is a simple statistic that tells us what portion of our income we put in the bank, invest, or use to purchase a home. Figure 1 shows the personal saving rate for the post–World War II period.

Data are from the National Bureau of Economic Research. As the chart shows, the saving rate began the post–World War II period at roughly 8 percent, peaked at about 11 percent in the early 1980s, and then dropped to nearly zero, where it hovers today. These numbers indicate that the American public has been putting away less and less money each year.

Fortunately, however, things are somewhat better than this statistic suggests because the official saving rate[1] is actually an incomplete indicator of wealth accumulation because it excludes *capital gains* on homes, stocks, and businesses. This is problematic because, over the last twenty-five years, rising asset values have significantly augmented many Americans' wealth, bubbles and crashes notwithstanding. For example, if an individual had put $5,000 in the S&P 500 at the beginning of 1980, the investment would have grown to a whopping $67,500 by Christmas 2007. Even as of October 2008, after the recent plummet in the stock market, the investment would still be worth $43,750. That gain of $38,750 would have constituted a very real addition to the individual's net wealth, but it would have been omitted from the official saving rate. Thus, we need to look beyond the saving rate to understand the true state of families' financial well-being.

If we bring capital gains and saving into the same picture (Figure 2), we can see that there has actually been a dynamic relationship between the two over the long term.

When asset values have risen, driving up net worth, the American public has cut back on its saving. This explains most of the drop in saving after 1985. When asset prices have fallen, saving has generally increased. (Although it is not evident in the graph, the saving rate has spiked in recent months as the housing bubble has popped and home prices have declined.)

Figure 1. The U.S. Personal Saving Rate, 1952–2007

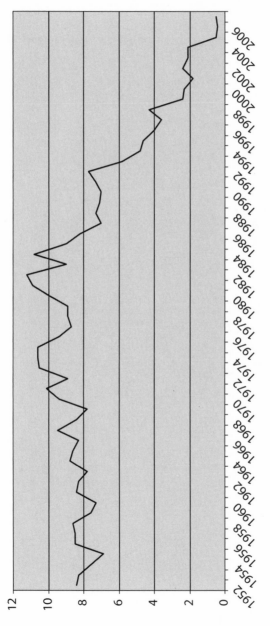

Data are from the National Bureau of Economic Research.

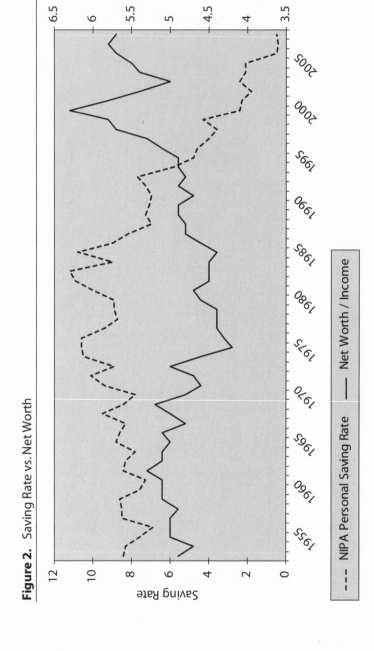

Figure 2. Saving Rate vs. Net Worth

--- NIPA Personal Saving Rate   — Net Worth / Income

Importantly, a number of studies have found that incorporating capital gains into the saving rate causes it largely to flatten out over time.[2] That is, the American public has been using both markets and traditional saving to build wealth at a fairly steady pace. Table 1 shows that mean and median family net worth has been rising over time.

Table 1. Family Net Worth (Dollar figures are in thousands of 2004 dollars.)

	1989	1992	1995	1998	2001	2004
Median family net worth	68.8	65.2	70.8	83.1	92.2	93.1
Mean family net worth	272.6	245.7	260.8	327.5	422.9	448.2

Data are from the Surveys of Consumer Finance.

In sum, then, the aggregate picture tells us that the average American family has, despite hard times like these, been doing well in the long term in recent years by saving and collecting capital gains.

But even if the American household writ large appears to be doing well, it does not necessarily follow that each family is doing well individually. Indeed, we know that many are struggling. The questions then become the following: who is in this American financial mainstream we have been discussing, who is outside it, and why?

WHO IS THRIVING, AND WHO IS FALLING BEHIND?

To answer these questions, we have to move beyond the aggregate data and see how different parts of the population have been faring. Tables 2 and 3 show the saving habits and net worth of American households by income level.

As shown, families in the top two income quintiles have, not surprisingly, been doing fine. About 75 percent of households in this part of

Table 2.   Household Saving by Income Bracket

(Income Bracket)	Percentage of Families that Save Each Year[1]	Saving Rates[2]		
		1992	*2000*	*Change*
0 – 20 %	31.6	3.8	7.1	3.3
20 – 40 %	46.9	4.2	7.4	3.2
40 – 60 %	57.7	2.7	2.9	.2
60 – 80 %	69.2	4.7	2.6	- 2.1
80 – 100 %	78.1	8.5	- 2.1	- 10.6

1. *Average derived from the 1992–2004 Surveys of Consumer Finances.*

2. *Source: Dean M. Maki and Michael G. Polumbo, "Disentangling the Wealth Effect: A Cohort Analysis of Household Saving in the 1990s," Finance and Economics Discussion Series, working paper 2001-21 (2001): 25; available at http://www.federalreserve.gov/ pubs/feds/2001/200121/200121abs.html.*

the population have been saving money each year. Overall *rates* of saving have declined in recent years, but this decline has been more than offset by capital gains on houses and investments, as reflected in the soaring median and mean net worth of wealthier households. This is not where our nation's saving problem lies.

Families' fortunes begin to diverge as we travel down the income ladder.

First, the good news. As Table 3 shows, a majority of middle-class families have been saving each year, as have a significant minority of those with lower incomes. The sheer amount put away by some is worth highlighting: in 1992, roughly 40 percent of families in the bottom two income quintiles saved at least 4 percent of *all income* earned in those quintiles. In 2000, they saved at least 7 percent of that income. Immigrant workers have been especially thrifty. They typically earn less than native-born Americans; yet, each month, the average worker sends about $293 back to family in his or her country of origin and saves an *additional* $289; this means that the average immigrant worker is setting aside a full *one-third* of his or her income each month.[3] Clearly, there are some highly dedicated lower-income savers out there.

What's more, lower-income Americans have been investing in stocks, bonds, CDs, and life insurance plans at an increasing rate. For example, as of 2003, 11.7 percent of families in the lowest income quintile held stocks either directly or indirectly through funds and plans, as did 29.6 and 51.7 percent of families in the second and third income quintiles, respectively. These rates of stock ownership represent dramatic increases over just a decade earlier.[4]

Lower-income savers are more likely than their peers to have debt. As Table 4 shows, most have gone in debt for an asset, as opposed to, say, a consumer good or a vacation. Owing to this wise use of money, an impressive 26 percent of savers living *below the poverty line* have been able to purchase a house, and 53.1 percent have a car.

Thus, many poorer Americans have embraced thrift as a way to build wealth and overcome adversity. Despite having low income, these individuals have been saving and using credit wisely to invest in themselves and build wealth over time.

Due to this thriftiness, median and mean net worth generally increased for both middle- and lower-income families between 1989 and 2004 (see Table 3).

But the data also give clear cause for concern. In particular, despite the advances made by many lower-income Americans, we still see some quite low levels of median net worth in the bottom income quintiles; in 2004, the typical poor household had only $7,500 in equity—hardly enough to handle a serious emergency. There are also some wide and widening spreads between median and mean net worth in the lower income brackets, which suggests that there is a fair amount of wealth polarization going on and that some are being left behind as national wealth has been increasing. This divergence is not surprising, because, while many poorer Americans do save and invest, about *3 in 5* families in the bottom two income quintiles do not save anything at all

Table 3. Family Net Worth by Income Bracket (In thousands of 2004 dollars.)

Income Bracket		1989	1992	1995	1998	2001	2004
0.0 – 20 %	Median	2.6	5.2	7.4	6.8	8.4	7.5
	Mean	36.2	43.4	54.7	55.4	56.2	72.6
20.0 – 39.9 %	Median	35.3	36.6	41.3	38.4	39.9	33.7
	Mean	96.4	84.6	97.4	111.4	122.7	121.5
40.0 – 59.9 %	Median	61.1	52.1	57.1	61.9	67.8	72.0
	Mean	148.5	133.3	126.0	146.6	173.3	194.6
60.0 – 79.9 %	Median	97.5	99.3	93.6	130.2	152.6	160.0
	Mean	199.3	185.4	198.5	238.3	313.2	340.8
80.0 – 89.9 %	Median	193.5	151.8	157.7	218.5	280.3	313.3
	Mean	326.1	297.1	316.8	377.1	487.0	487.4
90.0 - 100 %	Median	569.5	479.3	436.9	524.4	887.9	924.1
	Mean	1,438.5	1,266.0	1,338.0	1,793.9	2,410.9	2,534.6

Data are from the Surveys of Consumer Finances.

each year. And many hold no productive financial assets such as stocks, bonds, or certificates of deposit.

To be sure, some of these households represent younger families that will move up the wealth ladder over time. But studies find that the low-income, low-saving population includes a large number of families that have not amassed sufficient resources to retire comfortably. Although it is difficult to pinpoint just how large this group is, the data suggest that about 15 to 35 percent of Americans are undersaving for retirement to some degree.[5] Many of the people in this category would also have a great deal of difficulty making it through a medical emergency, unemployment, or other income shocks without going deeply into debt. And, of course, it is likely that the situation has gotten even worse in the past two years as Americans have taken on record levels of debt and lost trillions of dollars of wealth in the real estate crash. Undersaving is, therefore, a serious problem that demands our utmost attention.

WHY DO SOME AMERICANS SAVE TOO LITTLE?

The reasons that some people save too little are complex. Income is obviously a major part of the story. To the extent that a poorer family must spend its income to meet basic needs, it will be unable to save or invest. Moreover, the less money one has, the more willpower it takes to divert each dollar from present consumption into savings. It is, therefore, no surprise that people who earn less, save less. Yet it is not clear why more low-to-moderate-income households do not save when some of the very poorest households are able to do so. Clearly, there are other factors at play. (I will ignore the limited income problem because questions of political economy and redistribution fall well outside this essay's focus on thrift and saving.)

Institutions are another major part of the story. Let's face it: investing in markets and saving for long-term goals are complicated, often daunting tasks. Left to ourselves, most of us would find it difficult to devise a sound investment plan and then carry it out in a disciplined fashion. When people are able to rely on institutions to simplify the investment process through plans and mechanisms, their chances of success increase greatly. Higher-income Americans have a clear advantage in this regard. They are much more likely to be courted by wealth managers and to have financial planners to shepherd them to a safe retirement. Lower-income Americans, for a variety of reasons, are much less likely to receive the same level of assistance or even a basic level of support. Take 401(k)s, for example. These accounts help make saving easy and automatic (through direct deposit) and are one of the primary vehicles through which American workers gain exposure to the stock market. But as of 2004, only 82 million of America's 153 million wage earners worked for an employer that offered a retirement plan (of any kind).[6] This means that about half of American employees do not have access to these wonderful wealth-building tools. Additionally, lower-income Americans are much more likely to live in neighborhoods where fringe financial institutions such as payday lenders are prominent.

While institutional factors are important, in many cases, motivation can be an even bigger problem. Some people fail to save money even when they receive substantial encouragement to do so. Case in point: although 401(k)s are popular in general, about 30 percent of eligible workers never bother to sign up for an account, even when generous employer matches are offered.[7] Matched saving programs for the poor have also had trouble recruiting and keeping participants. These findings indicate that some people's desire to consume now is so strong that it renders them indifferent to saving incentives. They simply do not take advantage of obvious opportunities to build wealth.

It seems that some people choose not to make saving or investing a priority. Why? Answering this question requires that we think in psychological or even philosophical terms.

We have already seen how many poorer Americans have embraced thrift as a way to get ahead in life. But thrift is not the only reaction one might have to difficult circumstances. Imagine that you earn the minimum wage and live in an area of entrenched poverty. Most of the people you know do not become affluent or upwardly mobile over time.

Crime and violence are prevalent. Perhaps you have been discriminated against. All in all, things seem kind of hopeless and uncontrollable, and your opportunities in life appear limited. While some individuals would strive hard to overcome these challenges, many likely would respond by lowering their expectations for the future and taking a more fatalistic, passive attitude toward life. They might avoid setting "big" goals to guard against the anticipated pain of failure.

This perspective would, by its very nature, strongly discourage one from saving. Saving, after all, is about deferring consumption now so that one can allocate capital toward some future use. If one lacks long-term objectives or believes them to be unattainable,[8] then it seems pointless to set aside money each month.[9] Why bother? And if one is skeptical that progress is possible, one will place greater value on immediate and seemingly attainable rewards. An individual might spend all of his or her discretionary income on, say, nice clothes, meals out, a new TV, and so on. He or she might be willing or even eager to use expensive credit to acquire such things.

My argument, in short, is that difficult circumstances and pessimism about the future have instilled in some lower-income individuals a myopic orientation that causes them to favor immediate consumption over saving.

Academic research yields support for this thesis. Several studies from Britain and the United States, for example, have found that lower-income individuals are more likely to say that it would be pointless for them to save, even though most report believing that saving is beneficial in general.[10] This suggests that these individuals believe that saving is for "other people," perhaps those with higher incomes or greater perceived chances of success. About 10 percent of lower-income individuals report having no reason to save at all.[11] Many more individuals have no saving strategy and do not plan for the long term.[12] These individuals save significantly less and have less wealth than their peers on average. Thus, there are indeed strong interconnections between low income, skepticism about personal advancement, and the choice not to save.

Studies also find that the poor—especially the nonsaving poor, one would assume—tend to be less patient than others and show a greater desire to spend money immediately.[13] They have higher rates of "time preference," as economists put it. In line with my argument above, this heightened propensity to consume appears to reflect a genuine preference, or orientation, as opposed to a simple lack of self-control. For example, Table 4 shows that a majority of lower-income nonsavers have *no debt* and do not use credit cards or fringe financial institutions.[14] Living paycheck to paycheck without debt or savings is an extraordinarily difficult lifestyle to maintain. It requires careful and attentive budgeting. It requires that one spend exactly what one takes in each month, no more, no less. Far from evincing weakness of will or victimization by predatory lenders, these data suggest that many nonsavers are financially disciplined people who are *opting* to spend rather than save. (Some, to be sure, simply have no extra money to save after expenses.) It is true that nonsavers are more likely than others to use fringe financers and owe money for consumer goods[15]—but this fact supports the idea that nonsavers have a high time preference and thus do not mind using expensive credit for discretionary purchases.

It is important to note that individuals' expectations for the future and saving habits are heavily influenced by their social, spatial, and historical contexts. We all look to our peers' actions to guide our own behavior, and, if our friends and family do not prioritize saving, then chances are we will not either. In this way, a disinclination to save can be absorbed from others and need not derive from individual level factors such as a negative assessment of one's future prospects.

But there are reasons to be hopeful even in cases where the motivation to save is lacking. As mentioned earlier, many people who do not save nonetheless believe that the practice of saving has value in general. When asked what they would do with a ten-thousand-dollar windfall, nonsavers are about as likely as savers to say that they would save it or use it to pay down debt, as opposed to spend it.[16] These findings imply that undersavers know that there is a better way but simply lack the confidence, hope, or tools needed to get on the right path. For the most part, these individuals do not need to be persuaded that saving is good. They just need to be encouraged to see themselves as savers and to be provided with the tools to help themselves.

Table 4. Debts and Assets among Savers and Non-Savers

	Savers	Non-Savers	Low-income[1] Savers	Low-income Non-Savers
Has any debt	50.5	39.1	39.7	32.3
.... Has a bank loan	12.9	3.4	8.0	1.7
.... Has a student loan	13.7	9.0	8.3	5.6
.... Has a car loan	17.9	7.3	11.9	4.3
.... Has a mortgage	9.3	1.8	5.6	2.4
.... Has other loan	3.5	8.8	1.9	8.1
Has credit card	69.7	26.5	45.7	20.2
.... Has a balance[2]	33.6	42.4	36.3	29.6
Has a car	73.4	41.0	53.1	25.3
Owns a home	44.1	17.5	26.0	11.9

Data are from a survey of 1,532 mostly lower-income households carried out in Chicago, Los Angeles, and Washington, DC in 2003 and 2004.[3]

1. *Income under $15,000.*

2. *Among those with credit cards.*

3. *The survey respondents represent a population of approximately 957,850 households; Seidman, Hababou, and Kramer.*

POLICIES TO ENCOURAGE THRIFT

How, then, can we best help undersavers make this transition into the American financial mainstream?

By and large, policymakers have proposed a "carrot and stick" approach to promoting saving. According to this strategy, the government should, on the one hand, provide tax subsidies to individuals who save and businesses that help them do so—and, on the other hand, it should clamp down on subprime lending and other practices deemed to be predatory. While I believe that there is some merit in many of the specific "carrot and stick" proposals currently discussed in policy circles, based on my understanding of the saving problem, I do not expect that those overall strategies will lead to any systemic improvement in the financial practices of lower-income Americans.[17] Among other things, the saving incentives most plans rely upon would likely be too weak and too diffuse in their effects to help undersavers get on a better path. They are not sufficient to create fundamental change.

I believe that the following two-pronged strategy to promote thrift stands a better chance of success.

First, the federal government should, as a public service, directly create institutions and products that facilitate saving and investment on a broad scale. This "prothrift infrastructure" should be ubiquitous and automate the wealth building process as much as possible. (These things need not be expensive or involve any major expansion of government power, as I will explain.)

Second, we must find creative and effective ways to draw people into this prothrift infrastructure. Possibilities include advertising the new saving opportunities to the public, integrating them into our existing state institutions, and automatically enrolling people in saving plans (but giving them the option to opt out). The goal of these efforts would be to make saving a kind of "default position" in our culture and institutional landscape—a normal behavior we carry out without having to think about it.

The principles behind this strategy are simple: most nonsavers, as we have seen, actually want to save but lack the conviction needed to start the process and keep at it. What these individuals most need is for someone—in this case, the government—to help them get the ball rolling and to make the saving process as easy as possible. Help people set aside money each month, and they will soon see themselves as savers. Cynics might smirk at this proposition. But scholars have long noted that when people experience success in saving money and making progress toward goals, it gives them a greater sense of self-efficacy and higher aspirations for the future; these sentiments, in turn, promote additional saving.[18] It is a virtuous cycle.

The following three policy recommendations are designed to put this strategy into action. If adopted, they could conceivably help millions of Americans to save more and build wealth for the future.

1. Create an "American Investment Plan" and Mandate Universal Automatic Enrollment.

As noted earlier, work-based retirement accounts are one of the primary vehicles through which Americans save and gain access to the market. But millions of workers are not offered a plan, and most people have no financial planner to help them invest on their own.

This is a shame because it is *technically* easier and cheaper than ever to gain diversified access to the market. There are now literally hundreds of low-cost index funds that are chopped up and sold as stocks, and they can be acquired for a one-time trading fee. All it would take for more people to gain access to these kinds of investment tools is an expansion of the retirement-account platform.

Actually, the government has already created a program that does just that: the retirement saving program offered to federal employees, the Thrift Savings Plan (TSP). Introduced in 1987, the TSP allows employees to divert a portion of their income into a few diversified stock, bond, and money market funds. The program is simple and facilitates safe investing. Participants can, for example, select "lifecycle" funds that are well diversified and shift into more conservative investments as retirement nears. These funds are managed by an independent board with oversight from the public and private sectors. The TSP is also cheap. The administrative fees on its funds are extraordinarily low at 0.06 percent, much lower than those for commercial funds.

Currently, the TSP has 3.8 million participants and manages $231.5 billion in assets. As a market-based program, it has generated tens of billions of dollars in returns for its participants without burdening taxpayers. So, there you have it: an inexpensive government program that has helped millions of average Americans access markets to build wealth—and demonstrated that, contrary to some claims, markets are not inherently too risky or too confusing for most people.

I propose that the federal government create a national investment trust—modeled on the TSP and open to *all* Americans—called the American Investment Plan (AIP).

The AIP would be simple and user friendly. It would consist of a money market and stock and bond index funds. Participants would be able to invest in specific funds (small cap, large cap, international, etc.) if they wished to do so. But they would also have the ability to choose an asset allocation fund that that would automatically select a stock/bond/cash mix suited to the customer's risk tolerance and investment time horizon.

Investors would be able to open up an account online or over the phone and fund it through mail-in or direct deposits. The plan would offer IRAs, but contributions would otherwise be after tax and could be withdrawn for *any purpose*. The AIP would, therefore, be a flexible saving program as opposed to a dedicated retirement saving vehicle like the TSP.

While people would be able to withdraw general funds for any purpose, the AIP would encourage members to invest for the long term. For example, the plan would explicitly be marketed as a longer-term saving tool, and customers would be forced to assess their risk tolerance when opening an account, which would reduce the chances of panicked withdrawals during market downturns. The money market might also pay interest only on the lowest balance held each month, which would discourage frequent account activity. In addition, withdrawing funds would take a few days, which would presumably discourage people from using the plan as a short-term saving vehicle.

The AIP would be funded like any other nonprofit investment fund: a tiny sliver of deposits and capital gains would be used to cover the plan's overhead and employees' salaries.

All funds in the plan would be independently managed and would belong solely to the individual investors at all times, so the government would not be able to dip into the plan to fund its projects. And because the AIP would use national and global index funds, it would not disrupt or unduly influence marketplace.

The real beauty of the American Investment Plan is that it could be leveraged in ways that take advantage of all the little tricks that help people to save. Consider the practice of automatic enrollment. Studies have shown that when companies automatically enroll workers in 401(k)s—giving them the option to opt out, of course—rates of participation absolutely soar, especially among poorer workers (from 10 percent to 80 percent!).[19] It is a practice that helps people snap out of their inertia and follow through on a decision they already want to make—and it does so far more effectively than employer matches and incentives. Unfortunately, automatic enrollment is rare at the moment, in part because many companies do not offer a retirement plan in the first place.

With the AIP in place, Congress could mandate that *all employers* automatically enroll workers in an opt-out saving plan (either with the company or the AIP). The default contribution would be conservative. Under the proposed law, employers might, for example, be required to deposit 1 percent of each worker's earnings into the worker's personal account where he or she would be invested in a money market fund. The law would give each worker ample time to modify his or her plan, or opt out, before it took effect. But barring any worker input, the default contribution would be made on his or her behalf by the employer.

Universal automatic enrollment, more than any other policy, has the potential to increase dramatically rates of saving among the public. If enacted, it would help millions of struggling Americans get on the path to a better financial future.

The AIP could be built upon and extended in numerous other ways as well. For example, the IRS might each year send people an approximate estimate of what they should be saving for retirement and then allow them to open up an AIP account on their tax return. We could also let people deposit any tax refunds or credits into their account. It is easier to do the right thing when you do not actually have the money in hand.

These kinds of policies are inexpensive and could further promote thrift and saving in the United States.

2. Create a Public Education Program to Promote Thrift.
Policymakers should strongly consider creating a new public education campaign to promote saving.

The cynic might again smirk at this idea. But campaigns to reduce drunk driving, reduce smoking, and encourage people to wear a seatbelt all had a significant impact on people's behavior. Consider, too, the tremendous surge in saving that occurred during World War II. At the height of the conflict, Americans saved about 25 percent of their income on average. This impressive display of thrift and sacrifice was driven largely by people's sense of patriotic duty, but it also had more proximal sources—the government actively stressed the importance of saving and provided a tool for people to do so in the form of war bonds.

Given that many Americans desire to save more, there is no reason to believe that a prothrift message would fall on deaf ears today.[20]

A prosaving campaign might begin with posters and media ads that focus on the benefits of saving in the American Investment Plan. A poster might convey the following information in some form:

Table 5.   Save $10 in an AIP account each week...[1]

	5 years	10 years	20 years	30 years	40 years
And you'll have put this much in	$2,600	$5,200	$10,400	$15,600	$20,800
But here's what you'll have in your account	$3,200	$7,700	$22,800	$52,600	$111,100

1. *These numbers are just rough approximations of returns, of course. They assume a 7 percent interest rate and that the interest is compounded on the first day of each year. The numbers have been rounded to the nearest hundred.*

Other ads might compare the life experiences of a hypothetical saver and nonsaver. Still others could point out the benefits of saving over high-cost financing and draw attention to the high fees one incurs by using payday loans and fringe transactions.

What is most important is that ads and messages not be overly abstract or general. They should not merely implore the viewer to save. They should use concrete examples to illustrate their points and always direct people to specific institutions and products that can help them. No viewers should be left wondering how they might act upon the message they have just seen.

It is particularly important that any such campaign strive to educate younger Americans. And there would be no better way to do that than by reintroducing financial education into our public schools.

While it is beyond the scope of this essay to suggest a specific curriculum, policymakers and educators could begin by looking to the successful but forgotten history of U.S. school-based saving programs[21] or to the more recent "Save for America" program.[22] These programs show that the most effective efforts to educate children on finance *actually help them to save money in school-based accounts.* Educators should, therefore, consider developing a model school bank program that could be replicated in districts across the nation. The school bank should be fairly realistic. It should accept students' deposits each week and provide account statements. It might also pay interest in lump sums to students who have kept money in their account for a specified period of time.

Aside from familiarizing students with banks and the process of saving, school bank programs would have an important psychological benefit. Research suggests that the ability to delay gratification—a skill needed for saving—can be learned in childhood and adolescence but not thereafter.[23] By helping children to develop this skill, school banks would be greatly increasing the chance that children will save in adulthood as well.

At the middle- and high-school levels, young adults should be required to take more detailed financial education courses that cover concepts such as compound interest and risk and that would familiarize students with financial products and institutions.

Given that financial knowledge and experience are some of the most important determinants of wise financial behavior, these school-based programs could dramatically improve the financial well-being of the American public.[24]

3. Create a "Save to Win Bond" to Compete with the Lotteries.

Every day state governments encourage citizens to gamble away their potential savings on the lottery. The amount of money frittered away on this new American pastime is staggering: $184 per year for the average person and a whopping $645 per year for households earning under $12,400.[25]

If we compare the returns on playing the lottery to the returns on investing, the wastefulness of the former becomes even more apparent. Let us suppose that a poor family spends that average sum of $645 per year on lottery tickets for forty years. Assuming a 53 percent payout rate,[26] the family will, after four decades, have spent $25,800 on tickets and lost $12,126 of that sum. The family will be left with $13,674. But what if the members of the same household had instead invested that same $645 each year? Assuming a 6 percent rate of return, they would have *earned* $86,645.04, leaving them with $112,445.04. If that does not demonstrate that lower-income Americans can save more and should be helped to do so, I do not know what does.

It is time to create a prothrift alternative to the lottery. I propose that the federal government create a "lottery bond," modeled on the successful "prize bond" programs of Britain and Pakistan,[27] which would compete with the state lotteries and help people to save.

A lottery bond—it could be called a "Save 2 Win" (S2W) bond or something along those lines—would at root be an interest-bearing government bond, a treasury bill. But, instead of paying out all interest to all bondholders in equal allotments, the S2W program would distribute some of its capital in the form of cash prizes to selected bondholders.

Here is how the process would work: In order to play the game, an individual would have to be over the age of seventeen and have an American Investment Plan account. Those conditions satisfied, he or she would be able to buy an S2W bond at a convenient location for fifty dollars or some other denomination. The customer would receive a receipt or certification confirming the purchase, but the "real" bond would be deposited into his or her AIP account. Each bond would have a number, and twice a month winning numbers would be randomly drawn from the list of outstanding bonds. At each drawing, there would be small and large cash awards and other prizes as well.

The bonds could be redeemed at any time, but a player would have a greater chance of winning a prize if he or she held onto the bond. Alternatively, a player would be able to exchange his or her bond for shares of an AIP index fund.

A S2W bond would, then, in essence, be a combination of a savings bond and a lottery ticket. It would attract customers (investors) looking for the excitement of playing the game, but it would encourage them to save and set aside wealth for the future at the same time.

If even a modest portion of the money spent on the lottery went into S2W bonds instead, it would mean millions of dollars in new savings for American families.

CONCLUSION

We face several serious challenges when it comes to the financial health of the American public. Too many people are not saving enough to live in financial freedom and security. Too many are skating by on a razor's edge of solvency, and too little is currently being done to improve the situation. It is now clearer than ever that we need a new national initiative to promote thrift and saving. Enacting the policies proposed in this essay would be a good start.

Chapter 8

Private Enterprise's Role in Increasing Savings

Ronald T. Wilcox

WELL-FORMED PUBLIC POLICY is a potent tool for increasing savings. It can lay the groundwork for coaxing people into making better decisions. But the front line in the battle to increase household savings is the workplace where people make many of the decisions that will affect their savings and long-term economic prospects. Private enterprise can also make substantial inroads here. A small business owner or senior executive in a large corporation can take some simple steps to increase the savings of his or her employees. If those steps become known as best practices, the effects could ripple throughout the U.S. economy.

This essay speaks mainly to those individuals who hold senior-level positions in U.S. companies or are small business owners. It appeals to some paternalistic instincts—beliefs that making life better for one's employees is a good use of time and energies.[1] If business executives do not have any paternalistic instinct toward their employees, they should, nevertheless, find this essay beneficial.

Broadening participation in and increasing employee contributions to employer-sponsored pension plans can directly benefit the company itself. It is clear that the old defined benefit pension plans common at many companies for most of the twentieth century increased employees' tendency to remain with a given company and, hence, effectively reduced employee turnover. There is increasing evidence that defined contribution pension plans have the same effect, although there is no obvious economic reason that this should be the case.[2] Employees vested in a defined contribution plan can always roll their pension money over into a private tax-deferred vehicle (e.g., an individual retirement account), suffer no financial loss, and seek employment elsewhere. But the interesting psychological effect of accumulating money within an employer-sponsored pension plan appears to extend well beyond that. In economic speak, the effect appears to stem from the fact that workers' discount rates and productivity rates are negatively correlated. This is just a very academic way of saying something business executives have probably known for a long time. Some employees have a strong work ethic, which extends beyond their desire for a weekly paycheck. They work hard because that is who they are; it is part of their worldview and defines for them what it means to be a good person. These are the same people who tend to take the long view of things, to put off immediate gratification in order to build slowly a better life for themselves some years down the road. Business executives want to keep these people on their payrolls. Such employees are very productive. They also happen to be motivated by well-funded, well-designed pension plans because they place a great deal of value on the future payoff of those plans.

Other workers want everything and want it immediately. They tend to be less productive workers; if they left, it would not be bad for one's business. Because they want everything immediately and have high discount rates, they tend to be unmotivated by generous pension plans.[3] These less productive workers are also more likely to leave the company to access the lump-sum distribution option offered by defined contribution plans. Therefore, in addition to making workers financially better off, a good pension plan has the effect of separating the proverbial wheat from the chaff, of retaining the better employees and implicitly coaxing the less-productive employees to leave.

Well-designed retirement plans are an important tool for increasing employee savings, and I will spend considerable time in this essay describing some important design features of a good plan. But even more basic than these ideas is the reality that if employees do not want to save, they certainly will not. We cannot make people save, but we do have the ability to change their attitudes toward savings, to make them want to save. This is not the realm of traditional economics. It is the world of peddling products and ideas, of consumer psychology, and the folk wisdom of tin men.

REPOSITIONING THRIFT

One story that I always tell my MBA students is about the demise of Oldsmobile. For many years, decades really, Oldsmobile was an aspirational car for the retired and almost-retired crowd. If you wanted a big luxury car with a little more of a sporty appeal than a Cadillac, then an Olds was the ticket. But, gradually, tastes for automobiles began to change, and General Motors (GM) found itself with a dying brand, a nameplate that was losing sales year after year.

What did GM do with Oldsmobile? Well, it tried to do what marketers call reposition the brand, to change consumers basic perceptions of the car. And a radical repositioning it was. GM executives wanted the public to think of Oldsmobile not as a big, dowdy ride but an exciting, sporty car for the younger driver. They were trying to reinvent its brand image totally. To do that, they brought out new, completely redesigned models with racy body lines and higher revolution engines. Accompanying this new engineering was a very expensive advertising campaign with the slogan "This is not your father's Oldsmobile." Even though those advertisements have been off the air for years now, you may remember that phrase—its exposure was so broad and so often repeated. Did it work? No. Oldsmobile was discontinued in 2004. Why did it not work? Well, GM certainly had and continues to have myriad problems, so I doubt there is only one answer. But here is an important part of the answer. No one believed that it was not his or her "father's

Oldsmobile." The nameplate had such strong perceptual associations with images and thoughts of being old, having the added problem that the word *old* was imbedded in the name of the vehicle, that no amount of reengineering and marketing communications could change it. In marketing, we understand that changing people's minds about a product or an idea or a political candidate is immensely difficult. And GM failed with Oldsmobile.

I think we are failing in how we communicate the goals and benefits of savings to younger workers. The average twenty-five-year-old person does not aspire to "retire." Much like the "old" in Oldsmobile, the word *retirement* brings with it a host of perceptual associations, often born of the stereotypes of "tired" old people. The twenty-something set does not look forward to the day when shuffleboard is its daily recreational activity. Even the word *thrift*, a word that is contained both in the title of my book on the subject, as well as this volume, conjures images of someone knitting while scanning the paper for coupons. These are not thoughts and images that inspire action. Retirement seminars, retirement planning sessions, online retirement calculators all suffer this important deficiency in the way they are presented or packaged.

Younger people do aspire to "financial independence." Rather than speaking of retirement, conversations and tools that help people determine how to save so that they will achieve financial independence earlier in life are likely to be better received. While the economics of a "financial independence calculator" or a "financial independence planning session" may be nearly identical to their retirement counterparts, the marketing is much better.

We need to begin speaking in new terms to the millennial generation, a group that on the whole saves very little. The language of "pensions," of "retirement," of "security," while certainly effective for those who remember the Great Depression, is less potent now than the language of "independence" and "self-determination." The math can remain the same, but the marketing needs to change.

And the younger crowd is indeed one of the groups on which we need to focus our attention. Our ability to change the economic circumstances of a sixty-five-year-old by altering attitudes and behaviors is far more limited than our ability to do the same with a twenty-five-year-old. It is also true that twenty-somethings save less than any current age cohort.[3] So, focusing on younger employees makes sense. It also makes sense to target more marketing and educational efforts toward women and minorities. Here is why.

FOCUSING ON WOMEN AND MINORITIES

Men are often overconfident and stubborn, to their detriment, when it comes to financial issues, whereas women are more accepting of advice that is given in financial education seminars. Men have two psychological characteristics that play havoc on their ability to save and invest money. First, they are overconfident in their own ability. This is not a characteristic confined to finance. They are overconfident in their ability with regard to almost anything. Evolutionary psychologists, those who study how our thinking patterns have evolved over time, have speculated that this tendency toward overconfidence arose because of the tasks men performed in early human societies. Men hunted, and, when hunting, it improves your survival chances if you are very confident when face to face with a wild animal. Today, we each face the market rather than wild animals. But, unlike the hunt, men's overconfidence often dooms them in this situation. They tend to trade stocks more actively because they are convinced they know what the next hot stock will be, what is likely to go up, and what is likely to go down. In so doing, they incur all of the transaction costs associated with trading (commissions, taxes, bid-ask spreads) but do not pick stocks any better than the woman in the office next to theirs. That woman, typically less confident in her own abilities, including finance, will trade stocks less often and, in so doing, generate risk-adjusted returns that are superior to her male counterpart.[4] Even in the more sedate world of mutual fund investing, the most common financial instrument found in defined contribution retirement plans, women seem to have a better ability to pick good funds because they concentrate on the fees a fund charges rather than what fund happens to be hot at any given moment.[5] And so, we have what amounts to a stark paradox in investing: men think they know what they are doing but often do not, and women think they do not know what they are doing but often do.

So, are women just better investors than men? Yes, they are. Women bring an emotional and psychological tool kit that is better adapted to decision making in modern financial markets. They listen, consider alternatives carefully, change their minds when necessary, and generally lack the hubris that leads men astray.

If we focus our workplace educational efforts on women, will it then produce a new cohort of women who are overconfident in the financial abilities and who themselves fall into the same traps as men? I doubt it. The psychological disposition of overconfidence is a deeply engrained one, and only at the margins are we likely to affect confidence. What we are more likely to produce is a group of women who know a bit more about reasonable savings rates, risk and return, and asset allocation, the basic tools that allow individuals to make good decisions about savings and investment. This is particularly important for women for two distinct reasons. First, women are more likely to share the knowledge they learn with others.[6] Men learn and internalize. Women learn and communicate. Executives cannot teach everyone in their company or organization everything they really should know about saving and investing, but if executives focus their early efforts on women, what is taught will diffuse through the employee population more quickly. Because of the importance of this knowledge diffusion effect, it is equally important that business executives do not target women from one social or economic strata of the company. People like to give and receive advice from others that they believe are a bit more knowledgeable in one particular area but who otherwise are like themselves. Information technology (IT) people are likely to give and receive advice from other IT people. They work with them, they talk to them, and in some respects, they think like them. Business leaders need to gather people together from different parts of their organizations to help this diffusion effect along.

The other reason it is important to target workplace educational efforts toward women is the hard reality that women generally outlive men, and because of this fact, their golden years are particularly at risk for financial shortfalls. Women are more likely to be left making serious financial decisions late in life. A little knowledge can go a long way in helping secure their financial future and avoiding being the victim of those who pretend to act as fiduciaries but do not.

Minorities should also be a target audience for financial education but for reasons that are quite different from those mentioned for women. The issue at hand here is one of overspending, of the propensity to consume too many of life's finer things now and to leave little for the future. This reason strikes directly at our moral understanding of thrift and at the question of why some people practice it with ease while others struggle. The most obvious, and most common, way to think about thrift is as an individual virtue. Within this broad framework, individuals receive pay for the work they have done and then decide how much money should be spent on housing, on clothes, and on discretionary items. Good people spend less than they earn, while bad people spend more than they earn. The moral superiority of the individual virtue of thrift is clear.

This simple and compact worldview has been the basis of many editorials about thrift and forms the philosophical underpinning for many of the questions I get when people ask me about issues related to the lack of savings we see in the United States. The individual moral vices of materialism and overconsumption are widely viewed as a major part of the problem.

But this view also has an important omission that has practical implications for the way we think about teaching thrift. Consumption, and particularly conspicuous consumption, takes on added social meaning when an individual feels powerless relative to others in society.[7] A Hispanic woman who speaks English with a Spanish accent may believe that others who meet her for the first time will assume that she is poor and less educated. A black man with a "black" accent may feel the same. And sometimes they are right. Even those who might view themselves as above constructing these types of instant perceptions do it.

How might this Hispanic woman compensate for this, an instant perception from which she is trying to flee? She may choose to purchase a Versace dress or drive a BMW in an attempt to counter this initial impression. Expensive luxury brands tell the world, "I am not as powerless as you think I am," and they appeal to some segments of the population who are least able to afford them. Even controlling for income differences, minorities spend a significantly higher proportion of their income on conspicuous consumption.[8] Look in the mirror. Will people meeting you for the first time assume by your appearance and speech that you are likely to be reasonably successful at life? If the honest answer is "yes," it is easier for you to practice thrift.

As we move forward to teach savings, investing, and thrift to others, it is important to understand why some people are better at these activities than others. We need to supplement the common moral narrative with the understanding that the psychological value of conspicuous consumption varies across individuals in accordance with their own self-perceptions of power and position. Lifting up those who feel powerless is more likely to change self-defeating spending behavior than recriminations that make them feel worse than they already do. Education in the workplace needs to project that tone in order to be effective.

What should be taught in these programs? Certainly, there are concepts that are central to employees' understanding of the benefits of savings, compound interest being prime among them. The basics of effective allocation (diversification) and an understanding of how this idea relates to the age of the employee are also important. The mechanics and particulars of an employer's tax-deferred retirement savings plan, 401(k), is the underlying decision environment in which many of the more important decisions are likely to take place. Employees need to have a detailed understanding of their company's plan.

But the hard reality here is that our state of knowledge in this area is woefully inadequate. It is not that we do not know what employees need to know. In general, we do. But many of the important topics, compound interest, for example, require a level of mathematical thinking that would escape many employees. What we need are simple rules of thumb that translate complicated mathematical ideas in savings and investing into ideas that people can actually learn, remember, and act on. Research that jointly uses the tools of economics and cognitive psychology to help bridge the gap between what employees know and what they need to know to secure their financial futures would go a long way toward helping construct a pragmatic workplace financial education curriculum, one likely to impart enduring benefits for the participants.

DESIGNING GOOD DEFINED CONTRIBUTION PLANS

Let's look at employee retirement savings and, in particular, the tax-deferred defined contribution plans that are ubiquitous among medium- and large-sized companies. These plans are a huge store of wealth for some employees and are virtually ignored by others. Nevertheless, there are simple mechanisms and design features that will allow these plans to work more effectively for all employees.[9] What follow are eight ideas or suggestions for business executives in charge of these plans. If you are simply a worker with a company retirement plan, you can glean some valuable insights. In addition, you could show this essay to your superiors and ask that they consider implementing my recommendations.

1. Choose a Pension Plan Provider with Low Fees.

The federal law governing private sector retirement plans, the Employee Retirement Income Security Act (ERISA), requires that those responsible for managing retirement plans (called fiduciaries) carry out their responsibilities prudently and solely in the interest of the plan's participants and beneficiaries. The fees assessed by the provider of your 401(k) plan are subtracted from the value of your employees' savings and are an important issue over which to exercise careful fiduciary oversight.

Mutual fund fees vary widely. Annual management fees for widely held equity funds commonly range between 0.2 percent and 2.0 percent. The fees for funds that concentrate their holdings in high-grade bonds vary somewhat less, but the differences among the fees charged by companies can be significant. There is no evidence that funds with high management fees provide a better net return to investors than funds with lower fees; in fact, there is a good deal of evidence that the opposite is true. Low fees are likely to be a reliable indication of higher net investment returns over the long run, and they affect the value of your employee's retirement account in economically significant ways.

Mutual funds held within an employee sponsored retirement plan may have all of the same fees associated with standard retail mutual funds: front-end loads, back-end loads, annual management fees, 12(b)-1 fees, and so on. In addition, investment management firms may charge a plan administration fee that would either be billed directly to the company or to individuals within the plan as a flat annual fee, or be deducted from the net return of employee shares, much in the same way the annual management fee is deducted. The point here is that these fee structures can get confusing, and, without careful attention, both your company and your employees can lose significant amounts of money before they even realize that they are in a bad financial situation relative to other marketplace offerings.

The U.S. Department of Labor offers a very useful template called a Uniform Fee Disclosure. This is a handy instrument for evaluating the fees assessed by alternative retirement plan providers and keeping fiduciaries from getting lost in the shuffle of complex and opaque fee structures. Although this kind of comparison work is detailed and tedious, there is no doubt that your employees' retirement wealth can be considerably enhanced by carefully scrutinizing fees charged by current and potential retirement plan providers.

2. Limit the Number of Mutual Funds in Your Plan.

Pension plans that contain a large number of investment choices work to the detriment of investors. Too many choices are more likely to confuse individual investors and delay both their participation and asset allocation decisions. When people become overwhelmed by too many funds and too much data, their natural tendency is to decide not to choose.[10]

If you do not believe that your employees may find the options in your defined contribution pension plan confusing, ask your human resources manager for the information new employees receive or attend their benefits orientation. If the prospectuses of the various mutual funds and annuity options are not included in the packet handed to you, ask for them. Assuming you can get them quickly, stack them up on your desk and then go through them. If you find yourself puzzling about the exact investment strategy of a given fund or the particular structure of an annuity that is being offered, just imagine what some of your employees are going through. You hired them because they each had a particular expertise. They may be very smart, but they are not likely to have a clue about the difference between Sallie Mae and U.S. Treasury bonds. The more options you throw at them, the more difficult this already daunting task becomes. You can simplify it for them.

A properly diversified portfolio does not require many choices. Basic needs can be covered by access to mutual funds specializing in (1) cash or cash equivalents, (2) fixed-income securities, and (3) domestic equities. It can be argued that it makes sense to include mutual funds that hold (4) foreign securities, (5) real estate, (6) small capitalization stocks, and (7) lifecycle funds that automatically adjust the asset mix of the portfolio as the employee moves closer to retirement. Some participants will also want access to an annuity product, but the above list just about spans the reasonable alternatives. Pension plans with many choices invariably have funds whose asset holdings overlap each other. The same underlying portfolio could be synthesized with far fewer funds and without the confusion that accompanies such a large set of choices.

Choose to offer the fewest number of investment options that span the necessary asset classes for a properly diversified portfolio. If there is more than one financial service provider offering products that are included in your deferred tax retirement plan, these companies will undoubtedly pressure you to offer more of their products to your employees. So that they will not miss out on the investment money that an employee might place with another provider, they will want to saturate the plan with all the possible products that any employee might find attractive. Remember: it is not in your employees' best interest to have a large number of inevitably overlapping products to choose from. Exercise your instincts to limit their options, and they will ultimately be better off.

3. Resist Payment-and-Product-Exchange Agreements.

Accepting payments in exchange for access to your employees' investment dollars is, in my view, a breach of the fiduciary responsibility required by the U.S. Department of Labor for companies that sponsor these types of plans. Nevertheless, I believe that this occurs with disturbing frequency. A plain reading of the law requires companies to act solely in their employees' best interest when designing a retirement plan. It is hard to construct a scenario under which accepting payments in exchange for the privilege of marketing financial products to employees enrolled in the plan would constitute a reasonable exercise of fiduciary responsibility. The monies transferred to the company could otherwise be used to reduce fees for products contained in the plan, which would certainly be in the best interest of employees.

4. Set the Default Asset Allocation in Thirds.

For many pension plans, if the employee does not elect an asset allocation, the "no choice" option or default is to place 100 percent of company contributions into a money market account. For the vast majority of employees, this asset allocation makes no sense.

Many companies use this as the default allocation largely for reasons of legal conservatism. Setting the default to all cash can be defended as the "safest" investment choice for employees, virtually guaranteeing that their principal will never decline in value. But this is only the safest portfolio allocation under the narrowest possible definition of safety—capital preservation. The real rate of return on that concentrated portfolio is likely to be below the rate of inflation, which leads to negative real returns for the investor. Employees who have all of their retirement savings in cash will indeed preserve their capital, but their spending power will not be preserved.

Also, many employees will leave their pension money in the default allocation of the plan.[11] Perhaps they are busy and do not want to take the time to change the asset allocation, even if the transaction costs associated with making such a change are generally low. It is also reasonable to assume that some employees believe the company is making decisions in their best interest. Because companies do have fiduciary responsibility with regard to employee pensions, this is not a completely unreasonable assumption; but it is often wishful thinking. It is also clear that a substantial proportion of employees do not understand what an allocation of 100 percent to a money market fund really means. Companies are not specifically required to use 100 percent cash as the default option in their pension plans. In recent years, the Securities and Exchange Commission has focused its regulatory attention on companies that aggressively market their own stock as an asset alternative for their employees' retirement plans. The abuses of this kind of behavior are well known (Enron, for example), but beyond the requirement that employers act in the best interest of their employees, they are largely free to set up retirement plan defaults however they see fit.

A default allocation divided into thirds between equities, bonds, and cash would better serve employees. This allocation would fall in line with common financial advice for many more employees than current pure cash defaults. It bears repeating that setting the default would in no way restrict the employee from choosing a different fund mix and asset allocation; it would simply occur if the employee decided not to choose. Barring a sudden and widespread uptick in financial acumen, we can rest assured that many people will not make a choice.

Another alternative to the equal division between stocks, bonds, and cash is the use of "life-cycle funds." These funds, which are marketed by a number of mutual fund complexes, automatically adjust the portfolio mix of the fund as the investor ages. Funds for individuals who are a long way from retirement typically are invested heavily in equities, while those whose investors are closer to retirement hold a greater proportion of fixed-income assets. In that sense, a fund is specific to a particular age group. A mutual fund complex that includes life-cycle-type funds will generally have several, each with a different target retirement date for the participant. Therefore, for a thirty-year-old employee, a life-cycle fund with a targeted retirement date of 2040 would be about right. Employers could set the default allocation of their pension plans to 100 percent in the life-cycle fund whose targeted retirement date most closely matched an employee's sixty-fifth birthday. That would generate asset allocations and projected retirement savings that are, in most cases, far better than the current practice allows.

5. Set Automatic Enroll Defaults on 401(k) Plans.

More troubling than the default allocation, however, is the reality that many employees will not enroll in the company 401(k) plan. My advice here is very simple: set up your human resource systems so that new employees are automatically enrolled in the 401(k) unless they specify otherwise. By law, companies that set an automatic enrollment feature for their defined contribution retirement plans must defer at least 3 percent of an employee's salary. The maximum is 10 percent. The minimum employee contribution steps up 1 percent each year for three years, so that a 6 percent minimum must be deferred in the fourth year. Also, employers must provide a contribution matching plan that contributes at least 3 percent to employee savings in addition to the deferrals of the employees themselves, and these contributions must vest in no more than two years. Consequently, automatic enrollment is not an option for companies that do not contribute to their employees' retirement plans, but it is an option for companies that currently either provide matching funds of at least 3 percent or contribute at least 3 percent, independent of employee contributions.

Setting the default to include a contribution on the part of the employee is a highly paternalistic approach with potential risks.

Financially naïve employees—or those who do not pay much attention to what is going on with their paychecks—would be unwittingly contributing money out of their regular pay to a pension plan that they had never considered or consciously joined. A few may be in financial situations where contributing to such a plan makes little sense, but because the default is set to include a contribution on their behalf and they are not paying close attention, they may end up somewhat financially worse off. For example, an employee trying to save money for a near-term business venture may want to keep as much of his or her savings out of age-restricted funds as possible. While this type of situation could certainly arise, I deeply suspect that only a very small minority of employees would be negatively impacted. Even those who were inattentive would not become financially worse off in tragic ways; the money would not disappear, and they would still get the match. On balance, it is clear that the benefit to employees who would otherwise not enroll or receive the matching funds far outweighs the risks to a comparatively small group of people.

6. Give Detailed, Personalized Financial Advice.

When I was hired by the University of Virginia, like many people starting a new job, I attended a benefits orientation session. It covered a lot of ground, but among the issues on the agenda was an explanation of the employer-based retirement plan, in this case, a defined contribution 403(b) plan. During the session, several people asked questions about the investment products offered in the plan. For the most part, these questions centered on mutual fund and annuity products offered by TIAA-CREF and Fidelity Inc. (the large mutual fund provider). Many questions focused on the differences among the various funds offered, what mix of funds made sense for a given individual, and whether it was wise to contribute additional money to the plan (beyond what the university would automatically contribute).

The facilitator, while certainly both prepared and wanting to be helpful, was obviously afraid to say anything that might even come close to helpful financial advice. When a new assistant professor in the

Sociology Department asked whether it made sense to contribute some of her income to the tax-deferred savings plan, the facilitator reluctantly said something like, "Well, it depends on your own individual financial situation." Of course, this is obviously true, but it also completely ignores the reality that, for the vast majority of people in a position similar to this thirty-something new assistant professor, the answer should be an unequivocal "Yes!" Unless she had large stores of wealth somewhere, of which she would be completely aware, putting some pretax money in this plan would make a lot of sense. At this point, one arrogant participant, a new faculty member at Darden, just could not take it any longer. He raised his hand and proceeded to answer her question in the affirmative. Everyone instantly began asking him questions and, perhaps foolishly, he began to answer them—very directly.

Answering people's questions on the spot was not nearly as daunting as it might sound. They were not asking about the subtleties of the average maturity or yield on a given bond fund. They wanted to know things like whether the retirement plan was good or bad. Should they make additional contributions to it? Should they just keep everything in a money market fund (the default allocation of the plan), or should they fill out one of the forms being offered to change the allocation? The facilitator could have offered some very concrete and sound advice in responding to these questions, such as "The retirement plan is indeed a good one. Yes, in most instances saving some additional money through the plan makes sense. No, an allocation of 100 percent to a money market account is probably not smart except in some special financial circumstances." The problem was not that we had an ignorant facilitator, but that the facilitator was afraid of being sued.

At that point in 2001, federal regulations issued by ERISA disallowed employers from giving financial advice to their pension fund participants. These regulations were well intentioned; there was a concern that employers would provide advice to employees that was in the best interest of the company and not the employees. For example, a company could advise employees to hold a large proportion of their retirement portfolio in company stock or to allocate money to mutual funds provided by an investment company that was paying the employer a kickback based on the amount of money employees invested in their funds. These were certainly reasonable concerns, but at the same time, disallowing any financial advice about retirement plan decisions to pass from employer to employee cut many people off from one of the best places they might receive good financial information.[12]

The Pension Protection Act of 2006 changed the landscape of federal regulation in this area, but it remains to be seen if businesses will implement many of the changes that this law allows. Particularly pertinent to this discussion, under the Pension Protection Act, ERISA-covered retirement plans can offer participants financial counseling through a registered investment company, registered broker or dealer, bank, or insurance company acting as a fiduciary. In short, this means that the companies you contract with to provide financial products and services to your plan are now allowed to give financial advice to individual employees.

To protect participants from the aforementioned conflicts of interest, any payments that occur between you (the employer) and the financial services provider must be independent of the product choices your employees make. Also, advice about a particular portfolio allocation must be based on a third-party-certified computer model. The employee provides information about his or her particular financial situation to the financial service provider, who must use that data and the computer model as the basis for recommendations. Advisors must also disclose compensation, potential conflicts, past performance of plan investment options, available services, how participant information will be used, and the fact that participants can get advice from an advisor not affiliated with the plan.

This new law is a very reasonable compromise between conflict of interest concerns and the realization that it is natural to receive financial advice about retirement plan choices from one's employer. It also allows one person to sit down and talk to another when seeking advice—and this tends to work.

7. *Implement Forward Contracts for Savings.*

In many respects, the crux of the savings problem in the United States revolves not around confusion with regard to the pricing structures of financial services or misplaced tax incentives, but rather the simple fact that people have trouble giving up immediate consumption. Saving is hard because it requires sacrifice, and sacrifice is a tough sell—even to yourself.

But what if we did not have to sacrifice today in order to make the decision to save more? Perhaps we could dampen the pain of going without by committing ourselves to save more—tomorrow. Tomorrow we will have more money, so it should not be as difficult. That is the logic behind an ingenious set of recommendations by Shlomo Bernartzi and Richard Thaler in their "Save More Tomorrow" plan.[13] In a nutshell, this plan offers employees the option of committing to a future increase in their contribution to their employer-sponsored retirement plan. The key is that the increase will take place at the time of their next scheduled raise in salary. So instead of taking an immediate pay cut to fund additional savings, employees are essentially committing to a smaller increase in their take-home pay so they can increase their savings. They are buffering the pain of sacrifice by pairing it with a larger increase in their ability to purchase. Bernartzi and Thaler implemented this plan at several companies, including a mid-sized manufacturing concern. In what is perhaps the most startling set of statistics of the entire implementation analysis, the preprogram pension contribution rate of those who took part in the program was 3.5 percent. Eighty percent of those who started the plan continued with it for at least four years. The average contribution rate of those who stayed with the plan rose to 13.6 percent. It is too early to tell if those results can be replicated in a large number of companies, but it is an understatement to say that the results are promising. The psychological effect of allowing people to commit to saving more in the future—when their income increases—appears to be powerful. Extending this logic to other situations is straightforward. While we often concern ourselves with the plight of those who have less money, we all know people who have perfectly reasonable incomes but cannot manage money or keep themselves out of debt. Sometime each year, everyone who earns more than about $90,000 gets what looks like a raise; this occurs when he or she hits the Social Security (FICA) tax ceiling. Suddenly, the worker's monthly or biweekly paycheck increases. Just like the raises of workers in manufacturing firms, the FICA tax limit could be used as the "gain" necessary to mask the pain of future sacrifice. I am not aware that this has ever been tried in any setting, but if it worked for raises, it would likely work in this situation as well. This is an amazingly simple thing that you could do with your own employees, requiring little more than the paperwork you already have on hand for employee retirement plan participation and allocation decisions.

8. Limit Your Own Conspicuous Consumption.

Your consumption matters in the savings rates of your employees. Like it or not, you are in their reference group, and some of them aspire to be like you. Your employees notice the kind of clothes you wear to work, the car you park in the lot, and the description of your last vacation. They know where you live. They know if you belong to the most expensive country club in town. You may not think they pay attention, but they do.

And when they see conspicuous consumption or relative frugality, they infer that you view others with similar consumption patterns more favorably.[14] This is a difficult concept to measure; to my knowledge, no one has done it with any degree of certainty, but we know from our experience as people that we tend to view those who have our same opinions and tastes as smarter than those who do not. It is hard for us to believe that a person who agrees with most of our ideas and choices is an idiot. Likewise, it is easy to believe that someone who comes to different conclusions than we do about life's choices is just a little less thoughtful and less intelligent. There are good reasons for employees to agree with their bosses, and not just on ideas expressed in the workplace but in taste and consumption decisions as well. You like people who are like you.

Furthermore, consumption decisions can form what some economists have termed an "information cascade" within the organization. If you are a CEO, a line worker may not know much about you. But those who immediately report to you know what club you belong to, what kind of house you live in, and what kind of car you drive; and they make consumption decisions based partly on their desire to seem more like you. That, in turn, can cause a ripple effect through the entire organization, as each person looks to his or her boss for consumption cues. It is well known that some companies have developed cultures of conspicuous consumption, whereas others are much more frugal. At which type of company do you think it is easier to save if you are an administrative assistant earning $30,000 a year?

9. Focus on Employee Savings.

Individuals in any workplace make decisions whether to spend or to save, whether to be sensible with their money or foolish. Much of this decision making is out of business executives' control. It is the workers' money. But some financial decision making is, if not within executives' control, then at least within their influence. Educating one's employees about savings and financial decision making can work if it focuses on the right issues, is delivered with the right tone, and targets those within the organization who are most likely to benefit from it. It will work even better if business executives have a well-structured retirement savings plan, one built for real human beings rather than idealized rational economic agents. The workplace can become a focal point for a return to thrift.

Conclusion

*David Blankenhorn, Barbara Dafoe Whitehead,
and Sorcha Brophy-Warren*

WE CONCLUDE THIS VOLUME with two parting thoughts. First, we
will wrap up with a brief summary of the themes we found most strik-
ing in our inquiry. Consider it our "take-away" lesson on thrift.

1. Thrift is a value and practice embraced by a striving and
    aspiring people. It has never held interest for the idle rich
    or for those who live lavishly on borrowed money or inher-
    ited privilege. To say it another way, the key principles of
    thrift—hard work, regular savings, and careful stewardship
    of resources—are central to flourishing middle-class societ-
    ies, while the same thrift principles are almost always dis-
    dained in societies dominated by aristocratic elites.

2. Thrift is broadly democratic in its ambition and reach. It
    aims to create mass prosperity. Toward that end, it seeks
    to bring new people, often immigrants and the working
    poor, into its compass and to unite such people in coop-
    erative institutions. Thrift is also democratic in its faith
    in the power of education. Thrift leaders and institutions

have consistently made it a priority to teach children about saving, conserving, and being generous to others.

3. Thrift is oriented to the future. One of the most persistent misconceptions about thrift is that it is stuck in the distant past. Nothing could be further from the truth. Every serious thrift advocate and every thrift movement has been future-minded, and often visionary, in its ambitions and efforts for social change.

4. Thrift is a renewable cultural resource. It offers a set of guiding ethical and social principles from which Americans today, no less than in the past, can draw upon in responding to the grave challenges we face today.

Our second parting thought has to do with recent events. As we write today, the economic news is grim. Powerful Wall Street institutions have fallen. Big banks are writing off billions in bad debt. Mortgage delinquencies and bankruptcies are at record levels. Job losses are the worst since 1974. Meanwhile, the public debt continues to climb into numbers so stratospheric as to be utterly incomprehensible to most of us.

No one knows for sure how long the current crisis will last, but what we can say for sure is that Americans are growing tired of the uncertainty and anxiety that come with burdensome personal and public debt. This may be one reason that thrift is creeping back into public consciousness and conversation. In recent months, it has become a hot topic on web sites and blogs and in books—including recent books by this volume's coeditor David Blankenhorn (*Thrift: A Cyclopedia*) and contributor Ronald Wilcox (*Whatever Happened to Thrift?*). New policy ideas to promote thrift, like those in the concluding two chapters of this volume, are being generated by credit union leaders, legislators, think tanks, and nonprofit organizations.

This, then, is a moment of potential receptivity to fresh ideas and leadership. Today's civic and philanthropic leaders have an opportunity to put forth a new case for thrift and to inspire others in civil society and government to join them. In this respect, the past can provide a useful guide to the future. As earlier generations succeeded in renewing and reinvigorating thrift for their times, there is reason to believe that we can succeed for our times as well.

Notes

INTRODUCTION

1. See, for example, David Blankenhorn, *Thrift: A Cyclopedia* (West Conshohocken, PA: Templeton Foundation Press, 2008).

CHAPTER 1: FRANKLIN'S WAY TO WEALTH

1. *Poor Richard: The Almanacks for the Years 1733–1758* (New York and London: Paddington Press, 1976). In this and subsequent references to Poor Richard's sayings, I have followed the convention of indicating the year of the *Almanack* issue in parentheses in text.

2. Warning his wife against overindulging his improvident nephew, Benjamin Mecom, and his large family, he wrote, "I hope they do not hang on you; for really as we grow old and must grow helpless, we shall find nothing to spare." *The Letters of Benjamin Franklin & Jane Mecom*, edited with introduction by Carl Van Doren (Princeton, NJ: Princeton University Press, 1950), 11.

3. Carl Van Doren, *Benjamin Franklin* (New York: Penguin Books, 1991), viii.

4. Gordon S. Wood, *Revolutionary Characters: What Made the Founders Different* (New York: Penguin Press, 2006), 74.

5. Franklin rarely used the word *thrift*. More often, he wrote of "industry and frugality," a commonplace phrase in the eighteenth century. Other founders—including John Adams, George Washington, Benjamin Rush, and

the famously unfrugal Thomas Jefferson—frequently called for "industry and frugality," But none of the founders did as much as Franklin, the oldest among them, to promote "industry and frugality" as a way to wealth for the vast population of Americans who were not born to it.

6. Wood, *Revolutionary Characters*, 76.

7. Claude-Anne Lopez and Eugenia W. Herbert, *The Private Franklin: The Man and His Family* (New York: W.W. Norton & Company, Inc., 1975), 32.

8. Stacy Schiff, *A Great Improvisation: Franklin, France, and the Birth of America* (New York: Henry Holt and Company, 2005), 85.

9. He pledged his own money to secure hundreds of horses and drivers for the western campaign in the French and Indian War; he pledged every penny he had to compensate the East India Company for losses sustained in the Boston Tea Party if Parliament would repeal the tax; he loaned Congress several thousand pounds and promised more if the Revolution needed it. Michael Zuckerman, "Doing Good While Doing Well: Benevolence and Self-Interest in Franklin's Autobiography," in *Reappraising Benjamin Franklin: A Bicentennial Perspective,* ed. J.A. Leo Lemay (Newark, DE: University of Delaware Press, 1993), 446.

10. Cited in Claude-Anne Lopez, *Mon Cher Papa: Franklin and the Ladies of Paris* (New Haven: Yale University Press, 1990), 9.

11. Schiff, *A Great Improvisation*, 161. Schiff further notes, "There was no word for 'industry' in 18th century France. ('*Assiduite*' was the closest equivalent Franklin could locate . . .)."

12. Abiah Folger, Franklin's mother, married Josiah Franklin, a widower with five surviving children. Franklin was the eighth of ten children born to Abiah and Josiah.

13. T. H. Breen, *The Marketplace of Revolution: How Consumer Politics Shaped American Independence* (New York: Oxford University Press, 2005), 136–37.

14. Bruce H. Mann, *Republic of Debtors: Bankruptcy in the Age of American Independence* (Cambridge, MA: Harvard University Press, 2002), 104.

15. Benjamin Franklin, *Benjamin Franklin's Autobiography and Selections from His Other Writings* (New York: Random House, 1950), 232.

16. Ibid., 223–24.

17. Ibid., 75.

18. Breen, *Marketplace of Revolution*, 137.

19. Franklin, *Autobiography and Selections*, 233.

20. Lopez and Herbert, *The Private Franklin*, 32.

21. Interestingly, Franklin's notion of the wifely virtue of thrift undercut the importance of a dowry. As he saw it, a prospective wife who had the habit of living simply and saving could contribute more wealth to a household than a prospective wife who simply brought family money into a marriage. This view was consistent with his belief that money earned through work and savings was more productive than money gained through inheritance.

22. Lopez and Herbert, *The Private Franklin*, 140–41.

23. Henry Fielding and Arthur Murphy, *The Works of Henry Fielding: With an Essay on His Life and Genius,* vol. 10 (London: J. Johnson, 1806), 357.

24. Franklin did not completely embrace good works as a means to salvation. In the same letter, he clarified his position: "You will see in this my Notion of Good Works, that I am far from expecting (as you suppose) that I shall merit Heaven by them. By Heaven we understand, a State of Happiness, infinite in Degree, and eternal in Duration: I can do nothing to deserve such Reward."

25. Van Doren, *Benjamin Franklin,* 428–29.

26. Nian-Sheng Huang, *Benjamin Franklin in American Thought and Culture, 1790–1990* (Darby, PA: Diane Publishing, 1994), 47.

27. Franklin, *Autobiography and Selections*, 108.

28. Lopez and Herbert, *The Private Franklin*, 86.

29. *Poor Richard,* 281–82.

30. Ibid., 283.

31. Schiff, *A Great Improvisation,* 363.

32. John Bigelow, ed., *The Works of Benjamin Franklin*, vol. 9 (New York and London: G.P. Putnam's Sons, 1904), 432–44. Published under Franklin's own name in England, this essay appeared anonymously in France and Germany so as not to damage the affectionate reputation he enjoyed among Europeans.

33. Ibid., 433.

34. Ibid., 433–35.

35. Lopez and Herbert, *The Private Franklin*, 35.

36. Bigelow, ed., *Works*, 438.

37. Franklin left his papers, including his *Autobiography*, to his grandson, William Temple Franklin, who was to have prepared them for publication. However, Temple did not hurry to the task, and the first part of the *Autobiography* appeared in French translation in 1791 and in two English translations of the French in 1793. One of the English translations appeared

serially in a Philadelphia publication in May 1790, and this piece was reprinted fourteen times between 1794 and 1800.

38. Bruce Sinclair, *Philadelphia's Philosopher Mechanic: A History of the Franklin Institute, 1824–1865* (Baltimore: Johns Hopkins Press, 1974), 9.

39. Huang, *Franklin in American Thought*, 47.

40. Ibid., 81–82.

41. Ibid., 83.

42. Gordon S. Wood, *The Americanization of Benjamin Franklin* (New York: Penguin Press, 2004), 236.

CHAPTER 2: U.S. MUTUAL SAVINGS BANKS AND THE "SAVINGS BANK IDEA"

1. William E. Knox, *The Ethics of the Savings Bank: Being an Address Delivered Before the Savings Bank Section American Bankers Association, at Its Annual Convention, Held in New Orleans, La., November 23, 1911* (New York: The Savings Bank Section, American Bankers Association, 1911), 3. For this essay, I rely mostly on bank documents (including charters, bylaws, advertisements, and commissioned bank histories) as well as papers, addresses, and histories published by self-declared "savings bank men." This is not a comprehensive essay on the history of thrift as exhibited by U.S. savings banks or their depositors but a compilation of and commentary on the ideologies as espoused by the banks. My sources include E. St. Elmo Lewis, "The Savings Idea and the People: An Address Delivered Before the Savings Bank Section of the American Bankers Association at Its Annual Convention in New Orleans, La., November 23, 1911," in *Thrift: How to Teach It, How to Encourage It: A Compilation of Leading Addresses on Thrift; Suggestive Outlines For Thrift Talks; Directions For Conducting A Thrift Campaign, and Statistical Information Relative to the Saving of Money. Issued by Savings Bank Section and American Institute of Banking Section, As Part of the Centennial Thrift Campaign of the American Bankers Association* (New York: Wynkoop Hallenbeck Crawford Co., 1916), 17.

2. Quote from a pamphlet by Duncan. Franklin J. Sherman, *Modern Story of Mutual Savings Banks: A Narrative of Their Growth and Development from the Inception to the Present Day* (New York: J.J. Little and Ives Company, 1934), 28.

3. Frank P. Bennett Jr., *The Story of Mutual Savings Banks* (Boston: F. P. Bennett & Co., Inc., 1926), 16. See also William H. Kniffen, *The Savings Bank and Its Practical Work: A Practical Treatise on Savings Banking, Covering*

the History, Management and Methods of Operation of Mutual Savings
Banks, and Adapted to Savings Departments in Banks of Discount and Trust
Companies (New York: The Bankers Publishing Company, 1928); Gertrude
E. Noyes, *The Savings Bank of New London at 150, 1827–1977: Published in
Commemoration of the One Hundred and Fiftieth Anniversary of the Savings
Bank of New London* (New London, CT.: The Bank, 1977). Alternate dates
for the first savings bank include a bank opened by Elizabeth Wakefield in
Tottenham in 1803 or 1804, Swiss banks at Geneva and Basel in 1792 or
earlier, a 1765 Hamburg institution, and a 1697 invention by Daniel Defoe.
See Bennett, *The Story of Mutual Savings Banks* and Frederic C. Nichols,
*The Operation of the Mutual Savings Bank System in the United States, and
the Treatment of Savings Deposits* (Philadelphia: The American Academy of
Political and Social Science, 1910).

4. Bennett, *The Story*, 15.

5. This chapter examines only banks within the United States, though
the invention of savings banks is hardly American. The values demonstrated
by United States thrift institutions throughout the period studied were ideas
exported from thrift institutions abroad. As such, the observations in this
essay yield insight into thrift ideologies of other parts of the Western world.
Yet, some of the identified tensions and paradoxes are characteristically
"American"—in part because they are tied to American social institutions
and social dynamics and in part because they identified themselves with
the spirit of Americanism. As a result, they developed with a distinctly
nationalistic identity and reflect American values about money, capitalism,
thrift, and fiscal morality.

6. Kniffen, *The Savings Bank*, 14. The Philadelphia Saving Fund Society
was actually the first savings bank to open in the U.S., on December 2,
1816, but it was not incorporated under Pennsylvania law until 1819.
*Mutual Savings Banks, Cornerstones of American Life: A Handbook of
Information* (New York: National Association of Mutual Savings Banks,
1943).

7. S. W. Straus, *History of the Thrift Movement in America* (Philadelphia:
J. B. Lippincott Company, 1920), 31.

8. Kniffen, *The Savings Bank*, 20.

9. Federal Deposit Insurance Corporation, *History of the Eighties—Lessons
for the Future, vol.1: An Examination of the Banking Crises of the 1980s and
Early 1990s* (Washington D.C.: FDIC, 1997), 212, available at www.fdic.
gov/bank/historical/history.

10. Bennett, *The Story*, 83–84.

11. See Knox, *The Ethics*.

12. Kniffen, *The Savings Bank*, 20–22.

13. Bennett, *The Story*, 13.

14. Knox, *The Ethics*, 7.

15. Henry Duncan, *An Essay on the Nature and Advantages of Parish Banks, for the Savings of the Industrious: Second Edition, Greatly Altered, And Enlarged by an Account of the Rise and Progress of the Scheme, And Remarks on the Propriety of Uniting These Institutions with Friendly Societies; together with an Appendix, containing a Copy of the Rules of the Dumfries Parish Bank, an Account of Such Banks as Differ from That of Dumfries, and Some Cursory Observations on Friendly Societies, &c.* (Edinburgh: Oliphant, Waugh, & Innes, 1816), 1.

16. Kniffen, *The Savings Bank*, 27.

17. Ibid.

18. Knox, *The Ethics*, 6.

19. N. J. Howard Savings Institution, *Gateway of Progress, 1857–1957*, ed. Muir and Company (Newark, NJ: Howard Savings Institution, 1957), 25. John P. Townsend, "Savings Banks in the United States," a paper read before the American Social Science Association at Saratoga Springs, September 7, 1888: prepared for the Universal Scientific Congress of Provident Institutions at Paris, July 4, 1889 (New York: 1888), 14.

20. *Fiftieth Anniversary* (New York: East River Savings Institution, 1898), 19, 24–26.

21. Knox, *The Ethics*, 3.

22. Henry Lee, *A Massachusetts Savings Bank: Being an Account of the Provident Institution for Savings: Together with a Discussion of Some Problems of Savings-Bank Management and Legislation* (Boston: Committee on Charities and Correction to Massachusetts Board of Managers, World's Fair, 1893), 3.

23. Nichols, *The Operation*, 168.

24. See Kniffen, *The Savings Bank*, and Lewis, "The Savings Idea and the People."

25. Alvin J. Schmidt, *Fraternal Organizations, The Greenwood Encyclopedia of American Institutions*, vol. 3 (Westport, CT: Greenwood Press, 1980), 3. Fraternal organizations are no longer a widely regarded part of the conscious American identity but served important social functions for a long period of U.S. history. Fraternal secret orders (e.g., the Masons, the Elks, Knights of Pythias) provided ritual content and moral teaching to members, while fraternal benefit societies (e.g., Catholic Knights of America)

were established primarily to provide members with life insurance. Schmidt credits these organizations with teaching Americans democratic processes and providing economic security and a sense of belonging and identity. See Schmidt's introductory chapter, "The Fraternal Context," for an exposition on the role and influence of American fraternal organizations. See also Alexis de Tocqueville, *Democracy in America*, trans. Arthur Goldhammer, chronology by Olivier Zunz, notes by Zunz and Goldhammer (New York: Literary Classics of the United States, Inc., 2004).

26. Knox, *The Ethics*, 6. In the case of savings banks, advocates throughout the nineteenth and early twentieth centuries often referred to the institutions as "sister" organizations. I would argue that the relationship between these organizations (as with the sense of cooperation or mutuality that existed in other societal organizations throughout the century) was fraternal in nature—as masculine voices dominated the public square, so societal ideologies were dominated by the masculine. Throughout the period, the term *fraternal* is used in exclusion to *sororal* to refer to a sense of camaraderie or mutual aid, even in cases where the term is applied to a social group or movement made up of women (as in the case of female fraternal organizations, who, "without exception . . . consistently appl[ied] the term 'fraternal' to themselves, and with pride." [Schmidt, 3]). Here I will use the term *fraternal* to refer to this sense of mutuality because I believe it accurately reflects the spirit of a male-dominated era in which women were excluded from a number of social roles and environments.

27. Kniffen, *The Savings Bank*, 73.

28. J. Frome Wilkinson, *Mutual Thrift* (London: Menthuen, 1891), 2.

29. Bennett, *The Story*, 12.

30. Noyes, *The Savings Bank of New London*, 13.

31. Robert N. Bellah et al., *Habits of the Heart: Individualism and Commitment in America* (Berkeley and Los Angeles: University of California Press, 1996), 147.

32. Samuel Smiles, *Thrift; or How to Get On in the World* (New York: John B. Alden, 1884), 7. Smiles's version of the well-known fable actually speaks of bees, rather than ants.

33. Quoted by Knox, *The Ethics*, 2.

34. Ibid.

35. J. H. Thiry, *The History, Rules and Regulations of the Penny School Savings Bank of the Public Schools of Long Island City, N.Y.* (Long Island City: Press of Daily and Weekly Star, 1886), 29.

36. Kniffen, *The Savings Bank*, 29. Quote from John Ruskin, *A Joy Forever*, lecture 1, p. 7.

37. Kniffen, *The Savings Bank*, 35.

38. Ibid., 31.

39. Quoted by Sara Louise Oberholtzer, *School Savings Banks, United States Bureau of Education Bulletin 1914 No. 46, whole number 620* (Washington: Government Printing Office, 1915), 10.

40. Kniffen, *The Savings Bank*, 39.

41. Ibid., 32.

42. Edward L. Robinson, *1816–1916, One Hundred Years of Savings Banking, Including Comprehensive Bibliography on Thrift Co-operation and Good Management as it Relates to Thrift* (Savings Bank Section, American Bankers Association, 1917), 8.

43. Ibid.

44. James Henry Hamilton, *Savings and Savings Institutions* (New York and London: Macmillan Company, 1902), 21.

45. Tocqueville, *Democracy in America*, 72, 612, 618. Bellah, *Habits*, viii.

46. Tocqueville, *Democracy in America*, 618.

47. I use the term *myth* only to describe the American Dream as an orienting narrative that helps people locate themselves within society.

48. *How to Buy a House: A Story that Will Interest You* (New York: Excelsior Savings Bank, 1877), 8–9.

49. Ibid., 11.

50. Kniffen, *The Savings Bank*, 25.

51. By 1943, mutual savings banks were still in operation in only seventeen (of the then forty-eight) states. *Mutual Savings Banks, Cornerstones of American Life*, 1.

52. *History of the Eighties—Lessons for the Future*, 1:212.

53. I do not, in this essay, give attention to the savings (building) and loan association (S&L), though the institution has an important role in the history of American thrift. Concurrent with the massive popularity of mutual savings banks (MSB) was the rise of what would become the modern savings and loan industry. Like MSBs, savings and loan associations were owned by depositors, though they were initially not technically banks. Rather, they were corporations organized by individuals who would pool their resources to make purchasing property a reality. Like those that established MSBs, the founders of these associations believed that self-help was the key to upward mobility and personal security. These individuals saw the pooling of resources as a means for achieving the American dream of

a better life. Though there are certainly similarities between mutual saving banks and savings and loan associations, I do not explore the ideology of the S&L here for two reasons: the first is simply limitations of space and resources. The savings and loan industry has a long and complicated history—this short chapter could not do justice to an exploration of the ideologies of both mutual savings banks and the savings and loan industry. Second, MSBs and S&Ls were started with very different social functions in mind. Savings and loan associations arose from within the lower and middle classes in response to the need for capital to purchase their own homes. Unlike the mutual savings banks, these institutions were not organized with the same overarching philanthropic and social goals in mind but with the intention of meeting very practical needs. As a result, they are not accompanied by an ideology as cohesive as the "savings bank idea." This becomes less true as the twentieth century approached. At that point, S&Ls began to offer the functions of the mutual savings bank. As the distinction between the two institutions became less apparent (the mutual savings bank had also begun to offer home loans), the ideology of the two institutions became increasingly similar. A comprehensive study of the relationship between the ideologies of the mutual savings bank and the savings and loan association would certainly enrich our understanding of the context within which Americans digested information about savings and thrift. See Paul Zane Pilzer, *Other People's Money: The Inside Story of the S&L Mess* (New York: Simon and Schuster, 1989); Kurt F. Flexner, *The Role of Savings and Loan Associations in the Banking Community of the State of New York* (n.p: The Savings Association League of New York State, n.d.); Knox, *The Ethics;* Kniffen, *The Savings Bank.*

54. Kniffen, *The Savings Bank*, 25.

55. Bennett, *The Story*, 73.

56. Townsend, "Savings Banks in the United States," 10.

57. Bennett, *The Story*, 73.

58. Thiry, *The History*, 5.

59. *History of the Eighties—Lessons for the Future*, 1:213.

60. Yehoshua Arieli, *Individualism and Nationalism in American Ideology* (Cambridge, MA: Harvard University Press, 1964), 2.

61. Ibid., 2.

62. Kniffen, *The Savings Bank*, 37.

63. When compared with their European counterparts, Americans were very often acknowledged to be relatively unthrifty. See Straus, *History of the Thrift Movement in America*, and Lewis, "The Savings Idea and the People."

64. Knox, *The Ethics*, 4.

65. Ibid.

66. Ibid.

67. Nichols, *The Operation*, 175.

68. Kniffen, *The Savings Bank*, 35.

69. Hamilton, *Savings and Savings Institutions*, 36.

70. Oberholtzer, *School Savings Banks*, 7.

71. Thiry, The History, 14.

72. Ibid., 10.

73. Oberholtzer, *School Savings Banks*, 7.

74. Tocqueville, *Democracy in America*, 610–11.

75. Thiry, *The History*, 5.

76. Townsend, "Savings Banks in the United States," 11. Quotation within text from the New Testament—Acts 17:5, King James Version.

77. Walter Russell Mead, *Power, Terror, Peace, and War: America's Grand Strategy in a World at Risk* (New York: Knopf, 2004), 49–50.

78. I use the word *temperance* here to stress the importance of restraint, moderation, and discipline to the savings bank idea, rather than to equate the movement with the concurrent Temperance Movement, the early twentieth-century campaign to restrict alcohol consumption. Because the movements proclaim the same virtues, many advocates affirm the importance of both. See W. Espey Albig, *A History of School Savings Banking in the United States and Its European Beginnings* (New York: Savings Bank Division, American Bankers Association, 1928), 24; and Sara Louisa Oberholtzer, *The Relation of Thrift Teaching to Prohibition* (Evanston, IL.: National Women's Christian Temperance Union, 1915).

79. Lewis, "The Savings Idea and the People," 24.

80. Quoted in Kniffen, *The Savings Bank*, 22. Emphasis in Kniffen's text.

81. E. St. Elmo Lewis, *Financial Advertising, for Commercial and Savings Banks, Trust, Title Insurance, and Safe Deposit Companies, Investment Houses* (Indianapolis: Levey Bros. & Compant, 1908), 52. I should here note the cynicism with which Lewis approaches the decision of bankers to employ traditional advertising tactics: "It was not until advertisers became bankers, as directors and officers, that bank advertising became a real thing. That the departure was due to a desire to serve any high ethical ideals, I may not be charged with being unduly cynical when I say, there can be little doubt but what ethics had nothing to do with it" (52). The trend toward the use of traditional "commercial" forms of advertising was not without opposition— the directors of a number of "passive" banks considered it unethical to

advertise the services of the bank (Kniffen, *The Savings Bank*, 40). These voices, however, became quieter as competition for savings deposits continued to increase. "Former Vice President, Campbell-Ewald Company," Advertising Hall of Fame. http://www.advertisinghalloffame.org/members/member_bio.php?memid=692 (Retrieved 8/15/2006).

82. Quoted by Mary B. Reeves, *Beyond the Counter* (New York: M.B. Reeves, 1927), 73.

83. Lewis, "The Savings Idea and the People," 24.

84. Ibid., 18.

85. Ibid., 24.

86. Reeves, *Beyond the Counter*, 10.

87. George E. Allen, "Sociology of Savings (Delivered at the Savings Bank Section Meeting, St. Louis Convention, American Bankers Association, 1906)." *Thrift: How to Teach It, How to Encourage It*, 26.

88. Lewis, "The Savings Idea and the People," 24.

89. Ibid.

90. Reeves, *Beyond the Counter*, 11, 33–36, 50.

91. Ibid., 48–49.

92. Ibid., 12.

93. Ibid., 50.

94. Ibid.

95. Lewis, "The Savings Idea and the People," 19–20, 23.

96. Reeves, *Beyond the Counter*, 25–26.

97. Advertising was not a new science, but the twentieth century brought changes in the way that content was communicated. The advertising industry, rather than the businesses and organizations that utilized advertising services, came to have a greater role in determining the mode of the message communicated.

98. Though I speak of the "rise of the middle class," I do not mean to suggest that the middle class did not exist in the U.S. prior to the mid-twentieth century. I recognize the ambiguity of the term—in the words of historian Sven Beckert, "There are few terms in American English that have been as often misused, poorly defined, and politically operationalized as the term 'middle class.' To historians, political scientists, and sociologists, as well as those without academic credentials, the term has denoted so many different aggregations of Americans past and present that it has essentially lost any distinct meaning it may have had." Yet, I employ the term because, at this point in American history, it took on new meaning in the conscious identity of Americans. By the year 1940, the vast majority of Americans

identified themselves as middle class. Sven Beckert, "Propertied of a Different Kind: Bourgeoisie and Lower Middle Class in the Nineteenth-Century United States," *The Middling Sorts: Explorations in the History of the American Middle Class*, ed. Burton J. Bledstein and Robert D. Johnston (New York: Routledge, 2001), 285. Jeffrey M. Hornstein "The Rise of the Realtor®: Professionalism, Gender, and Middle-Class Identity," *The Middling Sorts*, 218.

99. From *The Hackettstown Gazette*, Hackettstown, N.J., for the Old First National Bank of Washington, N.J. Quoted by Lewis, "The Savings Idea and the People," 22.

100. *Mutual Savings Banks, Cornerstones of American Life*, 1–2.

101. In his 1975 history of the Bowery Savings Bank, Oscar Schisgall provides a segment from a *New York Times* editorial printed near the opening of the bank: "This is the Poor Man's Bank. . . . Let the friends of the poor, who cry out against the monopolies of the rich, give the poor their iron chest, where they too may get interest on their money no matter how small the sum may be." Oscar Schisgall, *Out of One Small Chest: A Social and Financial History of the Bowery Savings Bank* (New York: Amacom, 1975), 11.

102. *Mutual Savings Banks, Cornerstones of American Life*, 2.

103. *It Began With a Little Leather Chest* (New York: The Bowery Savings Bank, 1929), 5.

104. Ibid., 9.

105. Edgerton Grant North, *The First Hundred Years, 1851–1951; an Account of the Founding and Growth of the Williamsburgh Savings Bank, Together with a Brief History of the Communities Served by This Bank through Its First Hundred Years* (Brooklyn: Williamsburgh Savings Bank, 1951), 66.

106. Federal Deposit Insurance Corporation, *Federal Deposit Insurance Corporation: The First Fifty Years, A History of the FDIC 1933–1983* (Washington DC: FDIC, 1984), iii.

107. In fact, MSBs during this period were so stable and so unaccustomed to bank runs that less than 12 percent of the nation's mutual savings institutions had joined the FDIC by 1935. It was not until forty years later that almost all of the U.S. mutuals had deposit insurance. *History of the Eighties—Lessons for the Future*, 1:213.

108. Ibid., 1:211.

109. *Federal Deposit Insurance Corporation: The First Fifty Years*, iii.

110. Disintermediation: "the withdrawal of funds from interest-bearing accounts or thrifts when rates on competing investments, such as Treasury

bills or money market finds, offer the investor a higher return." *History of the Eighties—Lessons for the Future*, 1:214.

111. Quotes from Saul B. Klaman, ibid., 1:218.

112. Ibid., 1:233.

113. It has been the intention of this chapter to set forth an exploration of the ideologies of U.S. savings banks during a period of time when the virtue of thrift was widely recognized by the American public—a thorough exploration of the twentieth-century factors that contributed to the demise of the culture of thrift, though an important next step, is beyond the scope of this project. I will here make a few preliminary connections between ideologies that I believe to play the most significant roles in eclipsing the position of thrift in the national consciousness—namely, consumerism and individualism. These ideas play a considerable role in structuring American identity, and attention given to them here is generalized; it must be considered to be in every way preliminary.

114. *History of the Eighties—Lessons for the Future*, 1:233.

115. Also for this reason, I take seriously the task of identifying the inherent biases of the savings bank idea. These are parts of the legacy of thrift that cannot be neglected if we are truly curious about the potential for "thrift" to have resonance today. We must demand a "thick description" of the cultural ideologies and values attached to the history of the savings bank idea. If we desire a thorough cultural ecology, it is necessary to identify these connections because they may help explain the ways that different communities have related to the thrift mentality, the institution of the savings bank, and the savings bank idea. How has the saving bank idea excluded some?

CHAPTER 3: THRIFT FOR A NEW CENTURY

1. Sara Louise Oberholtzer, *Thrift Tidings* 7, no. 2 (April 1913): 3.

2. T. D. MacGregor, *The Book of Thrift: Why and How to Save and What to Do with Your Savings, A Book of Inspiration and Practical Help* (New York: Funk and Wagnalls, 1915), 34.

3. Franklin J. Sherman, *Modern Story of Mutual Savings Banks: A Narrative of Their Growth and Development from the Inception to the Present Day* (New York: J. J. Little & Ives, Co., 1934), 93.

4. Ibid., 107.

5. Mary Wilcox Brown, *The Development of Thrift* (New York: Macmillan Company, 1899), 35.

6. Ibid., 141.

7. Sherman, *Modern Story*, 89.

8. Edmund Dane, *The Value of Thrift: The Golden Thread of the World's Life and Activity, Talks for Young People on the Saving of Talent, Effort, Time and Money* (New York: G.P. Putnam's Sons, 1927), 106.

9. W. H. Carothers, "Thrift in the School Curriculum," in Roy G. Blakely, ed., *The New American Thrift*, vol. 28, *Annals of the American Academy of Political and Social Science* (Philadelphia, 1920), 224.

10. Adolph Lewisohn, Adolph Lewisohn to C. Bascom Slemp, January 13, 1925, letter from Library of Congress, Prosperity and Thrift: The Coolidge Era and the Consumer Economy, 1921–1929, < http://memory. loc.gov:8081/cgi-bin/query/r?ammem/coolbib:@field(NUMBER+@band(amrlm+mc18))> (June 30, 2008).

11. Bolton Hall, *The New Thrift* (New York: B. W. Huebsch, 1916), 154.

12. Ibid.

13. MacGregor, *The Book of Thrift*, 7.

14. Brown, *The Development of Thrift*, 129.

15. Alvin Johnson, "The Promotion of Thrift in America," in Blakely, ed., *The New American Thrift*, 237.

16. S. W. Straus, *History of the Thrift Movement in America* (Philadelphia: J. B. Lippincott Company, 1920), 97.

17. Dane, *The Value of Thrift*, 3.

18. Straus, *History of the Thrift Movement*, 20.

19. Ibid., 215.

20. T. N. Carver, "The Relation of Thrift to Nation Building," in Blakely, ed., *The New American Thrift*, 785.

21. Straus, *History of the Thrift Movement*, 59–60.

22. S. W. Straus, "Promotion and Practice of Thrift in Foreign Countries," in Blakely, ed., *The New American Thrift*, 191.

23. Dora Morrell Hughes, *Thrift in the Household* (Boston: Lothrop, Lee, and Shepard, Co., 1918), 13.

24. Straus, *History of the Thrift Movement*, 146.

25. Dane, *The Value of Thrift*, 89.

26. NEA, *Thrift Education: Being the Report of the National Conference on Thrift Education, Held in Washington, D.C., June 27 and 28, 1924, Under the Auspices of the Committee on Thrift Education of the National Education Association and the National Council of Education* (Washington, DC: National Education Association, 1924), 39. This theme was hit on by

several speakers at this conference alone. See, for example, Olive Jones on page 51 and H. R. Daniel, the secretary of the American Society for Thrift, who quoted the United States League of Saving and Loan Associations: "Children, while being taught to save, must also be taught the relationship between the mere function of saving *versus* true, progressive thrift" (45).

27. Hall, *The New Thrift*, 11.

28. NEA, *Thrift Education*, 38.

29. Hall, *The New Thrift*, 11.

30. Anna Steese Richardson, *Adventures in Thrift* (Indianapolis: The Bobbs-Merrill Company, 1915), 6. *Adventures in Thrift* was originally serialized in *Woman's Home Companion*.

31. Straus, *History of the Thrift Movement*, 52.

32. Dane, *The Value of Thrift*, 81.

33. Calvin Coolidge, *Notes from Calvin Coolidge*, from Library of Congress, Prosperity and Thrift: The Coolidge Era and the Consumer Economy, 1921–1929, <http://memory.loc.gov:8081/cgi-bin/query/r?ammem/coolbib:@field(NUMBER+@band(amrlm+mc18))> (June 30, 2008).

34. Carothers, "Thrift in the School Curriculum," 223.

35. See, for example, MacGregor, *The Book of Thrift*, 71–93.

36. See also ibid., 99: "Saving a dollar a week is to the common laborer a task requiring perseverance. But it is the ladder on which he climbs out of the laboring class."

37. Straus, *History of the Thrift Movement*, 43; MacGregor, *The Book of Thrift*, 22.

38. Milton Harrison, "The Development of Thrift Facilities," in Blakely, ed., *The New American Thrift*, 168.

39. William Mather Lewis, "Freedom through Thrift," in Blakely, ed., *The New American Thrift*, 9.

40. George F. Zook, "Thrift in the United States," in Blakely, ed., *The New American Thrift*, 206.

41. S. S. Huebner, "Life Insurance in Its Relation to Thrift," in Blakely, ed., *The New American Thrift*, 186.

42. Ibid., 187.

43. Hall, *The New Thrift*, 64.

44. Carver, "The Relation of Thrift to Nation Building," 785.

45. Hughes, *Thrift in the Household*, 11.

46. Edward L. Thorndike, "Psychological Notes on the Motives for Thrift," in Blakely, ed., *The New American Thrift*, 212, 216.

47. *Girl Scout Leader* 3, no. 12 (Dec. 1926): 1; NEA, *Thrift Education*, 52.

48. William Schooling, "National Saving in the United Kingdom," in Blakely, ed., *The New American Thrift*, 204.

49. NEA, *Thrift Education*, 38.

50. Harrison, "The Development of Thrift Facilities," 171.

51. Dane, *The Value of Thrift*, 93.

52. Benjamin R. Andrews, "Thrift as a Family and Individual Problem," in Blakely, ed., *The New American Thrift*, 13.

53. Hughes, *Thrift in the Household*, 12.

54. Hall, *The New Thrift*, 51. See also Straus, "Promotion and Practice of Thrift in Foreign Countries," 194.

55. Carver, "The Relation of Thrift to Nation Building," 785.

56. As quoted in Straus, *History of the Thrift Movement*, 102.

57. MacGregor, *The Book of Thrift*, 9.

58. Hartley Withers, "The Consumer's Responsibility," in Blakely, ed., *The New American Thrift*, 226. For a more business-centered version of this argument, see George W. Dowrie, "Thrift and Business," in *The New American Thrift*, 54: "The thriftless spender . . . injures business in two ways: first, by his failure to act in providing adequate working capital for business activity, and second, by his unwise demands being responsible for the diversion of business activity into lines which will not result in the achievement of a maximum of social satisfaction."

59. NEA, *Thrift Education*, 64.

60. MacGregor, *The Book of Thrift*, 161.

61. Hughes, *Thrift in the Household*, 11.

62. H. L. Baldensperger, "The Garbage Pail, a National Thrift Barometer," Blakely, ed., *The New American Thrift*, 135.

63. Carothers, "Thrift in the School Curriculum," 222.

64. Mrs. Arthur G. Learned, as quoted by MacGregor, *The Book of Thrift*, 164.

65. Thorndike, "Psychological Notes," 217–18.

66. Sara Oberholtzer, *The Relation of Thrift Teaching to Prohibition* (Evanston, IL: National Women's Christian Temperance Union: 1915), 1.

67. Straus, *History of the Thrift Movement*, 136.

68. MacGregor, *The Book of Thrift*, 47.

69. Dane, *The Value of Thrift*, 20.

70. Hall, *The New Thrift*, 14–15.

71. Johnson, "The Promotion of Thrift in America," 233.

72. Hall, *The New Thrift*, 61.

73. Straus, *History of the Thrift Movement*, 190.

74. Ibid., 186.

75. Warren G. Harding, *Speech from Warren G. Harding*, From Library of Congress, Prosperity and Thrift: The Coolidge Era and the Consumer Economy, 1921–1929, < http://memory.loc.gov:8081/cgi-bin/query/r?ammem/coolbib:@field(NUMBER+@band(amrlm+mc18))> (June 30, 2008).

76. MacGregor, *The Book of Thrift*, 36.

77. Straus, *History of the Thrift Movement*, 214.

78. NEA, *Thrift Education*, 9.

79. *Savings Bank Journal* 2, no. 3 (May 1921): 16.

80. Johnson, "The Promotion of Thrift in America," 237.

81. Flynn, "The Insurance of Thrift," in Blakely, ed., *The New American Thrift*, 26.

82. NEA, *Thrift Education*, 16.

83. Baldensperger, "The Garbage Pail," 135. And yet, the thrift movement in the United States never took on the cooperative character that was present in many European nations, to many thrift advocates' disappointment.

84. Alvin Johnson, "Influences Affecting the Development of Thrift," *Political Science Quarterly* 22, no. 1 (June 1907): 237.

85. Ibid., 241.

86. Ibid., 243.

87. Ibid., 244.

88. NEA, *Thrift Education*, 35.

89. L. P. Behens quoted in MacGregor, *The Book of Thrift*, 313. This sentiment was also expressed by a teacher at the NEA's 1924 national meeting on thrift education; in describing her students, she explained, "They don't need any great urging to get money. What they need is rather understanding in the wise use of money." NEA, *Thrift Education*, 51.

90. Straus, "Promotion and Practice of Thrift in Foreign Countries," 195.

91. Zook, "Thrift in the United States," 205–6. See also Lewis, "Freedom through Thrift," 9.

92. NEA, *Thrift Education*, 36.

93. Straus, *History of the Thrift Movement*, 49.

94. There were, of course, a few exceptions, such as Frank McVey, the president of the University of Kentucky, who struck an unusually pessimistic note: "The world is poorer, much poorer than it was in 1880. The generation now coming on faces a less pleasing prospect than the one that is passing. What is more disturbing is the lack of habits in the new generation for hard work and thrift." Frank L. McVey, "The Nation's Call for Thrift," in Blakely, ed., *The New American Thrift*, 31.

95. J. H. Thiry, *School Savings Banks in the United States: A Manual for the Use of Teachers* (New York: The American Banker, 1890), 10.

96. Roy G. Blakely, "Foreword," in Blakely, ed., *The New American Thrift*, 1.

97. Sherman, *Modern Story*, 142.

98. MacGregor, *The Book of Thrift*, ix.

99. "Economic Mobilization of the United States," *Historical Outlook* 10, no. 1 (January 1919): 40.

100. Woodrow Wilson, "Do Your Bit for America," April 15, 1917, <http://www.firstworldwar.com/source/doyourbit.htm> (June 30, 2008).

101. "Economic Mobilization," 38.

102. Ibid., 41.

103. Straus, *History of the Thrift Movement*, 71. Straus had encouraged greater local and household production of foodstuff well before the outbreak of World War I; in particular, he encouraged schools to have their students plant and tend gardens in nearby empty lots.

104. "Economic Mobilization," 41.

105. Ibid., 43.

106. Zook, "Thrift in the United States," 209.

107. Joseph E. Cummings, "United States Government Bonds as Investments," in Blakely, ed., *The New American Thrift*, 159.

108. Straus, *History of the Thrift Movement*, 175–76.

109. Ibid., 171.

110. Frank E. Wolfe, "Organized Labor's Attitude toward the National Thrift Movement," in Blakely, ed., *The New American Thrift*, 50–51.

111. NEA, *Thrift Education*, 3.

112. Zook, "Thrift in the United States," 211.

113. NEA, *Thrift Education*, 3.

114. W. Espey Albig, *A History of School Savings Banking: In the United States and Its European Beginnings* (New York: American Banking Association, Savings Banks Division, 1928), 14, 18–19. Actually, while

Thiry's school savings bank was the first to show staying power, it was the second to be started in the United States. The first was founded in 1881 by another immigrant, Sereno Taylor Merrill, superintendent of Beloit, Wisconsin. However, his successor was uninterested in the program and discontinued it a mere five years later.

115. Ibid., 21.
116. Thiry, *School Savings Banks*, 5.
117. Albig, *A History*, 22.
118. Ibid., 22–23.
119. Oberholtzer, *The Relation of Thrift Teaching to Prohibition*, 1.
120. Albig, *A History*, 23–24.
121. Brown, *The Development of Thrift*, 57–58.
122. Sara Louise Oberholtzer, *How to Institute School Savings Banks* (privately printed, 1891), 2.
123. Sara Louise Oberholtzer, *Thrift Tidings* 26, no. 1 (Jan. 1923): 1; Sara Louise Oberholtzer, *Thrift Tidings* 26, no. 2 (April 1923): 1.
124. Albig, *A History*, 25.
125. Oberholtzer, *Thrift Tidings* 6, no. 1 (Jan. 1912): 4.
126. Albig, *A History*, 37.
127. NEA, *Thrift Education*, 47–48.
128. Straus, *History of the Thrift Movement*, 124–25, 166–67.
129. Albig, *A History*, 32.
130. Ibid.
131. Ibid., 28–31.
132. Sara Louise Oberholtzer, "School Savings Banks," *Annals of the American Academy of Political and Social Science* 3 (July 1892): 14–29.
133. American Bankers Association (ABA), *Title of Report*, tenth annual report, (1929), 3.
134. ABA, *Recession in Industry Affects School Savings Banking*, eleventh annual report, (1930), 3.
135. Albig, *A History*, 35.
136. ABA, tenth annual report, 3.
137. *National Thrift News* 9, no. 2 (Sept. 1927): 5.
138. For all the reshaping thrift advocates had attempted, note how consistent these principles are with the ones Mary Wilcox Brown wrote about in 1899: "Spend less than you earn; pay ready money; never anticipate uncertain profits; keep regular accounts." Brown, *The Development of Thrift*, 30.

139. C. Bascom Slemp, C. Bascom Slemp to M.S. Sherman, February 27, 1924, letter from Library of Congress, Prosperity and Thrift, <http://memory.loc.gov:8081/cgi-bin/query/r?ammem/coolbib:@field(NUMBER+@band(amrlm+mc18))> (June 30, 2008).

140. Lewisohn, letter to C. Bascom Slemp.

141. *National Thrift News* 9, no. 2 (Sept. 1927): 8.

142. Ibid. The months and their themes were as follows: October—"Have a Bank Account"; November—"Invest Safely"; December—"Share with Others"; January—"Carry Life Insurance"; February—"Keep a Budget"; March—"Pay Bills Promptly"; April—"Own Your Home"; the respective slogans were "Don't Spend It All"; "Before You Invest—Investigate"; "It Is More Blessed to Give than Receive"; "Live to Win"; "Spend Time and Money Wisely"; "Preserve Your Credit"; and "Build a Home First."

143. Edith McClure-Patterson, Edith McClure-Patterson to Everett Sanders, December 11, 1925, letter from Library of Congress, Prosperity and Thrift, <http://memory.loc.gov:8081/cgi-bin/query/r?ammem/coolbib:@field(NUMBER+@band(amrlm+mc18))> (June 30, 2008). Also, Herbert Lord, "director of the U.S. budget," argued that the creation of the federal budget in response to World War I had stimulated interest in budgeting throughout the nation. NEA, *Thrift Education*, 57.

144. NEA, *Thrift Education*, 11.

145. Richardson, *Adventures in Thrift*, 14.

146. Hughes, *Thrift in the Household*, 17.

147. Richardson, *Adventures in Thrift*, 42.

148. MacGregor, *The Book of Thrift*, 182.

149. Richardson, *Adventures in Thrift*, 44.

150. Ibid., 115–16.

151. Ibid., 136.

152. Gifford Pinchot, *The Fight for Conservation* (New York: Page and Co., 1910), 48.

153. Ibid., 106, 108.

154. Arthur H. Chamberlain and James F. Chamberlain, *Thrift and Conservation* (Philadelphia: J. B. Lippincott Company, 1919), 17.

155. Ibid., 18.

156. See, for example, MacGregor on coal smoke, *The Book of Thrift*, 118.

157. NEA, *Thrift Education*, 10.

158. Ibid., 24.

159. Ibid., 42.

160. Chamberlain and Chamberlain, *Thrift and Conservation*, 41.

161. Harrison, "The Development of Thrift Facilities," 168–69.

162. Sherman, *Modern Story*, 149.

163. MacGregor, *The Book of Thrift*, 130.

164. *Savings Bank Journal* 10, no. 5 (July 1929): 60.

165. *Savings Bank Journal* 2, no. 3 (May 1921): 15.

166. One savings bank president noted in 1929, "It is only within the past half dozen years that savings banks themselves have recognized this need or conceded their right to appropriate funds for the consistent promotion of new business." *Savings Bank Journal* 10, no. 5 (July 1929): 65.

167. *Savings Bank Journal* 10, no. 2 (April 1929): 54. Apparently, according to Mr. Blodgett, the thrift movement's long-standing efforts to emphasize that thrift is not merely about saving had not taken hold.

168. Sophie Wenzel Ellis, "Why Not Aid 'Spending Youth'?" *Savings Bank Journal* 10, no. 4 (June 1929): 52.

169. *Savings Bank Journal* 10, no. 5 (July 1929): 68.

170. Ibid., 60.

171. Ibid., 61.

172. Ibid.

173. Ibid, 64. William M. Hayden, president of Eutaw Savings Bank in Baltimore, MD, had complained in a 1921 article for the *Savings Bank Journal*: "That which would create a wonderfully philanthropic system *is liberty of human judgment, of the banks' judgment*. The mere broadening of the limit [on the size of deposits] will not fill the want; *it is the human touch that is needed*; a comprehensive and sympathetic benevolence now dwarfed because denied by law." *Savings Bank Journal*, 2, no. 3 (April, 1921): 8. (emphasis in original).

174. "Girl Scouts Are Teaching a Lesson in Thrift," editorial from Library of Congress, Prosperity and Thrift, < http://memory.loc.gov:8081/cgi-bin/query/r?ammem/coolbib:@field(NUMBER+@band(amrlm+mc18))> (June 30, 2008).

CHAPTER 4: A CENTURY OF THRIFT SHOPS

1. Anne Tyler, *The Accidental Tourist* (New York: Knopf, 1986), 182.

2. Goodwill Industries, International, Inc., "Our History," http://www.goodwill.org/page/guest/about/whatwedo/ourhistory (accessed October 2, 2007).

3. William Booth, *In Darkest England and the Way Out* (London: The Salvation Army, 1980), part 2, chapter 2, section 4.

4. Ibid., 87.

5. E. H. McKinley, *Somebody's Brother: A History of the Salvation Army Men's Social Service Department, 1891–1985* (New York: The Salvation Army, 1986), 42.

6. Louise A. Tilly, "Women, Women's History, and the Industrial Revolution," *Social Research* 61, no. 1 (Spring 1994).

7. Gordon M. Fisher, "From Hunter to Orshansky: An Overview of (Unofficial) Poverty Lines in the United States from 1904 to 1965," paper presented October 28, 1993, at the Fifteenth Annual Research Conference of the Association for Public Policy Analysis and Management, in Washington, DC (revised August 1997), U.S. Census Bureau, Housing and Household Economic Statistics Division, http://www.census.gov/hhes/www/povmeas/papers/hstorsp4.html.

8. Undated statement by Calvin Coolidge, enclosed in letter from C. Bascom Shemp, secretary to the president to Mr. Earl R. Obern, *Evening Herald*, Los Angeles, September 22, 1923; Images 6 and 7, Calvin Coolidge Papers, "Thrift—Encouragement, 1923–29" (http://memory.loc.gov:8081/cgi-bin/query/D?cool:24:./temp/~ammem_IgTT); Prosperity and Thrift: The Coolidge Era and the Consumer Economy, 1921–1929, (http://memory.loc.gov:8081/ammem/coolhtml/coolhome.html), American Memory, The Library of Congress, http://memory.loc.gov:8081/cgi-bin/ampage?collId=amrlm&fileName=mc18page.db&recNum=6&itemLink=r?ammem/cool:@field(NUMBER+@band(mc18))::&linkText=8 and http://memory.loc.gov:8081/cgi-bin/ampage?collId=amrlm&fileName=mc18page.db&recNum=5&itemLink=r?ammem/cool:@field(NUMBER+@band(mc18))::&linkText=8. In the same collection, there are letters showing that Shemp sent this same statement to others, including on April 29, 1924.

9. Simon William Straus, *History of the Thrift Movement in America* (Philadelphia: J. B. Lippincott Co., 1920), 97.

10. Ibid., 131.

11. Ibid., 134.

12. Benjamin R. Andrews, *Economics of the Household: Its Administration and Finance* (New York: Macmillan, 1923), 39–40.

13. Gordon M. Fisher, "Poverty Lines and Measure of Income Inadequacy in the United States Since 1870: Collecting and Using a Little-Known Body of Historical Material," paper presented October 17, 1997, at the twenty-

second meeting of the Social Science History Association, Washington, DC, appendix, http://aspe.hhs.gov/poverty/papers/since1870.htm#appendix.

14. Andrews, *Economics*, 419.

15. Anne Rittenhouse, *The Well-Dressed Woman* (New York: Harper & Brothers, 1924), 48.

16. Ibid., 192.

17. "Miscellany, Books and Periodicals," *Journal of Home Economics* 20, no. 4 (April 1928): 295.

18. McKinley, *Somebody's Brother*, 88.

19. B. R. Andrews and Lucy F. James, "Second-Hand Furniture for Beginning Housekeeping," *Journal of Home Economics* 23, no. 4 (April 1931): 351–53.

20. McKinley, *Somebody's Brother*, 181.

21. Rosemary T. Specian, "An Interdisciplinary Approach to Teaching Homemaker Aides," *Journal of Home Economics* 61, no. 5 (May 1969): 347.

22. McKinley, *Somebody's Brother*, 181.

23. Pamela Klaffke, *Spree: A Cultural History of Shopping* (Vancouver, BC: Arsenal Pulp Press, 2003).

24. Hillary Chura, *The New York Times*, June 24, 2006, C5.

25. U.S. Census Bureau, "Statistics of U.S. Businesses: 1999 Used Merchandise Stores by Employment Size of Enterprise," http://www.census.gov/epcd/susb/1999/us/US4533.HTM#table1 (accessed October 2, 2007); U.S. Census Bureau, "Used Merchandise Stores: 2002 Economic Census" (U.S. Department of Commerce, June 2004), Table 1.

26. http://www.salvationarmy.ca/2006/06/08/salvation-army-thrift-stores%E2%80%A6recycling-since-1890/.

27. Melanie Rysik, "Walk a Mile in My Shoes (and My Shirt), *New York Times*, "Sunday Styles," July 9, 2006, 2.

28. Russ Baruffi '04, in an essay in the Brown University *The College Hill Independent* (2003), makes this point and also writes, "And while critics would say that thrift-shopping has largely become as trendy as the mall, there remains a certain inevitably creative element to assembling an outfit that is indeed unique to you, not mass produced. For these reasons, thrift stores have been beacons for people trying to avoid the general plague of consumerism or seeking something different that you can't find in the strange cloned netherworld that is the American mall." http://www.brown.edu/Students/INDY/alpha/article.php?id=22&issue_id=184.

29. Suzanne Horne, *Charity Shops: Retailing, Consumption & Society* (Florence, KY: Routledge, 2002), 25.

30. McKinley, *Somebody's Brother*, 105.

31. Virginia Postrel, *The Substance of Style* (New York: Harper Perennial, 2004).

32. Andrews, *Economics*, 79.

CHAPTER 5: IN SAVINGS WE TRUST

1. This quotation and the subsequent account of the early credit union movement are drawn from Ian MacPherson, *Hands Around the Globe* (Victoria, BC: Horsdal & Schubart Publishers Ltd. and World Council of Credit Unions, 1999), 1–9.

2. The University of Southern Mississippi, Department of Marketing and Public Relations, *Miss McCarty's Major Awards, Appearances, Interviews, and Scholars Information,* available at http://www.usm.edu/pr/oolaward.htm.

3. "Louise McCarren Herring," http://en.wikipedia.org/wiki/Louise_McCarren_Herring.

4. National Federation of Community Development Credit Unions, *World View: NFCDCU @ 25* (New York: National Federation of Community Development Credit Unions, 1999), 4.

5. Faith Community United Credit Union, Inc., *50th Annual Meeting of Shareholders* (Cleveland, OH: Faith Community United Credit Union, Inc., 2002).

6. "National Credit Union Foundation Names 2009 Wegner Awards Winners," *Credit Union Times,* September 3, 2008, 16.

7. Credit Union National Association, *People Not Profit: The Story of the Credit Union Movement* (Madison, WI: CUNA, 2005), 11.

8. National Credit Union Administration, *Annual Report* (Alexandria, VA: National Credit Union Administration, 2008), 76.

9. Sharon Wertz, "Oseola McCarty Donates $150,000 to Southern Miss," Southern Miss Archives, June 16, 1995, available at http://www.usm.edu/pr/oola1.htm.

10. Ibid.

11. Ibid.

12. Clifford N. Rosenthal and Joseph Schoder, *"People's Credit": A Study of the Lending of the Lower East Side People's Federal Credit Union, 1986–89* (New York: National Federation of Community Development Credit Unions, 1990).

13. Michael Sherraden, *Assets and the Poor: A New American Welfare Policy* (Armonk, NY: M. E. Sharpe, 1991).

14. Ibid.

15. Musette Bracher, telephone interview by Clifford Rosenthal, GECU of El Paso, TX, July 23, 2008.

16. Callahan and Associates, *2008 Credit Union Directory* (Washington, DC: 2008), 12.

17. Credit Union National Association, *People, Not Profit*, 75.

18. Callahan & Associates, *Peer to Peer Financial Analysis Software: First Quarter, 2008* (Washington, DC: 2008).

19. National Credit Union Administration, data for March 31, 2008.

20. Federal Deposit Insurance Corporation, Division of Insurance and Research, *Online Institution Directory*, 2008, available at http://www4.fdic.gov/IDASP/index.asp, and Callahan & Associates, 2008.

21. According to the National Credit Union Administration (NCUA), using data provided by Datatrac, Inc., as of January 2008, credit unions paid on average from 0.20% to approximately 0.60% more than banks on various savings products. On loans, credit unions charged rates averaging typically 1.20% to 1.6% lower than banks on nonmortgage loans. See www.NCUA.gov.

CHAPTER 6: CONFRONTING THE AMERICAN DEBT CULTURE

1. This essay originally appeared in *The American Interest* 3, no. 6 (July/August 2008): 8–17, and was titled "A Nation in Debt: How We Killed Thrift, Enthroned Loan Sharks and Undermined American Prosperity." It is used here by permission. Sources for all data can be found in the report from which the article was adapted: *For a New Thrift: Confronting the Debt Culture* (New York: Institute for American Values, 2008). See also www.newthrift.org.

2. References to all data cited in this essay are available from the editor upon request. Or interested readers can consult the full report by the Commission on Thrift, *For a New Thrift: Confronting the Debt Culture* (New York: Institute for American Values, 2008), available from www.newthrift.org.

CHAPTER 7: CRAFTING POLICIES TO ENCOURAGE THRIFT IN CONTEMPORARY AMERICA

1. What I call the "official savings rate" is that calculated by the Bureau of Economic Research using National Income and Product Account (NIPA) data. The NIPA-based savings rate also underestimates personal wealth accumulation because it captures taxes on capital gains as spending (while excluding the capital gains as income) and treats spending on durable goods and education as consumption when it is often an investment.

2. Kevin J. Lansing, "Spendthrift Nation," *FRBSF Economic Letter*, no. 2005-30 (Federal Reserve Bank of San Francisco, 2005); F. Thomas Juster, Joseph P. Lupton, James P. Smith, and Frank Stafford, "The Decline in Household Saving and the Wealth Effect," *The Review of Economics and Statistics* 87, no. 4 (2005) 20–27; Dean M. Maki and Michael G. Palumbo, "Disentangling the Wealth Effect: A Cohort Analysis of Household Saving in the 1990s," *Finance and Economics Discussion Series*, no. 2001-21 (Board of Governors of the Federal Reserve System, 2001), http://www.federalreserve. gov/pubs/feds/2001/200121/200121abs.html; Milt Marquis, "What's Behind the Low U.S. Personal Saving Rate?" *FRBSF Economic Letter*, no. 2002-09 (Federal Reserve Bank of San Francisco, 2002).

3. Inter-American Development Bank, "Sending Money Home: Leveraging the Development Impact of Remittances," October 18, 2006; Janice Fine, Lauren Leimbach, and Katy Jacob, "Distributing Prepaid Cards through Worker Centers: A Gateway to Asset Building for Low-Income Households" (The Center for Financial Services Innovation, October 2006), http://www.cfsinnovation.com/research-paper-detail.php?article_id=2772.

4. Surveys of Consumer Finance.

5. Eric M. Engen, William G. Gale, Cori E. Uccello, Christopher D. Carroll, and David I. Laibson, "The Adequacy of Household Saving," *Brookings Papers on Economic Activity* 1999, no. 2 (1999): 65–187; John Karl Scholz, Ananth Seshadri, and Surachai Khitatrakun, "Are Americans Saving 'Optimally' for Retirement?" *Journal of Political Economy* 114, no. 41 (2006): 607–43; Paul A. Smith, David A. Love, and Lucy C. McNair, "Do Households Have Enough Wealth for Retirement?" FEDS Working Paper No. 2007-17 (The Federal Reserve Board, 2007); Damon Darlin, "A Contrarian View: Save Less and Still Retire with Enough," *New York Times*, January 27, 2007, section A, page 1.

6. Mark Iwry and David C. John, "Pursuing Universal Retirement Security through Automatic IRAs," White Paper no. 02122006 (The

Heritage Foundation, 2006), http://www.heritage.org/research/
socialsecurity/wp20060212.cfm.

7. Olivia S. Mitchell, Stephen P. Utkus, and Tongxuan (Stella) Yang,
"Turning Workers into Savers? Incentives, Liquidity, and Choice in 401(k)
Plan Design," NBER Working Paper 11725 (National Bureau of Economic
Research, 2005).

8. My arguments here should not be taken to mean that poor nonsavers
are creating their own problems by simply imagining that they are
constrained. Rather, in my view, pessimism-based aversion to saving is a
somewhat common phenomenon that often has some rational basis. For
example, during the cold war, Americans saved significantly less when they
believed the threat of nuclear war to be high because the perceived greater
possibility of death shortened people's time horizon; they may also have cut
back on capital accumulation because catastrophic upheaval would have
caused assets to become worth less. (See Joel Slemrod, "Saving and the Fear
of Nuclear War," *The Journal of Conflict Resolution* 30, no. 3 [1986]: 403–19;
Bruce Russett, Jonathon Crowden, David Kinsella, and Shoon Murray,
"Did Americans' Expectations of Nuclear War Reduce Their Savings?"
International Studies Quarterly 38, no. 4 [1994]: 587–603.) These decreases
in saving might look irrational in hindsight since nuclear war never broke
out and was probably unlikely barring an accident; yet the threat seemed
real to people at the time, and so they modified their behavior accordingly.
Other studies have discovered that expectations of sociopolitical upheaval
inhibit saving across the globe. (See Yiannis P. Venieris and Dipak K.
Gupta, "Income Distribution and Sociopolitical Instability as Determinants
of Saving," *The Journal of Political Economy* 94, no. 4 [1986]: 873–83).
In short, uncertainty and risk—real and perceived—cause future assets
to be devalued. Thus, because lower-income individuals are more likely
than others to experience a variety of difficulties—crime, unemployment,
destruction of property, incarceration, early death, etc.—it makes sense that
many would be skeptical of the idea that they could improve their condition
in life or reap the rewards of delayed consumption; at the same time, the
expectation or anticipation of failure undoubtedly creates a self-fulfilling
prophecy by causing many to adopt a self-defeating passive orientation.

9. Some might argue that people would not live paycheck-to-paycheck
unless forced to do so because it would render them helpless in the
event of an emergency or economic downturn. But there are at least two
important safety nets for low-income Americans that reduce the risk of
living on the financial edge. The first is welfare. If a person loses his or

her job, governmental assistance will provide for his or her basic needs. One interesting study found that asset restrictions in means-tested welfare programs actually cause potential program recipients to save at a lower rate. (Sondra Beverly, "How Can the Poor Save? Theory and Evidence on Saving in Low-Income Households," working paper [St. Louis: Center for Social Development, Washington University, 1997], 36.) This finding clearly suggests that many low-income Americans do consider welfare when deciding how to save and spend their money. Second, studies find that lower-income Americans often lend and borrow from one another in the event of an emergency. This is a second safety net that lowers the risk of not saving. (Ellen Seidman, Moez Hababou, and Jennifer Kramer, "A Financial Services Survey of Low- and Moderate-Income Households" [The Center for Financial Services Innovation, 2005], 19; Stephen Brobeck, "Making Household Saving a Priority" [Consumer Federation of America, 1999]).

10. Seidman, Hababou, and Kramer, "A Financial Services Survey"; Adrian Furnham, "Why Do People Save? Attitudes to, and Habits of, Saving Money in Britain," *Journal of Applied Social Psychology* 15, no. 5 (1985): 354–73.

11. Jeanne Hogarth, Amberly Hazembuller, and Michael Wilson, "How Much Can the Poor Save?," white paper presented at the Closing the Wealth Gap Policy Research Forum, September 2006, http://www.frbsf.org/community/research/assets/HowMuchCanthePoorSave.pdf.

12. Ibid.

13. Emily C. Lawrance, "Poverty and the Rate of Time Preference: Evidence from Panel Data," *The Journal of Political Economy* 99, no. 1 (February 1991): 54–77; Shlomo Maital and Sharone Maital, "Time Preference, Delay of Gratification and the Intergenerational Transmission of Economic Inequality," in *Essays in Labor Market Analysis in Memory of Yochanan Peter Comay,* ed. O. C. Ashenfelter and W. E. Oates (New York: Wiley, 1977), 179–99.

14. Not shown in the table: the survey found that only about 35 percent of nonsavers had used a nontraditional source of credit (e.g., payday or auto title loan, rent-to-own, pawned an item, etc.) in the past five years. Seidman, Hababou, and Kramer, "A Financial Services Survey," 22.

15. Ibid.

16. Ibid.

17. For example, it is unclear whether saving incentives have any effect on the average person's behavior (see sources at the end of this note). This ambiguity might seem odd since people are generally eager to take advantage of incentives. Common sense tells us that if we increase the value of saved

dollars, then people will opt to save more and spend less. But think about this perspective: saving is not really an alternative to spending in the long run. It is the *delaying of* consumption, the allocation of capital toward some future end. We do not save primarily because there are interest rates and returns on investment but because we will need the money in the future. Now let us assume that a certain man wants to amass $1,000,000 for retirement. If he has articulated this goal to himself, then chances are good that he will be saving already. Now assume that the federal government informs him that he can put up to $5,000 per year into a tax-free saving account to build wealth for retirement. What will his response be? He might *not* spend less and save more. He might just divert cash flows already pegged for saving into the tax-advantaged account *without saving more overall*. In this way, he can take advantage of the incentive without altering his overall saving rate. Regardless of whether this scenario accurately reflects the behavior of most people, it provides an explanation for why saving incentives might be ineffectual. In any event, we saw earlier that undersavers are quite prone to ignore saving incentives, and thus incentives are not a compelling policy solution to the challenges discussed in this essay. For studies concluding that saving incentives do not work, see Eric M. Engen, William G. Gale, John Karl Scholz, B. Douglas Bernheim, and Joel Slemrod, "Do Saving Incentives Work?" *Brookings Papers on Economic Activity* 1994, no. 1 (1994): 85–180; William G. Gale and John Karl Scholz, "IRAs and Household Saving," *The American Economic Review* 84, no. 5 (1994): 1233–60; Eric M. Engen, William G. Gale, and John Karl Scholz, "The Illusory Effects of Saving Incentives on Saving," *The Journal of Economic Perspectives* 10, no. 4 (1996): 113–38. For studies finding that saving incentives have a positive effect, see R. Glenn Hubbard and Jonathon S. Skinner, "Assessing the Effectiveness of Saving Incentives," *The Journal of Economic Perspectives* 10, no. 4 (1996): 73–90; James M. Poterba, Steven F. Venti, and David A. Wise, "How Retirement Saving Programs Increase Saving," *The Journal of Economic Perspectives* 10, no. 4 (1996): 91–112; Steven F. Venti and David A. Wise, "Have IRAs Increased U.S. Saving? Evidence from Consumer Expenditure Surveys," *The Quarterly Journal of Economics* 105, no. 3 (1990): 661–98.

The proposal that government should offer subsidies to financial institutions that help lower-income Americans to save is also problematic. For one, if the idea is that financial firms will court small savers by passing along the subsidy to the customer, then this policy is just a different iteration of the problematic one discussed above. For another, small saving products are not particularly profitable. It is unlikely that any reasonably sized subsidy would prompt financial firms actively to seek customers for these products. This is precisely the reason it has almost always been the case that only benevolent and philanthropic institutions—e.g., mutual savings banks and credit unions—ever bother to encourage those of lesser means to save. Finally, clamping down on subprime lending might also do little to promote saving. If the majority of people who use subprime credit do so because they have a strong preference for immediate consumption or fail to save in the first place, then restricting such credit is unlikely to improve people's financial well-being (though there are other reasons one might take this course of action). For example, one study finds that banning payday lending only causes a corresponding surge in overdraft fees as customers switch to using their checking account as a line of credit: Donald P. Morgan and Michael R. Strain, "Payday Holiday: How Households Fare after Payday Credit Bans," Staff Report no. 309 (Federal Reserve Bank of New York, 2008).

18. Kurt Lewin, Tamara Dembo, Leon Festinger, and P. S. Sear, "Level of Aspiration," in *Personality and the Behavior Disorders*, ed. J. M. Hunt (New York: Ronald Press Company, 1944), 1:333–78; George Katona, *Psychological Economics* (New York: Elsevier, 1975); Albert Bandura, "Self-Efficacy Mechanism in Human Agency," *American Psychologist* 37, no. 2 (1982), 122–47; Albert Bandura, *Social Foundations of Thought and Action: A Social Cognitive Theory* (Englewood Cliffs, NJ: Prentice-Hall, 1986).

19. Brigitte C. Madrian and Dennis F. Shea, "The Power of Suggestion: Inertia in 401(k) Participation and Savings Behavior," *Quarterly Journal of Economics* 116, no. 4 (2001): 1149–87.

20. Paul Taylor, Cary Funk, and April Clark, "We Try Hard. We Fall Short. Americans Assess Their Saving Habits" (Pew Research Center, 2007).

21. Ashley Cruce, "School-Based Savings Programs, 1930–2002," Working Paper 02-7 (St. Louis: Center for Social Development, 2002).

22. http://www.saveforamerica.org.

23. Beverly, "How Can the Poor Save?"

24. Jeanne M. Hogarth, Sondra G. Beverly, and Marianne Hilgert, "Patterns of Financial Behaviors: Implications for Community Educators and Policy Makers," paper presented at the 2003 Federal Reserve System Community Affairs Research Conference (February 2003).

25. Institute for American Values, *For a New Thrift: Confronting the Debt Culture* (New York: Institute for American Values, 2008), 28; Alicia Hansen and Gerald Prante, "Lottery Taxes Divert Income from Retirement Savings,"

Fiscal Fact No. 45 (The Tax Foundation, January 19, 2006), http://www. taxfoundation.org/research/show/1302.html

26. Hansen and Prante, "Lottery Taxes Divert Income."

27. See http://www.nsandi.com/products/pb/index.jsp and http://www. savings.gov.pk.

CHAPTER 8: PRIVATE ENTERPRISE'S ROLE IN INCREASING SAVINGS

1. See Richard H. Thaler and Cass R. Sunstein, "Libertarian Paternalism," *The American Economic Review* 93, no. 2 (2003): 175–79 and Richard H. Thaler and Cass R. Sunstein, *Nudge* (New Haven, CT, and London: Yale University Press, 2008).

2. See Kim Burham, "401(k)s as Strategic Compensation: Align Pay with Productivity and Enable Optimal Separation," PhD diss., University of Notre Dame, 2003).

3. Scott I. Rick, Cynthia E. Cryder, and George Loewenstein, "Tightwads and Spendthrifts," *Journal of Consumer Research* 34 (April 2008): 767–82.

4. This is the central result of Brad M. Barber and Terrance Odean, "Boys Will Be Boys: Gender, Overconfidence, and Common Stock Investment," *Quarterly Journal of Economics* 116, no. 1 (February 2001): 261–92.

5. See my article, "Bargain Hunting or Star Gazing: Investors, Preferences for Stock Mutual Funds," *Journal of Business* 76, no. 4 (October 2003): 645–63.

6. See Esther Duflo and Emmanuel Saez, "Implications of Pension Plan Features, Information and Social Interactions for Retirement Savings Decisions," *Pension Design and Structure: New Lessons from Behavioral Finance*, ed. O. S. Mitchell and S. Utkus (Oxford: Oxford University Press, 2004), 137–57.

7. Derek D. Rucker and Adam D. Galinsky, "Desire to Acquire: Powerlessness and Compensatory Consumption," *Journal of Consumer Research* 34 (April 2008): 767–82.

8. Kerwin K. Charles, Erik Hurst, and Nikolai Roussanov, "Conspicuous Consumption and Race," working paper, University of Pennsylvania, 2007.

9. The explanations in the remaining sections of this essay are borrowed from my book, *Whatever Happened to Thrift? Why Americans Don't Save and What to Do About It* (New Haven, CT, and London: Yale University Press, 2008).

10. Sheena Sethi-Iyengar, Gur Huberman, and Wei Jiang, "How Much Choice Is Too Much? Contributions to 401(k) Retirement Plans," *Pension Design and Structure*, 83–95.

11. Shlomo Bernartzi and Richard H. Thaler, "Naïve Diversification Strategies in Defined Contribution Savings Plans," *The American Economic Review* 91, no. 1 (2001): 79–98.

12. Douglas Bernheim and Daniel Garrett found that advice delivered on a person-to-person basis was much more effective than printed brochures or other company-produced literature. See their article, "The Effects of Financial Education in the Workplace: Evidence from a Survey of Households," *Journal of Public Economics* 87 (2003): 1487–1519.

13. Shlomo Bernartzi and Richard H. Thaler, "Save More Tomorrow: Using Behavioral Economics to Increase Employee Savings," *Journal of Political Economy* 112, no. 1 (2004): S164–S187.

14. Anne S. Tsui and Charles A. O'Reilly, "Beyond Simple Demographic Effects: The Importance of Relational Demography in Superior-Subordinate Dyads," *Academy of Management Journal* 32, no. 2 (1989): 402–23.

Contributors

David Blankenhorn is the author of *Thrift: A Cyclopedia* (Templeton Press, 2008), *The Future of Marriage* (Encounter Books, 2007), and *Fatherless America* (Basic Books, 1995) and the coeditor of eight volumes on issues of marriage, fatherhood, and civil society. He is the founder and president of the Institute for American Values—a nonpartisan research organization devoted to strengthening families and civil society in the United States and the world. He earned an MA with distinction in comparative social history from the University of Warwick in Coventry, England. He has been profiled in *USA Today*, the *New York Times*, and the *Los Angeles Times*. He lectures and speaks internationally on issues of marriage, families, and civil society. He lives in New York City.

Sorcha Brophy-Warren is a doctoral student in sociology at Yale University. Previously, she was an affiliate scholar at the Institute for American Values, where she researched thrift and wrote a literature review of business ethics curricula. Prior to joining the institute, she was a fellow at the Trinity Forum Academy. She graduated with high honors in the comparative study of religion, earning an AB degree from Harvard University. She lives in New York City and New Haven, Connecticut.

Alison Humes is a magazine editor and writer who lives in New York City. Currently the features editor at *Condé Nast Traveler*, she previously worked at *Vogue* and *The Atlantic*.

Sara Butler Nardo is a doctoral student in American history at the University of Chicago. Formerly, she was a research associate at the Institute for American Values, having earned a BA from the University of Chicago. She lives in Chicago with her husband and son and has been known to wash and reuse zippered plastic bags.

Alex Roberts is an affiliate scholar with the Institute for American Values, where he focuses on economic policy, family sociology, and Islam–West relations. He is coeditor of *The Islam/West Debate: Documents from a Global Debate on Terrorism, U.S. Policy, and the Middle East* (Rowman and Littlefield, 2005) and coauthor of *The Consequences of Marriage for African Americans: A Comprehensive Literature Review* (Institute for American Values, 2005). Prior to joining the institute, Mr. Roberts earned a BA from Wesleyan University with departmental honors in history. He lives in Chicago.

Clifford N. Rosenthal is president and chief executive officer of the National Federation of Community Development Credit Unions, a position he has held since 1983. The federation represents and serves more than two hundred credit unions that specialize in serving low-income communities across the United States. Under his leadership, the federation has invested more than sixty-million dollars in low-income credit unions. Having served on numerous advisory boards, including for the Federal Reserve System as well as J. P. Morgan Chase Bank, Mr. Rosenthal was appointed in 2008 by Mayor Michael Bloomberg to the advisory board of New York City's Office of Financial Empowerment. Mr. Rosenthal holds a BA and an MA from Columbia University and lives in New York City.

Barbara Dafoe Whitehead is an award-winning journalist, having written about social and family issues for numerous national publications. She was the lead researcher and writer of a report to the nation by the Commission on Thrift, titled *For a New Thrift: Confronting the Debt Culture*. Her 1993 *Atlantic Monthly* cover story, "Dan Quayle

Was Right," was named by *Policy Review* as one of the ten most influential pieces of the late twentieth century and was recently reprinted in *The American Idea: The Best of the Atlantic Monthly*. Her books include *Why There Are No Good Men Left: The Romantic Plight of the New Single Woman* (Broadway, 2003) and *The Divorce Culture* (Knopf, 1997; Vintage, 1998). She holds a PhD in American social history from the University of Chicago and lives in Amherst, Massachusetts.

Ronald T. Wilcox, professor of Business Administration, teaches Marketing Intelligence and Investor Behavior and Imperfect Markets at The Darden School of Business, University of Virginia. His research, focused on the marketing of financial services and its interface with public policy, has appeared in leading marketing and finance journals. He is the author of the book *Whatever Happened to Thrift? Why Americans Don't Save and What to Do About It* (Yale University Press, 2008). Professor Wilcox joined the Darden faculty in 2001. He was formerly an assistant professor at the Carnegie Mellon Graduate School of Industrial Administration and an economist for the U.S. Securities and Exchange Commission.

Index

ABA. *See* American Bankers
Association
Adams, John, 8–9
Adventures in Thrift (Richardson),
65–66, 88, 89
advertisements, 45–46
by banks, 220n82
by credit unions, 133–34
government, 182–83
to immigrants, 47–48
to middle-class, 49–50
by payday lenders, 156–57
psychology of, 48–49
by Salvation Army, 118
in twentieth century, 221n97
to youth, 92–93
Advice to a Young Tradesman
(Franklin, B.), 10, 12
AFI. *See* Assets for Independence
African Americans, 131
age, 191
aggressive conservation, 46
Aguilar, Gloria, 137

AIP. *See* American Investment Plan
Albig, E. Epsey, 82, 83–84, 85
alcohol, 72, 220n78
Allen, George E., 47
America Saves, 137
American Bankers Association
(ABA), 58, 83–84
American Dream, 37–38, 51,
218n47
American Federation of Labor, 80
American Investment Plan (AIP),
180–83, 181
American Political Science
Association, 62
American Society for Thrift, 58, 84
Andrews, Benjamin, 69, 105
on luxury, 123
on thrift shops, 106–7
Annie Hall, 116
antithrift, institutions of, xi
apprenticeship, 13
assets, 177
CDCU, 140–41

pension plan, 198–200
Assets and the Poor (Sherraden), 138
Assets for Independence (AFI), 138
Autobiography (Franklin, B.), 3–4,
    12, 16, 17
    persona in, 24–25
    publication of, 213n37

Bache, Richard, 13
Baldensperger, H. L., 71
Bank for Savings, 35
    bankruptcy
    in eighteenth century, 149
    U.S., 10, 149
banks. *See also* mutual savings bank;
    school savings bank
    advertisements by, 220n82
    runs on, 222n107
    savings, 33, 51–52
    U.S., 90, 215n5
Baruffi, Russ, 233n28
Beckert, Sven, 221n98
Bellah, Robert, 34
Bergengren, Roy F., 128
Bernartzi, Shlomo, 204
Beyond the Counter (Reeves), 47–48
Booth, Evangeline, 103–4, 114
Booth, William, 102
Bowery Savings Bank, 41, 51,
    222n101
Breen, T. H., 12
Brown, Mary Wilcox, 62
    The Development of Thrift by, 59,
        60
    on school savings banks, 83
    on spending, 229n138
Bureau of Economic Research,
    236n1

caisse populaire. *See* credit unions
Cammerer, Arno B., 89
capital gains
    for AIP, 181
    saving and, 166, 169, 170
    tax on, 236n1
capitalism, 75–76
Capra, Frank, 145
Carothers, W. H., 61
Carver, T. N., 63, 69
CDCUs. *See* community
    development credit unions
CFED. *See* Corporation for
    Enterprise Development
Chamberlain, Arthur, 89
Chamberlain, James, 89
charity, 58. *See also* philanthropy
    attitude of, 103
    Franklin, B., on, 14–15
    organizations, 31–32
    Straus on, 64
*Charity Shops Retailing, Consumption
    & Society* (Horne), 119
checking accounts, 132
Church of Stop Shopping, 118
citizenship, 73
clothing swap, 118–19
Cobain, Kurt, 117
cobweb economics, 94
The College Hill Independent, 233n28
college students, 150, 157–58
Commercial Economy Board, 79
community development credit
    unions (CDCUs), 135–36
    assets of, 140–41
    GECU, 137–38
    purpose of, 140
COMO, 125

conservation, 89–90
conspicuous consumption, 193–94,
    205–6
Consumer Federation of America,
    137
consumerism. *See also* conspicuous
    consumption
    after World War II, 113–14
    critique of, 71–72
    thrift movement and, 67–68
    U.S., 54–55
Coolidge, Calvin, 66–67, 104
Corporation for Enterprise
    Development (CFED), 138
Craigslist.org, 120
credit
    in eighteenth century, 10
    Franklin, B., on, 12
    saving and, 238n14
credit cards, 150–51, 157–58
credit unions, x. *See also* community
    development credit unions
    advertisements by, 133–34
    of African Americans, 131
    interest rates of, 235n21
    members of, 132
    origins of, 127–28
    payday lenders and, 160, 161
    poverty and, 130
    purpose of, 160, 161
    U.S., 139

Dane, Edmund, 61, 72
Daniel, H. R., 224n26
debt
    burdensome, 148–49
    in eighteenth century, 10
    Franklin, B., on, 11

saving and, 177
    U.S., 148–50, 151
democracy, 43, 73–75
Democracy in America (Tocqueville),
    43
Department of School Savings and
    Thrift, 83
Depression. *See* Great Depression
Desjardins, Alphonse, 127–28
Desjardins, Dorimene, 127–28
The Development of Thrift (Brown),
    59, 60
disintermediation, 222n110
The Dollar Stretcher, 118
Van Doren, Carl, 5, 16
Dowrie, George W., 226n58
dowry, 213n21
Duncan, Henry, 29
Duplain, George, 110

eBay, 120
*The Economics of the Household: Its
    Administration and Finance*
    (Andrews), 105–6, 123
education, financial, 192–93. *See also*
    school savings bank
    on 401(k), 194–95
    in Massachusetts, 84
    through school savings bank,
        183–84
efficiency, 71–72
Ellis, Sophie Wenzel, 92–93
Employee Retirement Income
    Security Act (ERISA), 195–96,
    202, 203
equality, 77
ERISA. *See* Employee Retirement
    Income Security Act

Europe, 23, 219n63
Excelsior Savings Bank, 37

Faith Community United Credit
    Union, 132
family, 84. *See also* marriage
    of Franklin, B., 7, 8, 12–13,
        211n2, 212n12, 213n37
    management of, 7, 12–13, 105–6,
        123, 213n21
Father Abraham, 18–19
FDIC. *See* Federal Deposit Insurance
    Corporation
Federal Credit Union Act, 129
Federal Deposit Insurance
    Corporation (FDIC), 222n107
Federal Reserve, 148
FICA. *See* Social Security
Fielding, Henry, 14
Filene, Edward, x, 128
Fisher, Gordon M., 103, 106
Food Administration, 79–80
401(k), 174
    education on, 194–95
    opt-out, 134, 181, 200–201
France, 8, 19–20
Franklin, Benjamin
    books by, xi, 3–4, 7, 8, 10, 11, 12,
        14–15, 16, 17–19, 20–21, 22,
        23, 24–25, 213n37
    on charity, 14–15
    on credit, 12
    on debt, 11
    family of, 7, 8, 12–13, 211n2,
        212n12, 213n37
    on frugality, 21–22, 211n5
    generosity of, 212n9
    on good works, 213n24

on industry, 20–21, 211n5
laziness of, 8–9
loan fund of, 8, 15
luxuries of, xi, 110
on marriage, 23, 213n21
persona of, 24–25
symbolism of, 6
on U.S., 22–24
wealth of, 6–7
Franklin, Deborah, 7
Franklin Typographical Society of
    Journeyman Printers, 26
Franklin, William Temple, 213n37
fraternalism, 33, 216n25, 217n26
Frazier, Raymond, 45
frugality, 21–22, 211n5
fur coats, 115–16

GECU, 137–38
gender, 191–92. *See also individual
    genders*
General Federation of Women's
    Clubs, 87
General Motors (GM), 189–90
General Society of Mechanics and
    Tradesmen of New York, 25
generosity, 14–15, 212n9
gentleman, 13–14
Gilliam, James, 131, 140
GM. *See* General Motors
Gold, Cookie, 118
Gold, Michael, 118
Gompers, Samuel, 80
good works, 213n24
Goodwill Industries, 101, 120
government. *See also* United States
    advertisements by, 182–83
    budget, 230n143

Grace Loans, 132
Great Britain, x, 185
Great Depression, 52, 94, 129

habit, 66
Habits of the Heart (Bellah), 34
Hall, Bolton, 61, 69, 70, 72, 73
Harding, Warren, 73, 104
harmonic convergence, 44
Harrison, Milton, 68
Hayden, William M., 231n173
Haynes, Rita, 132
Helms, Edgar James, 101–2
Henry, O. H., 93–94, 95
Herring, Louise, 130, 131
*History of the Thrift Movement in
    America* (Straus), 104
Hoover, Herbert, 79
Horne, Suzanne, 119
Household Salvage Brigade, 102
Housing Works, 120
How to Institute School Savings Banks,
    83
Huey, John, 15
Hughes, Dora Morrell, 64, 69, 70,
    71
Hun v. Cary, 45

IDAs. *See* Individual Development
    Accounts
immigrants
    advertisements to, 47–48
    saving of, 170–71
    to U.S., 22–24, 41–42
    using MSBs, 41–42
In Darkest England (Booth, W.), 102
income
    net worth and, 172

saving and, 170–71, 173–77,
    237n8, 237n9
independence, 68
Individual Development Accounts
    (IDAs), 132, 138
individualism
    MSBs and, 34
    Tocqueville on, 36–37
    in U.S., 34–35
Industrial Revolution
    mass production after, 114
    thrift movement and, 60–63
    thrift shops and, 100–101
industry, 20–21, 211n5, 212n11
inflation, 198–99
"Information to Those Who Would
    Remove to America" (Franklin,
    B.), 22
insolvency, 10
installment plans, 91–92
interest rates
    of credit unions, 235n21
    of payday lenders, 152, 153
investment, 179
    diversification of, 197–200
    by gender, 191–93
    U.S., 171
investor class, 147–48
It's a Wonderful Life, 145, 146

Johnson, Alvin, 73, 75–76
Jordan, Daniel, 70
Journal of Home Economics, 109–10,
    114–15

Kelso, Robert, 159
kinderwhore, 117
Klaffke, Pamela, 116–17

Klaman, Saul, 53
Kniffen, William, 34, 36, 42
Knox, William E., 31, 32, 41

language, 190
Lawrence, D. H., 5
Lewis, E. St. Elmo, 46, 48, 220n81
Lewisohn, Adolph, 86
Liberty Bonds, 80
life insurance, 68–69, 91, 216n25
lifecycle funds, 179–80, 197,
    199–200
Lord, Herbert, 230n143
lottery, 147
    funding by, 155–56
    repurposing of, 163, 184–85
    spending on, 154–55, 156,
      184–85
    Texas, 157
    U.S., 154–55, 184
lottery bond, 185
lottery class, 147, 148
Love, Courtney, 117
luxury
    Andrews on, 123
    of Franklin, B., xi, 110
    fur coats as, 115–16
    at vendues, 18–19
    Withers on, 71

MacGregor, T. D.
    on efficiency, 72
    on saving, 62
    on shopping, 88
    on spending, 70–71
    on thrift as virtue, 73
Madonna, 116–17
Make a Budget Day, 87

marriage, 23, 213n21
Massachusetts, 84
mass-production, 114
Maxwell, Dora, 130
McCarty, Oseola, 135
McKinley, E. H., 115
McVey, Frank, 228n94
Mead, Walter Russell, 44
Mecom, Benjamin, 211n2
Melville, Herman, 5
men
    investments of, 191, 192–93
    in thrift shops, 124–25
Mennonite Central Committee, 101
Merrill, Sereno Taylor, 228n114
middle-class
    advertisements to, 49–50
    MSBs as, 50–51
    in thrift shops, 113
    in twentieth century, 221n98
middling ranks, 9–10, 25, 26. *See
    also* middle-class
Miller, Daniel, 125
minorities
    credit unions for, 131
    spending of, 193–94
miserliness, 63–64
moneylending, 10–11, 60. *See also*
    payday lenders
morality, 193
    of poverty, 11, 103, 105
    of saving, 35, 40–41, 42, 46,
      54–55, 63, 71, 73
mornings, 8, 20–21
mortgage, 91
MSB. *See* mutual savings bank
mutual funds, 191–92, 196. *See also*
    lifecycle funds

mutual savings bank (MSB), 30–31
  in 1910, 40
  bank runs on, 222n107
  competition with, 39–40, 52–53
  crises of, 54
  in Great Depression, 52
  identity through, 40–41, 42–43
  immigrants using, 41–42
  individualism and, 34
  as middle-class, 50–51
  Northeastern, 38
  as philanthropic organizations, 52,
    59
  as "Poor Man's Bank," 50, 51
  saving deposits in, 93
  S&L's and, 218n53
  trustees of, 32–33
Mystic Women's Club Thrift Shop,
  126

National Association of Resale and
  Thrift Shops, 117
National Bureau of Economic
  Research, 166
National Conference of Mutual
  Savings Banks, 93
National Credit Union
  Administration (NCUA), 132,
  235n21
National Education Association
  (NEA), 58, 81, 84
National Federation of Community
  Development Credit Unions,
  136, 140
National Housewives' League
  (NHL), 88
National Income and Product
  Account (NIPA), 236n1

National Park System, 89
National Thrift Committee, 58, 86
National Thrift Week, 52, 86
National Thrift Week, 86
National Women's Christian
  Temperance Union (NWTCU),
  82–83, 103
Navy Federal Credit Union, 139
NCUA. *See* National Credit Union
  Administration
NEA. *See* National Education
  Association
net worth
  income and, 172
  in U.S., 168, 169
The New American Thrift, 68,
  226n58
New York Times, 117
NHL. *See* National Housewives'
  League
Nichols, Frederic, 41–42
NIPA. *See* National Income and
  Product Account
nuclear war, 237n8
NWTCU. *See* National Women's
  Christian Temperance Union

Oberholtzer, Sara Louise
  passbook system of, 84–85
  on school savings banks, 42–43
  Temperance Movement and,
    82–83
*Observations Concerning the Increase
  of Mankind* (Franklin, B.), 23
Oldsmobile, 189–90

Pakistan, 185
Palmer, George, 74

pawnbrokers, 60
payday lenders
    advertisement by, 156–57
    banning of, 238n17
    credit unions and, 160, 161
    income and, 151
    interest rates of, 152, 153
    rollover loans of, 152–53
    Social Security and, 152
    in U.S., 158
payroll deduction, 134
Pennsylvania, 82
Pennsylvania Gazette, 7
pension plans, 187–88
    asset allocation in, 198–200
    choices in, 196–98
    financial advice for, 201–3
    forward contracts in, 204–5
    providers of, 195–96
    targeting of, 206
    U.S. Department of Labor on,
        196, 198
Pension Protection Act, 203
Peterson, Christopher, 160–61
philanthropy, 31, 32
    MSBs as, 52, 59
    thrift as, 35, 58–59
Poor Richard, x
Poor Richard's Almanack (Franklin,
    B.), 3, 7, 16, 17, 22
    on charity, 14–15
    on frugality, 21
    on generosity, 14–15
    on indulgence, xi
    on industry, 20–21
    on leisure, 14
    on making money, 4
    on mornings, 8, 20–21

on religion, 15, 19
on reputation, 11
on social divisions, 20
The Way to Wealth and, 18–19
poverty
    credit unions and, 130
    morality of, 11, 103, 105
Principles of Scientific Management
    (Taylor), 72
prize bond, 185
"A Program of Thrift for New York
    State" (Rose and Renssalaer),
    105
Provident Institution for Savings in
    Boston, 30
psychology, 48–49
public service, 14
purchasing power, 61–62

Real Simple, 118
*Recession in Industry Affects School
    Savings Banking*, 85
Red Cross, 109
Red Cross Courier, 109
Reeves, Mary, 47–48, 49
regionalism, xi
religion, 19
Renssalaer, Martha Van, 105
reputation, 11–12
resources, natural, 75–76, 89–90
"Resume of Banking in the
    United States as It Exists at
    the Present Time and Its Past
    History, Together with Future
    Outlook and Possible Future
    Requirements," 93
retirement, 173
Reverend Billy, 118

Rhoades, John Harsen, 59
Richardson, Anna Steese, 65–66,
   88, 89
Rittenhouse, Anne, 107–8
Rittenhouse, Mr., 50
rollover loans, 152–53
Roosevelt, Franklin D., 52
Roosevelt, Teddy, 65
Rose, Flora, 105

S2W. *See* Save 2 Win
salary lenders. *See* payday lenders
Salvation Army, 102–4
   advertisements by, 118
   collection by, 114
   merchandising in, 109, 110
Saunders, Richard. *See* Poor Richard
Save 2 Win (S2W), 185
"Save More Tomorrow," 204
saving. *See also* school savings bank
   by age, 191
   banks, 33, 51–52
   capital gains and, 166, 169, 170
   credit and, 238n14
   debt and, 177
   deposits, 39–40
   factors in, 236n1
   incentives for, 178, 238n17
   income and, 170–71, 173–77,
      237n8, 237n9
   MacGregor on, 62
   morality of, 35, 40–41, 42, 46,
      54–55, 63, 71, 73
   opt-out, 134, 152, 178, 181
   for retirement, 173
   self control for, 65
   spending as, 69
   Straus on, 64

   in U.S., 55, 76, 95, 137, 162, 166,
      167, 168–70, 236n1
   welfare and, 237n9
   by women, 69–70
   during World War II, 162, 182
Savings and Friendly Society, 29
savings and loan association (S&L),
   218n53
Savings Bank Journal, 92, 231n173
Savings Challenge '07, 137–38
"The Savings Idea and the People"
   (Lewis), 48
"Savings Outweigh Any Stigma at
   Upscale Consignment Shops,"
   117
Schiff, Stacy, 20
Schisgall, Oscar, 222n101
school savings bank
   under ABA, 83–84
   Brown on, 83
   education through, 183–84
   in Great Depression, 85
   Oberholtzer on, 42–43
   passbook system for, 84–85
   start of, 82, 228n114
*The Science of Good Richard, or The
   Easy Way to Pay Taxes* (Franklin,
   B.), 8
Second Mt. Sinai Baptist Church,
   131–32
Securities and Exchange
   Commission, 199
Seerley, Homer, 71
Sherman, Franklin, 59, 91
Sherraden, Michael, 138
shopgoodwill.com, 120
shopping, 122
   comparative, 114–15

MacGregor on, 88
in thrift shops, 107, 109–10, 114–15, 117–19, 125–26, 233n28
by women, 88–89, 125
S&L. *See* savings and loan association
Slemp, C. Bascom, 86
small loans, 159–60
Smith, Herbert, 90
social policy, 43–44, 47, 67, 73
Social Security
benefits from, 152
payday lenders and, 152
tax limit, 205
Somebody's Brother (McKinley), 115
Sparks, Jared, 25
Specian, Rosemary, 114–15
spending
alcohol, 72
Brown on, 229n138
lottery, 154–55, 156, 184–85
MacGregor on, 70–71
minority, 193–94
as saving, 69
in thrift movement, 69–72
value of, 70–71
Spree: A Cultural History of Shopping (Klaffke), 116–17
St. Luke Credit Union, 131
St. Mary's Bank, 128
stock ownership, 171, 179–80
Straus, S. W., 58
on charity, 64
on democracy, 73
on efficiency, 72
on habit, 66
History of the Thrift Movement in America by, 104

on miserliness, 63–64
on saving, 64
on thrift as virtue, 63, 74, 104, 105, 110
on war gardens, 80, 228n103
subsidies, 238n17
Swap-O-Rama Rama, 118–19

tax, 182
on capital gains, 236n1
FICA limit on, 205
Taylor, Frederick Winslow, 72
temperance, 220n78
Temperance Movement
Oberholtzer on, 82–83
thrift and, 220n78
Texas Lottery, 157
Thaler, Richard, 204
A Theory of Shopping (Miller), 125
thethriftshopper.com, 118
Thiry, J. H., 35–36, 42
on equality, 77
school savings banks of, 82
Thorndike, Edward, 69, 71–72
thrift
broader, 35–36
citizenship and, 43
in Great Depression, 129
as lifestyle, 35–36, 63
negative view of, ix, 5
as philanthropy, 35, 58–59
as social policy, 43–44, 47, 67, 73
Temperance Movement and, 220n78
as virtue, 73, 74
in World War I, 57, 73, 77, 78–79, 81

Thrift in the Household (Hughes), 64, 70
thrift institutions, 145–47
thrift movement
  consumerism and, 67–68
  democracy and, 73–75
  future orientation of, 77–78
  Industrial Revolution and, 60–63
  origins of, 58–60
  school savings banks, 82
  self control in, 64–67, 104
  spending in, 69–72
Thrift Savings Plan (TSP), 162–63, 179–80
The Thrift Shop, 108
thrift shops. *See also* vintage shops
  Andrews on, 106–7
  functions of, 119
  Industrial Revolution and, 100–101
  location of, 119–20
  men in, 124–25
  middle-class in, 113
  origination of, 97–103
  shopping in, 107, 109–10, 114–15, 117–19, 125–26, 233n28
  U.S., 117
  women in, 102–3, 124
Thrift Tidings, 83
ThriftOn, 118–19
Tilly, Louise, 103
time preference, 176
Tocqueville, Alexis de, 36–37, 43
Townsend, John P., 43–44
TSP. *See* Thrift Savings Plan
Twain, Mark, 5

Uniform Fee Disclosure, 196

Uniform Small Loan Act, 160
Unit Plan, 86–87
United States (U.S.)
  bankruptcy in, 10, 149
  banks in, 90, 215n5
  consumerism in, 54–55
  credit unions in, 139
  debt in, 148–50, 151
  Department of Labor, 196, 198
  eighteenth century, 10, 16–17
  Europeans and, 219n63
  Forest Service, 90
  Franklin, B., on, 22–24
  immigration to, 22–24, 41–42
  individualism in, 34–35
  investment rates in, 171
  lottery in, 154–55, 184
  net worth in, 168, 169
  payday lenders in, 158
  recession of, 4, 141, 208
  Savings rate in, 55, 76, 95, 137, 162, 166, 167, 168–70, 236n1
  thrift shops in, 117
  Treasury Department, 80
United States League of Saving and Loan Associations, 224n26
University of Southern Mississippi, 135
U.S. *See* United States
usury laws, 153, 159–61

The Value of Thrift (Dane), 61
vendues, 18–19
vintage shops, 116

Wall Street Journal, 152
Wallace, Thomas F., 93
war gardens, 80, 228n103

War Industries Board, 79
War Savings Stamps, 80
The Way to Wealth (Franklin, B.), 3,
   16, 22
   debt in, 11
   Father Abraham in, 18
   religion and, 19
Weber, Max, 5
welfare, 237n9
The Well-Dressed Woman
   (Rittenhouse, A.), 107–8
Wheaton, H. H., 92
"Why Not Aid 'Spending Youth'?",
   92–93
Wilkinson, J. Frome, 34
Willard, Frances E., 82–83
Wilson, Woodrow, 79
Withers, Hartley, 71
women
   clubs for, 87–88
   household management by, 7,
      12–13, 105–6, 123, 213n21

investments of, 191–93
saving by, 69–70
shopping by, 88–89, 125
in thrift shops, 102–3, 124
Wood, Gordon S., 26
World War I
   cost of, 78–80
   federal budget in, 230n143
   thrift in, 57, 73, 77, 78–79, 81
World War II
   consumerism after, 113–14
   saving during, 162, 182
Worth, Jean, 107

YMCA. *See* Young Men's Christian
   Association
Young Men's Christian Association
   (YMCA), 58, 86
youth, 92–93

Zook, George, 81